Flirting
with
Disaster

Bureaucracies, Public Administration, and Public Policy

Kenneth J. Meier
Series Editor

Bureaucracies, Public Administration,
and Public Policy

Flirting with Disaster

Public Management in Crisis Situations

SAUNDRA K. SCHNEIDER

M.E. Sharpe
Armonk, New York
London, England

Library of Congress Cataloging-in-Publication Data

Schneider, Saundra K., 1952–
Flirting with disaster : public management in crisis situations /
Saundra K. Schneider.
p. cm. — (Bureaucracies, public administration,
and public policy)
Includes bibliographical references and index.
ISBN 1-56324-570-1 (hardcover : alk. paper). —
ISBN 1-56324-571-X (paperback : alk. paper)
1. Emergency management—United States. 2. Crisis management
in government—United States. I. Title. II. Series.
HV551.3.S38   1995
363.3'456'0973—dc20   95-17904
CIP

Printed in the United States of America

The paper used in this publication meets the minimum requirements of
American National Standard for Information Sciences—
Permanence of Paper for Printed Library Materials,
ANSI Z 39.48-1984.

BM (c)   10   9   8   7   6   5   4   3   2   1
BM (p)   10   9   8   7   6   5   4   3   2   1

To the memory of my father, Jacob W. Schneider

Contents

Part Three: Summary, Implications, and Conclusions

Foreword

The M.E. Sharpe series Bureaucracies, Public Administration, and Public Policy is designed as a forum for the best work on bureaucracy and its role in public policy and governance. Although the series is open with regard to approach, methods, and perspectives, especially sought are three types of research. First, the series hopes to attract theoretically informed, empirical studies of bureaucracy. Public administration has long been viewed as a theoretical and methodological backwater of political science. This view persists despite a recent accumulation of first-rate research. The series seeks to place public administration at the forefront of empirical analysis within political science. Second, the series is interested in conceptual work that attempts to clarify theoretical issues, set an agenda for research, or provide a focus for professional debates. Third, the series seeks manuscripts that challenge the conventional wisdom about how bureaucracies influence public policy or the role of public administration in governance.

Flirting with Disaster: Public Management in Crisis Situations breaks new theoretical and empirical ground. A truism of public administration is that bureaucracies handle large-scale tasks of a routine nature especially well. For effective performance, political elites need merely to set clear goals, provide sufficient resources, and let bureaucracy develop its own routines and expertise. What the field of public administration does not know much about is how to manage catastrophic events. Professor Schneider offers the first comprehensive look at the process of managing natural disasters. The management task is made even more complex by a federal system that requires that local governments, which generally lack the experience, be in the front line of managing disasters while the federal bureaucrats, who have a great deal of expertise, are restricted in their range of authority. By looking at a series of case studies guided by a solid theoretical framework, Professor Schneider fills a major void in public administration and public management. Her insights, both empirical and normative, could be applied to organizational disasters as well as natural ones.

Professor Schneider finds that structure interacts with task demands in disaster management. Whether the situation is a success or a failure depends on how well the public's response fits with bureaucratic expectations. Where emerging public norms in a disaster do not fit bureaucratic norms, major management problems occur. The size of the gap between public norms and bureaucratic norms is the key variable in determining how well a disaster is managed.

Flirting with Disaster is an important book for public administration; it explores a rarely examined dimension of bureaucracy—crisis management—and thus merits reading in any introductory, intermediate, or advanced course. Students of federalism will also find much new material in *Flirting with Disaster* because it examines a high stress point in contemporary federalism. Finally, students of public management would greatly benefit from the book's unique focus on how to deal with crisis situations.

Kenneth J. Meier

Preface

There is nothing like personal experience to spark one's interest in a topic. That is certainly the case with this study, which began and ended in the midst of natural disasters. I started to think about the main ideas presented in this book shortly after sitting through Hurricane Hugo's onslaught of the southeastern states in September of 1989. Having moved to South Carolina just one month prior to this time, I was struck by the government's apparent inability to respond to the needs and demands of the hurricane victims. So I began investigating the causes and consequences of governmental actions during these traumatic times, as well as the kinds of dilemmas that naturally arise when public officials try to restore order in the aftermath of natural catastrophes.

Like most other research projects, this one turned out to be larger than I originally anticipated. I spent the next five years collecting information on a variety of natural disasters and the governmental actions that took place in each one. As my research proceeded, I was increasingly impressed with the enormity of the problem, the pressures faced by virtually everyone involved in the disaster-relief process, and the seemingly constant criticism of the government's response. Juxtaposed against these pressure-ridden aspects of the subject matter, I was also pushed toward a fairly clear conclusion: the system usually works quite well.

Then, just as I was about to complete the manuscript for this book in January 1995, I had another firsthand experience with a natural disaster. This time, a small and compact, but nevertheless violent, tornado touched down in my backyard (literally). Thankfully, my own home was largely spared, but the brief storm left a swath of damage clearly visible through my neighborhood. It toppled dozens of tall loblolly pine trees, tore the roofs off several houses, and rearranged just about everything that happened to get in its path. To say the least, this provided me with a potent reminder about the forms of human behavior that occur whenever a disaster strikes.

January 1995. Disasters can (and do) strike in your own backyard. This photo shows some of the damage caused by a tornado that ripped its way through the author's neighborhood in Columbia, South Carolina.

The tornado vividly demonstrated just how unsettling and traumatic even a small natural disaster can be, particularly for those who experience it directly. It also reinforced in my mind the difficulties faced by the relief organizations that are responsible for addressing the concerns, problems, and demands of disaster victims. In short, my research both began and ended with opportunities to observe directly the conceptual principles that I develop in this book.

The central question of this study is a straightforward one: why does the government handle some natural disasters successfully but fail miserably in other cases? The answer to this question does not really lie in the factors that most people would identify, the magnitude of the disaster and the amount of governmental resources spent on relief efforts. Instead, the success or failure of an emergency response depends on the size of the inevitable gap between the collective behavior of disaster victims and the bureaucratic procedures of public officials. The case studies presented in this book demonstrate that this relatively simple principle appears again and again in a wide variety of natural disaster situations.

I believe that the topic of this book is both interesting and intrinsically important. Of course, natural disasters attract a great deal of attention from both journalists and scholars. But most of the journalists' accounts are descriptive and anecdotal in nature, containing little systematic or comprehensive coverage of the topic. And the scholarly treatments have been segmented by academic discipline; thus, the emergency management studies in public administration and the collective behavior field in sociology remain largely separate and distinct research traditions. Moreover, there has been little, if any, attempt to integrate broader principles of bureaucratic behavior and policymaking into research on disaster relief. My purpose in this book is to overcome these limitations. I employ information from journalistic and scholarly sources, along with my own research, in order to develop a general theoretical framework for analyzing governmental performance in disaster situations.

This book is intended to contribute to our understanding of disaster management in the United States. It should appeal to a broad audience beyond American scholars and practitioners in the field of emergency management.

First, the basic principles espoused in this study should be applicable to disaster relief in other nations. For example, two disasters that occurred when I was completing this study—a major earthquake in Kobe, Japan, and massive flooding in the Netherlands—clearly demonstrate the relevance of the gap between victims' expectations and bureaucratic performance. Consider the Kobe earthquake of January 17, 1995: The Japanese have a well-developed administrative structure for dealing with emergency situations, but it failed, at least in the initial periods after the disaster struck. Accordingly, the Japanese press, public, and governmental officials have criticized their own system for being slow, ineffective, and nonresponsive to offers of outside help. The floods in the Netherlands represent a somewhat different situation. The Dutch are all too familiar with flooding, and they have routinized procedures for dealing with these situations. The floods that occurred in early February 1995, however, were so massive and widespread that the nation was caught off guard; the preparations and response procedures that had worked so well in the past simply failed this time. Once again, the Dutch public officials charged with emergency management responsibilities were subjected to intense criticism. Both situations, the Dutch and the Japanese, along with literally hundreds of others throughout the world, illustrate the importance of the gap between collective behavior and bureaucratic norms for understanding the success or failure of governmental responses to natural disasters.

Second, the findings of this study may also provide insights into public policymaking during other stressful situations. A natural disaster is certainly not the only event or problem that can generate a conflict between governmental planning and public expectations. For example, environmental protection agencies at both the national and state levels monitor air and water quality, issue regulations to maintain environmental standards, and oversee compliance with many kinds of environmental protection laws. Most of the time, these agencies carry out their responsibilities in a routine manner, attracting little if any public attention. Occasionally, however, they come into direct conflict with the public, with powerful interest groups, or with both—people who become incensed when economic development is halted because of such factors as endangered species, wetlands, and pollution-control standards. As another example, consider the state and local social service agencies that are responsible for placing children in foster care. Usually, their activities proceed smoothly, and the results provide positive benefits for everyone concerned. Occasionally, however, foster children suffer injuries, abuse, and even death; when this occurs, the agencies that place and protect the children come under intense public scrutiny and criticism. These two examples represent very different substantive policy situations, and they affect very different population groups. But both of them provide perfect illustrations of a gap between the standard operating procedures of governmental bureaucracies and the norms and expectations of the general public. Thus, the explanatory factor that accounts for governmental responses to natural disasters is directly applicable to policy performance in other areas as well.

Third, the findings of this study should have broad relevance to the general fields of public policy and public administration. Although the book focuses specifically on disaster relief, it still addresses such general issues as policy implementation, program evaluation, bureaucratic politics, and public management. The study also deals with some of the central dilemmas in American policymaking—that is, intergovernmental relations, governmental accountability, and public- and private-sector interactions. Therefore, it should be useful to political scientists in many of the subfields associated with American government, as well as to scholars in other disciplines, particularly sociology and economics. Finally, and most obviously, this book should be relevant to scholars and practitioners in the field of emergency management. After all, these individuals focus directly on the governmental response to disasters.

I am grateful to the many people who have assisted throughout this project. Kenneth Meier provided helpful comments and suggestions on an earlier draft of the manuscript. In addition, his continuous support of the project over the past three years has been invaluable. Indeed, he convinced me that the study was worthwhile and encouraged me to carry it on to a successful completion.

Several graduate students at the University of South Carolina helped collect important and voluminous information about the natural disasters discussed in this study. In this respect, I would particularly like to thank Sherral Brown Guinyard, Shawn Benzinger, and Teresa Spires.

It is also appropriate that I acknowledge the invaluable assistance provided to me by dozens of national, state, and local disaster-relief officials. The information and materials that they supplied constitute much of the raw material and data on which this study is constructed. I would also like to thank B.D. Publishing Company for its generous permission to use photographs of Hurricane Hugo's destruction in Charleston, South Carolina.

At M.E. Sharpe, Inc., I would like to acknowledge my appreciation to Michael Weber, who has helped me get the book into print.

Finally, a special thanks goes to William G. Jacoby, who provided me with insightful comments, invaluable support, and continuous help throughout the entire time I worked on this book. Without his assistance and encouragement, I would not have been able to undertake or complete this study. I am deeply appreciative of all his efforts.

Saundra K. Schneider

Part One

Analytical and Theoretical Frameworks

1

The Varied Success of the Governmental Response to Natural Disasters

Over the past few years, a series of major natural disasters have struck the United States. On September 17, 1989, a massive hurricane named Hugo blasted the U.S. Virgin Islands at full force. On the following day, the storm ripped its way across the northeast portion of Puerto Rico. After a brief respite in the Atlantic Ocean, Hugo hit the U.S. mainland about forty miles northeast of Charleston, South Carolina. The huge storm pounded the coastal areas for several hours; then it moved quickly and violently in a northwesterly direction, carving a destructive path across half the state of South Carolina. Hugo made one last stop at Charlotte, North Carolina, before it finally turned north and diminished in strength. During its brief but violent life, Hugo left thousands of people without shelter, water, food, sewer facilities, electricity, or telephone services. Overall, it was responsible for fifty-six deaths and damages estimated at more than $11 billion. Hurricane Hugo was clearly one of the most destructive storms of the twentieth century.

A month later, on October 17, 1989, a major earthquake rocked the San Francisco Bay area. The quake, called Loma Prieta by geologists, shook the earth for about fifteen seconds with a force measuring 7.1 on the Richter scale. Severe damage was reported within a hundred-mile radius around the quake's epicenter (located eight miles northeast of Santa Cruz). Tremors were felt several hundred miles beyond that point in all directions. The earthquake destroyed or damaged thousands of buildings. Roads were cracked open and bridges crumbled. Natural gas and power lines snapped apart, and water pipes exploded. In all, the quake caused more than sixty deaths, thousands of injuries, and an estimated $7.1 billion in damages. It was the second most lethal earthquake recorded in American history.

Almost three years after these incidents, a major hurricane called Andrew smacked into the U.S. coastline about thirty-five miles south of Miami, Florida. On August 23, 1992, Andrew blasted the southern tip of Florida with sustained winds of 140 miles per hour and gusts of up to 164 miles per hour. The storm traveled quickly across the Florida peninsula, leveling virtually everything in its path. It continued to move in a west-northwesterly direction over the Gulf of Mexico. Early on August 25, Andrew made landfall again. This time it hit a sparsely populated section of southern Louisiana. Later that same day, the hurricane finally lost its punch as it moved northward, up through the south-central section of the United States. In its wake, Hurricane Andrew left hundreds of thousands of people homeless, and thousands more without power, water, communications, and sewer facilities. This compact but extremely fierce storm caused at least forty deaths and over $20 billion in property damages. Hurricane Andrew had earned the ominous distinction of being the most expensive natural disaster to date in U.S. history.

In 1993, another type of natural disaster hit the central portion of the United States. From April 1 to July 31, ten times the normal amount of rain fell in the central section of the nation, completely saturating the entire area. There was so much water that the Mississippi and Missouri rivers were simply incapable of handling it. The excess spilled over onto the surrounding land, creating enormous new lakes, rivers, and inland seas. Severe flooding was reported in nine states, stretching from Minnesota in the north to southeastern Missouri. The scope of the flooding was immense. Millions of acres of farmland were completely submerged; hundreds of highways, levees, and dams were washed away; thousands of residents were forced to leave their homes and farms. In all, the flooding caused forty deaths and between $10 billion and $15 billion in damages. The devastating overflow of the Mississippi and Missouri rivers is now generally known as the Great Flood of 1993.[1]

Then, early in 1994, Mother Nature struck again on the West Coast. On January 17, an earthquake jolted the Los Angeles, California, area at 4:21 in the morning. The tremors lasted for about forty seconds, reaching a level of 6.6 on the magnitude and intensity scales. Ironically, the quake occurred along a little-known, unnamed fault, in the northwestern section of the city. Nevertheless, it inflicted severe damage on one of the nation's most populated urban areas. Major freeways, bridges, and buildings crumbled into pieces; water pipes burst open; and electric wires snapped apart. The quake severed natural gas lines, which in turn set off a number of serious fires throughout the surrounding neighborhoods. Thousands of residents lost their homes and personal belongings. The damages to property, buildings, highways, and so on have been estimated at more than $30 billion. In addition, the quake killed sixty-one people and injured hundreds more. Experts say that this earthquake was not fierce enough to qualify as "The Big One." But it definitely sent a wake-up call to the citizens of Los Angeles, the state of California, and the rest of the nation.[2]

Major natural disasters, such as Hurricane Hugo, the Loma Prieta earthquake, Hurricane Andrew, the Great Flood of 1993, and the 1994 Los Angeles earthquake, place enormous and extraordinary burdens on the people who experience them. They generate problems and conditions that are difficult to anticipate, comprehend, and address. Individuals, families, and private organizations try to help citizens deal with the chaos and disruption. Their efforts are extremely important but are often woefully inadequate for disasters of these magnitudes. As a result, people turn naturally to the public sector for assistance. Government is the only institution with the resources and the authority to help citizens cope with such cataclysmic events.

In the United States, the government has developed a system to deal with major disasters. This system is designed to guide official activity before, during, and after a disaster situation occurs. It identifies the basic objectives of governmental activity in this area, as well as the policies and procedures that should be used to achieve these goals. The system also ties together the activities of all three levels of government and coordinates the operations of various public and private organizations. Overall, this governmental response system strives to provide the most effective and efficient utilization of available resources.

The government relies on this basic apparatus whenever and wherever a disaster strikes. In general, the system appears to work quite well. For the vast majority of disasters, the government is able to respond in a fairly routine manner. Public institutions use standard operating procedures to step in and provide relief to disaster-stricken areas, and there is little fanfare, commotion, or publicity surrounding these activities. In these situations, the governmental response is viewed as timely, appropriate, and successful.

Unfortunately, however, the governmental response does not always operate so smoothly or effectively. As Hurricane Hugo, the Loma Prieta earthquake, and Hurricane Andrew demonstrated, some natural disasters generate severe environmental and societal disruptions. Public institutions find it extremely difficult to handle such situations. So the government appears to react too slowly and haphazardly. In other instances, it mobilizes quickly, but subsequently cannot direct available resources to those who are truly in need. And in a few rare cases, the governmental response appears to be completely misguided. Public agencies fail to react swiftly or appropriately for the disaster situation at hand. In sum, the overall effectiveness of governmental efforts with major natural disasters is highly variable. This raises an interesting and important question: why is governmental performance in the area of disaster response so inconsistent? This book addresses precisely that question.

I argue that the answer to the preceding question does not lie solely in the structure of the governmental response system or the nature of the disaster. Instead, it is a combination of these two factors. More specifically, the key to a successful governmental response depends on the extent to which postdisaster human behavior corresponds to prior governmental expectations and planning. On the one hand, public organizations develop standard operating procedures, routine policies, and institutionalized processes that are supposed to address every possible contingency. These bureaucratic norms provide the foundation for the governmental response system. On the other hand, some disasters generate conditions that are unusually difficult, complicated, or stressful. During these situations, bureaucratic norms and institutionalized patterns of behavior simply do not seem to apply. Therefore, new or emergent norms develop to provide guidance and meaning to the affected population.

When the gap between these emergent norms and the preexisting bureaucratic norms of the governmental system is quite wide, the response process breaks down. This leads to widespread dissatisfaction with and criticism of governmental activities. When the disaster situation conforms to prior governmental expectations and planning, the gap between bureaucratic and emergent norms is relatively small. In these cases, public organizations are able to cope effectively with the disaster. The response and recovery activities proceed smoothly, and the entire governmental effort is perceived as successful. Thus, it is the *size of the gap* between the bureaucratic norms guiding governmental activity and the emergent norms arising within the affected population that determines the variability in governmental performance.

Varying sizes of the gap correspond to three alternative patterns of policy implementation. First, when the gap between emergent and bureaucratic norms is relatively small, governmental policies and procedures provide an appropriate guide to human behavior. There is little confusion or delay, and the government is able to react to the disaster situation in a relatively routine, straightforward manner. All relevant emergency management officials work together and perform their previously defined responsibilities. Governmental activity flows from the "bottom up," precisely as it was intended. The response "bubbles" up from the local level to the state and ultimately to the national government.

Second, there are other disasters that produce a moderately sized gap.

Bureaucratic and emergent norms do not exactly agree with each other, but they are not entirely contradictory either. This leads to a situation in which there is no clear guidance for, or support of, governmental activities. A number of different actors and agencies at each level of government may try to take action; however, there is little or no coordination to these efforts, and it is difficult to tell exactly which (if any) level of government is responsible for the various relief and recovery operations. The result is a "confused" pattern of governmental activity.

Third, in some situations, bureaucratic procedures and patterns of human behavior diverge entirely from one another; in such cases, the gap is extremely wide. In these disasters, the government simply cannot follow its standard operating procedures. The preestablished intergovernmental response framework is incapable of administering disaster relief. Local and state governments may be unable or unwilling to handle the crisis; the national government has to step in and take control of the entire effort. The normal bottom-up intergovernmental response pattern is supplanted by a top-down implementation process.

These three patterns of policy implementation for disaster relief—bottom up, confused, and top down—are extremely important. Although the specific nature and detail of natural disasters vary widely, almost all disaster response efforts conform to one of these patterns. They provide clear representations of the government's overall performance in this policy area. More specifically, the three patterns reveal the extent to which governmental plans match the needs and expectations of the affected population. Governmental responses that conform to the bottom-up process are most likely to be labeled successes; those that proceed in a confused, disorganized manner are usually viewed with mixed reactions; and those that follow the top-down pattern are generally perceived to be complete failures. Consequently, these three implementation patterns are used in this study to construct a framework for understanding the success or failure of the government's natural disaster relief efforts.

The rest of the book is organized as follows: In Part One, I present the fundamental theoretical and analytical frameworks of the study. Chapter 1 examines two basic questions: (1) Why are disasters viewed as legitimate *public* problems, requiring *governmental* action? and (2) What role *should* the government play in disaster-related activities? In order to answer these questions, Chapter 2 compares disasters to other public problems and issues. Unlike situations in many other policy areas, citizens expect *government* to act when disaster strikes. Public beliefs about governmental intervention have had a significant influence on the development of disaster-relief policy in the United States. Chapter 3 examines the basic governmental approach to disasters in the United States, and it provides a brief overview of the historical development of governmental activity in this area. It then discusses the basic framework and structure of the current governmental disaster-assistance system, focusing on the strengths and weaknesses of the government's policy approach.

Chapter 4 examines the two sets of norms that exist in every disaster situation: the bureaucratic norms that guide the governmental response process and the emergent norms that develop within the disaster-stricken population. Chapter 5 uses these two sets of norms to construct a general framework for explaining the government's disaster-assistance efforts. Here, I present the key concept of the study. I argue that it is the *size of the gap* between bureaucratic norms and emergent norms that determines the predominant policy implementation pattern for emergency relief. More important, the size of the gap accounts for the success or failure of the entire governmental relief effort.

In Part Two of the book (Chapters 6 through 13) I provide detailed examples of recent disaster situations. These case studies illustrate the extreme variability of governmental activity in this policy area. In addition, they show quite clearly the importance of the size of the gap for explaining the success or failure of the governmental response to natural disasters.

The last section of the book summarizes and expands on key points made earlier. Chapter 14 discusses the fundamental paradox of public policymaking in emergency management. When the government responds to disasters smoothly and effectively, its efforts receive little attention; when the response breaks down, governmental activity is highly publicized. Finally, Chapter 15 examines the most popular recommendations for improving the government's disaster relief operations. It also presents the broader implications of this study for understanding the general limitations of governmental activity when bureaucratic institutions confront extraordinarily stressful conditions.

Notes

1. The first three disasters—Hurricane Hugo, the Loma Prieta earthquake, and Hurricane Andrew—are used as case studies in this book, and additional references for each of these situations are provided in later chapters. For additional summary information on the Midwest floods of 1993, see U.S. Department of Commerce (1994); U.S. Senate (1994a); and U.S. Senate (1993b). There are also a number of excellent sources for more detailed, day-by-day accounts of the flooding; see the *New York Times,* the *Washington Post,* and *St. Louis Post-Dispatch* during the months of July and August 1993.

2. For an overview of the Los Angeles earthquake, see U.S. Senate (1994b); U.S. General Accounting Office (1994); "Shattered" (1994); and "State of Shock" (1994). For more detailed descriptions, see the *New York Times,* the *Washington Post,* and the *Los Angeles Times,* particularly during January 1994.

2

Natural Disasters as Public Policy Issues

When a natural disaster occurs, few people stop to ask if the government *should* intervene. Instead, citizens tend automatically to view the situation as a serious *public* problem requiring immediate *governmental* action. Part of this perception is inevitable. Government has a basic responsibility to restore public safety, utilities, and so on. But popular expectations go far beyond this to a widespread belief that government should take an active, positive role by helping private individuals and businesses in their recovery efforts. This raises an interesting question: why are natural disasters perceived to be *public* problems? After all, many private institutions, such as insurance companies, relief agencies, and charity organizations, could help resolve the kinds of disruptions caused by natural disasters. So why do these situations produce an almost automatic expectation of a *governmental* response?

The answer to this question is extremely important. Many social problems are never elevated to the status of political issues. Likewise, many political issues are never addressed by meaningful public policies. This is simply not the case with natural disasters, which garner immediate public attention and almost invariably become the target of large-scale governmental activity. Therefore it is essential that we determine why natural disasters seem to move through this usually slow, difficult process in a speedy and almost automatic manner.

Theoretical Perspectives on Agenda Building

The process through which social problems evolve into public and governmental concerns is called agenda building.[1] The notion of an agenda-building process is an abstraction. It does not exist in any concrete or officially designated form; there are certainly no statutes or regulations to guide the evolution of problems into issues. Instead, this concept is useful because it explains why certain problems become the focus of public attention, and why they become matters for governmental action. More broadly, the agenda-building process identifies how collective judgments are made about ideas, events, and activities. Therefore, it reveals a great deal about the values, priorities, and commitments that exist within a political system.

The agenda-building process has received a great deal of attention in the scholarly literature (Cobb and Elder 1983a; Eyestone 1978; Kingdon 1984; Baumgartner and Jones 1993). Researchers have devised many different explanations of how the process works, and they have identified different factors that affect an issue's placement on the policy agenda. Several of these factors have particular relevance for natural disasters: the objective dimensions of the problem, the symbolic elements of the issue, the political aspects of the situation, and the lack of private-sector solutions.[2] Taken together, these factors help explain why natural disasters are considered to be legitimate public problems requiring governmental solutions.

Objective Characteristics

Certain problems are so large and salient that they almost automatically attract public attention. Analysts have referred to such problems as "triggering mechanisms" (Cobb and Elder 1983a) or "focusing events" (Kingdon 1984). Some triggering mechanisms develop gradually over time. A series of technological breakthroughs might eventually create new situations and problems for governmental action. The industrial revolution and the attendant problems of urbanization and economic change illustrate this kind of triggering mechanism. Others can erupt instantaneously and unexpectedly. For example, an act of international aggression will almost certainly become an immediate policy issue.

All triggering mechanisms convert routine problems into important policy issues. But when does a problem become a triggering mechanism? Two basic factors determine this transformation from the mundane to the extraordinary: (1) the number of people affected by the situation, and (2) public perceptions of how important the event is.

The significance of triggering mechanisms is widely recognized in the agenda-building literature (Eyestone 1978; Cobb and Elder 1983a), and their role is perhaps most clearly explained by Anthony Downs (1972). He describes agenda building as a dynamic, highly unstable process that follows an "issue attention cycle." According to Downs, a triggering mechanism initiates the cycle: A dramatic event is responsible for catapulting an issue onto the agenda almost instantaneously. Once it is on the agenda, the issue receives intense public and governmental attention, but only for a brief period of time. As the public begins to realize the costs of addressing the problem, it loses interest in the issue and shifts its focus to other situations and problem areas. Governmental decision makers usually follow suit. So the issue "falls off" the agenda almost as quickly as it ascended to prominence.

Not all social problems will go through this issue attention cycle. But the cycle is more likely to occur if (1) the problem affects a sizable, noticeable minority, but not a majority, of the public; (2) the underlying causes of the problem actually benefit certain powerful groups within society; and (3) the problem initially appears to be "new" and/or "different," but it quickly loses its novelty and appeal. Thus the nature of the social problem itself—its objective dimensions as well as the manner in which these characteristics are transmitted across a society—determines public and governmental involvement in any particular policy area.[3]

Political Factors

Political forces also play a key role in pushing issues onto (or off) the policy agenda. Here, there are many different kinds of factors to consider. Some scholars focus on the general impact of public opinion (Key 1961; Page and Shapiro 1983). Others emphasize the role of political parties, interest groups, and the media in shaping policy preferences (Ginsberg 1976; Sinclair 1977; Walker 1977; Iyengar 1991). Still others look more directly at the individual motivations of political leaders (Light 1982; Riker 1986; Baumgartner 1987). Taken together, it is extremely difficult to deny the impact of political variables during the agenda-building process.

John Kingdon (1984) groups all these forces into one general category and calls it the "political stream." According to Kingdon, an issue becomes a prominent item on the policy agenda when a "policy window" opens in the political environment. Policy windows open when (1) there is a shift in public opinion, (2) there is organized pressure within the political system, or (3) administrative changes bring about personnel and procedure changes within government. These conditions allow policy advocates to push their preferred ideas and issues onto the policy agenda. Nevertheless, if policy entrepreneurs do not take advantage of these opportune situations, the policy window closes and the issue will not gain prominence on the policy agenda. Kingdon and others certainly view agenda building as an intensely *political* activity. According to this view, partisan forces, ideological forces, or both play a decisive role in the agenda-building phase of public policy development.

Deborah Stone (1988) takes this argument one step further. She states that it is simply impossible to think about policymaking without considering the role of politics. Public policies are generated in political communities, and they represent the struggle over political values and ideas. Issues are crafted images of political problems. They get placed on the policy agenda because individuals or groups of individuals are actively trying to define the boundaries of acceptable governmental activity. In this view, agenda building is not a rational, straightforward process of orderly governmental efforts to meet pressing social needs. Instead, it is an inherently irrational and unpredictable process—one that is always shaped by political preferences and values.

Symbolic Aspects

Some scholars (e.g., Edelman 1964, 1977, 1989; and Cobb and Elder 1983b) have argued that the symbolic elements of an issue are the most important aspects of agenda building. A symbol can be anything—a word, a phrase, a gesture, an object, a person, an event—that gives meaning or value to an issue beyond the objective content inherent in the issue itself (Cobb and Elder 1983b). Some symbols seem to emerge almost spontaneously. For example, the term "Watergate" was coined because of a specific political event (the illegal wiretapping of the Democratic National Party headquarters during the 1972 elections), but it quickly became a shorthand way of communicating more general concerns about governmental corruption and dishonesty. Other symbols seem to be more deliberately and carefully crafted.[4] Presidential programs are given labels, such as Woodrow Wilson's "New Freedom," Lyndon Johnson's "Great Society," and Ronald Reagan's "New Beginning," in order to describe their focus and to garner public and governmental support. Given the subjectivity of these phenomena, it is virtually impossible to predict precisely when a particular type of symbol will emerge; however, it is possible to identify the circumstances that contribute to the use of symbolism in the policy process.

Symbols are human inventions. They are created and used to impart varying degrees of significance to social problems. On the one hand, if a new issue can be tied to an enduring, acceptable societal value (e.g., freedom, liberty, or self-sufficiency in the American context), it is much more likely to receive serious attention by the general public and by governmental officials (Edelman 1977; DeNeufville and Barton 1987; Weiss 1989). For example, President Kennedy succeeded in making poverty a major issue in the 1960s by appealing to a traditional notion about "America, the land of opportunity." The poor were pictured as unable to pursue the American dream, and it was society's responsibility to help them. On the other hand, proponents of the status quo can also employ symbols to block the emergence of new issues (Schattschneider 1960; Baratz and Bachrach 1963; Bennett 1988). The recent health-care-reform debate in the United States illustrates this point clearly. Opponents of a more nationalized, public health-care system argue that such a system would violate the freedom of choice enjoyed by American citizens—their right to choose their own health-care providers and their own form of medical treatment. In either case, symbols are used to link relatively new social problems to enduring values and beliefs. This can, in turn, either propel or deter the placement of issues on the policy agenda. This makes symbolism a vitally important component of the agenda-building phase in public policy development.

Prevailing Beliefs about Legitimate Governmental Action

Closely related to the symbolic interpretation is the belief that certain issues systematically get mobilized into the policy process, while others do not. Here there are really two separate but related arguments to consider. First, some scholars contend that a set of prevailing values and beliefs within every political community shapes the scope and content of the policy agenda. If a new issue coincides with the prevailing values of the community, it has an excellent chance of getting on the agenda. If the issue conflicts with prevailing values, however, it is likely to become a "nonagenda item"—it will never be taken up for serious public consideration (Baratz and Bachrach 1963). On the one hand, this screen of bias works to the advantage of old agenda items. In many instances, governmental officials and the general public already know something about these issues, and they can rely on past governmental activities to guide their responses. This makes old issues both easier and safer to address; hence they tend to dominate policy agendas. On the other hand, the screen of bias works against the emergence of new issues that have not been addressed previously. These new issues may affect groups in society whose members lack status or access in the community, such as the poor, the mentally ill, or convicted criminals. Alternatively, these new issues may be dismissed because they are simply not considered to be legitimate topics for governmental discussion or action. Thus, governmental ownership of corporations and businesses has never received much serious attention or discussion in American politics.

Second, there are certain issues—for example, maintaining a sound economy and promoting national defense—that are widely accepted as being particularly appropriate, legitimate focuses for governmental action. These kinds of items are often called "public goods." Such goods are indivisible—that is, the consumption by one individual does not interfere with the consumption by another individual (Donahue 1989). Public goods are also nonexclusive, meaning that nobody can be excluded from the use and benefits of a public good (Savas 1982, 1987; Wolf 1988). Consequently, every individual has an economic incentive to become a "free rider"—to take advantage of public goods without paying for them (Savas 1987). In order to counter the free-rider problem, collective action is necessary (Olson 1965). More specifically, governmental involvement is usually considered justifiable when it is addressing issues that involve public goods. So citizens accept governmental regulations on highways and roadways (e.g., traffic signals and street signs) because all motorists benefit from them, but no one would volunteer to provide them in every location or across all jurisdictions.

Specific Characteristics of Natural Disasters

As we have seen, there are many different ideas about how the agenda-building process works. Analysts have identified several important factors that make it more likely that a particular problem will develop into a prominent policy issue. The agenda-building literature says that any *one* of these factors should be sufficient to propel an issue onto the policy agenda. Natural disasters present a relatively unusual situation because they possess all four of the characteristics necessary to attain immediate agenda status. Let us consider each one in turn.

Objective Dimensions

Natural disasters easily qualify as triggering mechanisms. They are, by definition, severe events (Silverstein 1992). When a tornado tears its way through a community, it can uplift homes, farms, and businesses. When excessive rains cause normally quiet, serene rivers to overflow their banks, buildings, roads, highways, and bridges can be washed away. The severity of these events is easy to calculate in terms of both the amount of physical destruction incurred and the economic costs involved. It is estimated that natural disasters are responsible for about $20 billion in property losses every year in the United States alone (National Research Council 1991). Natural disasters can also cause serious physical injuries, psychological trauma, and even death. The World Health Organization estimates that between 1964 and 1978, natural disasters killed nearly 2.5 million people and left an additional 750 million injured or harmed throughout the world. The number of deaths caused by extreme weather events increased about 50 percent during every decade from 1890 to 1950. There have been even more dramatic increases in fatality rates since the 1950s (Kreimer and Munasinghe 1990).

Second, natural disasters encompass an incredible range of sizes, circumstances, and effects (Fritz 1957; Dynes 1970; Drabek 1970; Kreps 1986). On the one hand, they can cause widespread destruction, affecting large numbers of people across an extensive geographic area. For example, droughts in the United States have destroyed thousands of acres of crops in states spanning the entire width of the country. On the other hand, they can strike in one small, isolated area. A tornado may touch down in a neighborhood and destroy a single house, leaving all others completely undamaged. Thus, natural disasters can have a limited, concentrated impact on small numbers of people, or they can inflict far-reaching damages on extensive sections of the population and the nation.

Third, natural disasters are highly visible problems. They can generate conditions that are difficult, and often impossible, for citizens to ignore (Hodgkinson and Stewart 1990). When an ice storm knocks out the electricity in a community, the people living in the affected area are definitely aware of the situation. When high winds tear the roofs off buildings and scatter personal belongings, the inhabitants of those buildings clearly recognize the existence of a problem. Moreover, these kinds of situations are easily and readily transmitted by the news media. Natural disasters are exactly the type of event that the media prefer to spotlight. They are unusual, different, spectacular, and at times even horrific. So, the problem is "visible" not only to those who are immediately affected by it but to the vast majority of the American population as well.

Each of these objective characteristics—severity, range, and visibility—affects how natural disasters are identified and described. Taken together, these attributes facilitate our general awareness of such situations. But several other important aspects must also be considered in order to understand completely why natural catastrophes are viewed as public issues and legitimate "targets" of governmental action.

Political Aspects

Disaster situations possess several significant political components. When a natural catastrophe occurs, the public's attention is riveted on that event. In Kingdon's (1984) terms, a natural disaster provides a window of opportunity for political action. In fact, a natural disaster is an almost perfect "win-win" situation. Public officials can use a natural disaster situation to demonstrate their leadership abilities and willingness to tackle tough, difficult problems. Their actions will almost always receive instant public consideration and (positive) media publicity. Moreover, it is virtually impossible to oppose or criticize an official who steps in and takes charge of the situation in order to help disaster-stricken citizens.

Natural disasters also produce conditions that allow political leaders to show their concern for citizens' needs and demands. Disaster victims often encounter problems that they have never before experienced. They may be unprepared or unequipped to handle these difficulties on their own. Public officials are simply in a much better position to channel necessary resources to help those who are truly in distress. Thus they have a perfect opportunity to demonstrate their responsiveness to the needs of the people. Political leaders who successfully address disaster-related problems are rewarded. They can dispense particularized benefits to constituents and use these as a resource to facilitate their reelection efforts (Mayhew 1974; Fenno 1978). In contrast, leaders who are unwilling or unable to act can suffer negative political repercussions because they appear to be unresponsive to the needs of their constituents (Abney and Hill 1966; Wolensky and Miller 1981).[5]

Symbolic Aspects

The issues surrounding natural disasters are imbued with highly symbolic content (Brown 1990). When an occurrence is identified as a "disaster," the term itself immediately signals that something terrible and calamitous has occurred. The urgency and severity of the situation are automatically understood. In addition, "disaster" implies an unusual, extraordinary event that private individuals cannot handle on their own. It represents a situation that will almost inevitably require broader public attention and action. Thus the term "disaster" is a strong metaphor.[6] Not only does it describe a complex, unusual event, but the word also carries the symbolic connotation that collective action is warranted (Ibarra and Kitsuse 1993; Rochefort and Cobb 1994).

In addition, natural disasters can occur without warning (Drabek 1986). They can strike at virtually any time (i.e., in any season, any month, or any time of day) and in a variety of different forms (e.g., as the consequence of too little rain—droughts—or too much rain—floods). The unpredictable and highly variable nature of these events contributes further to their symbolic appeal. More specifically, it provides additional justification for governmental intervention. If the government is there to protect its citizens, then it should certainly become involved when unexpected, unpredictable situations develop.

Finally, it is important to note that natural disasters can, and often do, hit innocent citizens. Some public problems develop because of the actions or inactions of the victims themselves. For example, teenage pregnancy, delinquency, and drug addiction are primarily the result of teen behavior and decisions. In most instances, teenagers are not forced to engage in sex, experiment with drugs, or get involved in criminal activity. They are at least partially to blame for the consequences of their actions. But the victims of disasters do not cause the natural occurrence. In many situations, the victims have virtually no control over the scope or severity of the event. Disaster victims are the innocent, helpless, and blameless targets of a natural catastrophe, and they deserve to be helped.

For all these reasons, natural disasters easily invoke all the symbolic elements that readily propel events onto the governmental agenda for action. Natural disasters are, by definition, unsettling, problematic situations; they are often almost impossible to predict with any accuracy (such as the timing of an earthquake or the path of a hurricane); they can affect innocent, blameless citizens; and they all seem to be extremely difficult to manage.

Absence of Private-Sector Solutions

Finally, natural disasters create problems that can realistically be addressed and managed only by government (Perry and Mushkatel 1984). When a severe thunderstorm causes massive damage in an area, private utility companies can repair broken electrical lines and (eventually) restore power. But they cannot deal with contaminated water supplies, broken telephone lines, or the disruption in sewer services. Similarly, when a fire destroys homes and property, private volunteer groups can effectively distribute clothing and food to fire victims. But they do not have the authority to tell local citizens to evacuate before the fire spreads or the resources to help people rebuild after the disaster occurs. Only the government has the technical capability, the appropriate resources, and the authority to coordinate a range of disaster-related responses. Thus a natural disaster situation tends to be viewed as a "public" responsibility because there are no real feasible alternatives in the private sector (Majone 1989; Kingdon 1984). Natural disasters inevitably involve problems that cannot be adequately addressed by private-market activities.

Another argument holds that the policies and procedures needed to address natural disaster situations can be produced only by the public sector. Everyone in society—regardless of age, sex, income, or occupation—could be affected by a natural catastrophe. And theoretically all citizens will benefit from the goods and services that decrease the impact of these occurrences. But there is no incentive for individual citizens to pay voluntarily for these services through the private sector if they will still reap the benefits. Stated simply, the policies and procedures required to address disaster situations qualify as nearly perfect examples of public goods (Downs 1957; Arrow 1963). And, like other public goods, they certainly fall within the purview of governmental responsibility.

In sum, there are a variety of reasons for the government to become involved in disaster situations. First, they can cause extraordinarily severe and patently obvious societal problems. The economic, physical, and emotional costs of these events can reach such high levels that they cannot be ignored or overlooked. Second, disaster situations can become highly "politicized" issues: They reveal the extent to which public figures are willing and able to respond to citizens' needs. Natural disasters also contain extremely important symbolic elements: individual people tend to view these events as cataclysmic, life-threatening, and beyond their control. Finally, many natural disasters, particularly the larger, cataclysmic events, generate problems that the private sector simply cannot or will not handle. Efforts to deal with these events fit the characteristics of a public or collective good.

As in any policy area, the definition of natural disasters is extremely important. It affects the level of attention that these events receive. The definition also determines the range and type of responses presented to address the problem. In theory, natural disasters could be described as individual-level problems requiring private-sector solutions. In fact, this was precisely the definition of natural disasters used in the early days of the American republic. Today, however, disasters are perceived quite differently. For all the reasons discussed earlier, natural disasters are now viewed as critical *policy* issues that require *governmental* attention.

Governmental Involvement in Disasters

If natural disasters are, in fact, policy issues, then this raises several further questions: How have public institutions in the United States dealt with disaster situations? When did the government first become involved in this policy area? Has the government's involvement changed over the years? What factors affect the nature and direction of governmental policy? How does governmental activity in disaster situations compare to governmental involvement in other policy areas? These questions are addressed in the remainder of this chapter.

Brief History of Governmental Disaster-Assistance Policy

It is impossible to say exactly when the American government first became involved in disaster issues. Even before the United States existed, public institutions in this country were providing assistance to victims of natural catastrophes. For example, local officials helped Boston residents affected by a major earthquake that struck the area in 1755. Disaster relief, however, was historically considered to be primarily a local responsibility (Bourgin 1983; Popkin 1990). When a natural catastrophe occurred, city and county officials were expected to help those in need. The actions of local governments were often supplemented by the efforts of private relief agencies, such as religious organizations and the American Red Cross. By and large, however, there was no expectation that higher levels of government would become directly involved in disaster situations.

State governments could be called in to help if local resources were exhausted. But most state-level organizations were ill equipped, unprepared, and even unwilling to intervene. They did not have the resources, capabilities, or inclination to supplement local efforts (Stratton 1989, 28). Disaster assistance simply was not considered a top priority among state governments.

Similarly, the federal government played a very limited role in early recovery efforts. Whenever events exceeded the capacities of subnational authorities, the federal government *could* be asked to step in and help. The U.S. Congress established the legal basis for federal intervention in 1803 when it granted special allowances to the victims of a natural disaster in Portsmouth, New York (May 1985b; Bourgin 1983). From 1803 to 1947, the federal government provided aid to the victims of some 128 disasters (Popkin 1990, 106). In each instance, specific legislation was passed to deal with a particular situation (May 1985b, 18).

Early federal disaster assistance was often uncertain and uncoordinated. There were no general policies or guidelines to shape governmental intervention, and it was never clear whether the federal government would intervene at all. Basically, it responded to each disaster on a piecemeal, case-by-case basis. Furthermore, federal intervention was often politically motivated as elected officials pushed through relief proposals in order to alleviate specific disaster-related conditions in their own states and congressional districts.

During this early period (pre-1950), governmental activities were primarily reactive in nature (May 1985b). Public institutions provided relief only in the aftermath of truly major disasters. The situation did change somewhat in the 1920s and 1930s, when the government initiated some preventive measures. For example, Congress passed a series of flood-control acts that authorized the financing, construction, and maintenance of thousands of miles of levees, flood walls, and channels throughout the nation. These initial proactive efforts were often passed for political rea-

sons, as the result of logrolling and pork-barrel tactics on the part of national legislators. In addition, these early measures stressed structural solutions to disaster-related issues. The emphasis was on building physical
barriers to contain disastrous situations and limit the scope of disaster-
related problems. Little if any attention was given to other, nonstructural
programs that would actually encourage citizens and communities to prepare for emergencies before they occurred.

The nature of government involvement in natural disasters changed dramatically during the middle decades of the twentieth century. This partially
reflected a much broader trend: After the 1930s, the national government
assumed more responsibility for a wide variety of domestic policy concerns.
Federal agencies were given greater authority to help individuals, families,
and businesses recover from economic losses. As part of this general trend,
specific legislation was passed making grants and loans available to industries and public facilities that incurred disaster-related damages (May
1985b). In 1950, Congress enacted legislation that made federal assistance
even more readily available to disaster-stricken communities. The Disaster
Relief Act of 1950 stated that federal resources could and should be used to
supplement state and local efforts when necessary. In addition, the act specified a standard process by which local and state authorities could request
federal assistance. In sum, it changed the entire tone and structure of disaster relief in the United States.

It is important to emphasize that the precedent-setting nature of the Disaster Relief Act of 1950 was not immediately recognized. The legislation
was passed as another limited response by the national government to a
particular disaster situation—severe flooding in the upper portions of the
Midwest. The act was not originally intended to surpass the scope or intent
of earlier efforts, and it received little attention or fanfare at the time
(Bourgin 1983). But the Disaster Relief Act followed a series of other
congressional provisions, which identified the responsibilities of various
federal agencies and established the intergovernmental context of disaster
relief. And perhaps more important, congressional leaders themselves soon
began to regard the act as a precedent-setting piece of legislation.

The 1950 Disaster Relief Act delineated the first general, national-level
policy for providing emergency relief (Bourgin 1983). As a result, it established a framework for governmental disaster assistance that has essentially
remained in place since that time. This act's provisions have had a tremendous impact on all subsequent governmental activity in this policy area.

Throughout the 1950s, 1960s, and 1970s, Congress passed a series of
laws that expanded the scope of national governmental responsibility in
disasters. Federal assistance was extended to additional population groups

(such as farmers living in rural areas and disaster victims living in the U.S. territories). Legislation also made new forms of relief available, including temporary housing, emergency shelters, legal services, unemployment insurance, food coupons, and small business loans.[7] In addition, the basic governmental approach to natural disasters shifted away from its earlier emphasis on "structural" controls to "nonstructural" measures. Instead of funding construction projects that would strengthen or rebuild physical barriers and frameworks, such as dams, levees, and sea walls, a greater emphasis was placed on keeping people out of hazard-prone, high-risk areas through zoning laws, building codes, and land-use regulations. By the late 1960s, existent public policies forced individuals (through zoning laws, building construction codes, etc.) to assume more responsibility for where and how they lived.

The shift in governmental policy was consolidated in the 1970s. Congress passed several major relief acts that integrated earlier efforts and expanded the scope of the government's responsibilities. In particular, the Disaster Relief Act of 1974, along with subsequent amendments, established the precedent for a new wave of federal policy. The 1974 act institutionalized efforts to mitigate against, instead of simply respond to, major disaster events. It also contained provisions requiring local, state, and federal agencies to develop strategies aimed at preventing future catastrophes. Furthermore, it stressed a "multihazard" approach to disasters. The latter perspective holds that instead of designing different policies for each particular kind of disaster, governmental efforts should be capable of handling *all* kinds of hazards—both natural and man-made.

By the late 1970s, a fairly comprehensive set of public disaster assistance programs existed. The very number of programs was problematic, however, because administrative responsibilities were divided among a variety of departments and governmental entities. This was particularly true at the national level, where many federal agencies were involved, at least in part, in some disaster relief activity (Popkin 1990). Criticisms of the existing system were common: There seemed to be little (if any) coordination of governmental efforts. It was also extremely difficult to determine exactly who was in charge of disaster relief. This was compounded by the fact that the responsibility for disaster relief at the national level had repeatedly shifted from one agency to the next. For example, in 1950 the Housing and Home Finance Administration (an independent agency) was placed in charge of disaster assistance; in 1953 disaster-relief activities were reassigned to the Federal Civil Defense Administration; in 1958 the Office of Civil and Defense Mobilization was created to handle the nation's emergency relief and response functions; in 1961 the Office of Emergency Planning (later renamed the Office of Emergency Preparedness) was established in the Executive Office of the President to coordinate the nation's civil defense and natural disaster efforts; then in 1973 major disaster-related responsibilities were divided up and distributed among three agencies—the Federal Disaster Assistance Administration, the Defense Civil Preparedness Agency, and the Federal Preparedness Agency (May 1985b). There was widespread support for developing a more organized, cohesive emergency management process (Stratton 1989).

Consequently, the Carter administration issued Reorganization Plan #3 in 1978. This plan focused directly on the structure, management, and operations of the government's disaster-relief programs. It created an entirely new administrative body, the Federal Emergency Management Agency (FEMA), to lead the governmental effort. The plan gave FEMA the primary responsibility for (1) mobilizing federal resources, (2) coordinating federal efforts with those of state and local governments, and (3) managing the efforts of the public and private sectors in disaster responses. For the first time, emergency management functions at the national level were centralized in one governmental agency.

Ten years later, in 1988, Congress passed the Robert T. Stafford Disaster Relief and Emergency Assistance Act. The Stafford act clarified inconsistencies in past policies—for example, it refined the definition of an "emergency" situation, and it expanded further the responsibilities and obligations of public institutions during natural emergencies. It emphasized the importance of mitigation and preparedness activities that would occur before a disaster struck, as well as the more traditional response and relief functions of governmental agencies that unfold after a disaster has occurred. In addition, the Stafford act established a process to guide when and how the government would become involved in disaster situations. More specifically, it delineated how the response would move from the local level, through the state, up to the national government.

Since the passage of the Stafford act, there have been no major legislative or statutory revisions in governmental policy;[8] however, there have been administrative elaborations and additions. In reaction to intense criticism in the late 1980s, the Federal Emergency Management Agency began working on a new set of guidelines and directives for the federal government. The guidelines, called the Federal Response Plan, were completed in April 1992 and presented as a cooperative agreement between twenty-six federal agencies and the American Red Cross.

The Federal Response Plan is a blueprint for coordinating and mobilizing federal resources in disaster situations. It provides more detail on the functions and activities of various federal agencies during large-scale natural disasters (FEMA 1992b). It also groups together the various kinds of emergency assistance available to public organizations and private citizens, and it identifies a lead federal agency for each of these functional areas. Moreover, it specifies a process whereby the resources of the federal government can be deployed more quickly and efficiently, particularly during large-scale natural disasters. Overall, the Federal Response Plan delineates the national government's roles and responsibilities when responding to a disaster or an emergency.

Clearly, both the level and scope of governmental activity in this policy area have changed dramatically over the years. Today the government provides a host of services and benefits so that public institutions, private companies, and individuals can cope with natural emergencies. A standard set of policies and procedures has been developed enabling the government to deal with any disaster, no matter where or when it occurs. Public institutions now play a direct role in helping citizens prepare for and respond to natural emergencies.

Parallels between Disasters and Other Policy Areas

The government's involvement in disaster relief parallels several broader trends in American politics and policymaking. Although we tend to think of natural disasters as unusual and unique events, they have a lot in common with other public policy issues. This is true in terms of both the nature of the events and the development of governmental actions intended to deal with them.

Unquestionably, the United States has undergone a tremendous growth in the size and scope of government. In 1942, public expenditures totaled $44,602 million (U.S. Bureau of the Census 1952); in 1992, governmental expenditures exceeded $2,488 billion (U.S. Bureau of the Census 1994). Not only does the government spend more today than it did at the midpoint of the twentieth century, it also allocates money toward many more issues and problems. Consequently, one could argue that the government's growing involvement in disasters is simply a manifestation of the larger trend toward greater public-sector responsibilities and obligations.

Another common feature of both disaster-assistance policy and other public activities is the trend toward greater involvement by the national government relative to the state and local levels. As explained earlier, the federal government began to play a more active role in disaster relief and recovery efforts during the 1930s. In 1950, a basic framework for public activity was established; as part of this, the federal government was allowed to direct and coordinate assistance efforts in extraordinarily severe disaster situations. By the late 1970s, it was necessary to consolidate and coordinate the national government's actions; in response, the Federal Emergency Management Agency was established in 1979. When the federal government creates a new administrative unit designed to deal with a particular kind of problem, it is a sign that the issue has become a permanent addition of the federal government's policy agenda (Seidman and Gilmour 1986). Therefore, the creation of FEMA reveals the extent to which national-level organizations are involved in disaster situations. Clearly, the focus of public policy activity has shifted away from subnational authorities to the federal government.

The history of governmental involvement in disasters also reveals the highly reactive nature of American public policymaking. Throughout American history, major disasters have been the prime stimulants of governmental relief activity. This was certainly true during the early years of the United States when disaster-assistance legislation was tied directly to specific disaster-related events. Funds and technical assistance were provided to the victims of a particular hurricane, flood, or tornado, and the programs disappeared as soon as their immediate mission was accomplished. More recent policy expansions and additions in this area have had more general objectives, but they still tend to be enacted following major natural disasters. For example, Congress passed PL 89-339 in 1965, which was commonly known as the Hurricane Betsy relief program. Similarly, PL 92-385, commonly referred to as the Hurricane Agnes relief program, was enacted in 1972 (May 1985b). Despite their names, both statutes established ongoing procedures and broader principles for the governmental-response process. They established standard operating procedures that remained in effect long after the disaster situations that created them had faded. Even though the specific content of federal disaster policy has broadened in scope, the evolution of these policies occurs in reaction to particular disaster events.

It is perfectly understandable that disaster relief policy has developed in this manner. Events such as hurricanes, floods, tornadoes, and earthquakes often receive a great deal of media attention. And they produce exactly the kinds of problems, issues, and conditions that are likely to prompt an immediate public-sector response. In sum, they easily qualify as "crisis" situations. The policy literature is filled with instances in which a specific crisis has triggered a governmental action. For example, a crisis in the late 1950s, the Soviet Union's orbiting of the first space satellite (*Sputnik*), led to the passage the National Defense Education Act in 1958. Similarly, the Love Canal crisis in the late 1970s prompted the enactment of the Compensation and Liability Act (the Superfund program) in 1980. Unfortunately, crisis situations usually do not sustain long-term public and governmental interest.

This is certainly the case with natural disasters. After the immediate problems and disruptions are resolved, the political system moves on to address different, more pressing concerns. Hence there are few demands or pressures on public officials to maintain ongoing relief programs.

In fact, natural disasters are precisely the kinds of issues that are likely to go through the issue attention cycle identified by Anthony Downs. They do not usually affect a majority of the population; they require substantial financial and physical resources in order to deal with them effectively; and they lose their fascination, uniqueness, and charm very quickly. Moreover, most people simply do not like to think about these events unless they are directly confronted with them. When a disaster occurs, the public wants "something" done immediately. But once action is taken, there is a tendency to put these problems out of mind in order to deal with other, more tangible, and less troubling situations.

Finally, the government's fundamental approach to disaster situations has evolved over the years. Initially, the content and objectives of policy were strictly reactive in nature; the government took action only after a disaster occurred, and its involvement was highly limited in scope and time. Current governmental policies place much greater emphasis on proactive measures, such as preparing American society and specific local communities for emergencies before they arise (Comfort 1988). In particular, the government tries to emphasize policies and procedures that will prevent or mitigate against the occurrence of severe disaster situations. Again, other public policy areas have shown comparable trends. For example, public health-care programs currently stress measures intended to prevent unnecessary and costly medical problems from developing. Similarly, many of the government's environmental policies aim to protect wildlife, plant life, and public lands so that they do not become endangered in the first place.

As is the case with all public policy areas, the government finds it extremely difficult to shift its focus in disaster-relief activities. To begin, there are the ever-present pressures of incrementalism on governmental decision making. Past policy responses become entrenched, and they provide the firm basis for subsequent governmental activity (Lindblom 1959; Wildavsky 1964). Incrementalism is a pervasive, conservative force on governmental disaster relief policymaking, as it is on virtually all public policymaking. In addition, public sentiment may deter public officials from pursuing alternative, more preventive strategies for emergency management. Citizens may not want the government to enact stronger zoning laws or building codes if these measures prohibit them from living or working in desirable (but hazard-prone) areas. Finally, natural disasters produce the kinds of situations that inhibit policy change. Disaster-stricken populations want the government to respond immediately to their conditions. There is simply no time to consider new or different policy alternatives. Consequently, public officials find it more expedient to pursue "old" policies" that enable them to make quick, almost automatic, decisions.

Nevertheless, a shift in the governmental approach to natural disasters has occurred across all governmental levels within the United States. This is true for two basic reasons. First, it is simply more cost effective to prevent a natural catastrophe from occurring than it is to deal with its consequences. Although mitigation programs require time, money, and resources, they can produce substantial economic payoffs. For example, the establishment of stricter building codes and regulations in disaster-prone areas has saved millions of dollars in property damages. Warning and evacuation procedures have also prevented the unnecessary loss of human life in a number of disaster situations. Thus the benefits—measured in both economic and physical terms—of preventive measures clearly outweigh their costs.

A second reason for the shift in governmental policy stems from changes in the definition of what constitutes a *disaster* situation. Events such as oil spills (the *Exxon Valdez* incident), toxic-waste mishaps (Love Canal), and chemical plant fires (the Union Carbide plant in Bhopal, India) are man-made situations; they are not the products of uncontrollable natural phenomena. In the past, human beings were simply incapable of causing situations comparable in scope and magnitude to natural catastrophes. As the previously mentioned events illustrate, however, this is no longer the case. Thus, modern relief efforts must anticipate "new" disasters as well as more traditional problems such as floods, droughts, and hurricanes. This, in turn, has placed new demands on the governmental agencies responsible for dealing with disaster situations (Kasperson and Pijawka 1985).

Government's Role in Addressing Natural Disasters

This chapter has addressed two major topics. First, natural disasters are discussed as major issues that are legitimate components of the policy agenda in the United States. Superficially, classifying natural disasters as "political" phenomena may seem strange, since their origins usually lie outside the realm of human capacity. Nevertheless, they share virtually all the characteristics of more traditionally recognized political issues. As a result, citizens naturally look to government for assistance when natural disasters strike.

The second concern addressed in this chapter has been the evolution of governmental disaster-response efforts. There have been two major trends in this area. One is the shift from limited, reactive relief programs to more comprehensive, proactive hazard mitigation policies. The other is the expansion of the federal government's role relative to states and localities. Both trends are fully consistent with more general principles and patterns of governmental decision making.

The major conclusion to be drawn from this chapter is a relatively simple one. Natural disasters can be viewed as public policy issues. As such, they can be treated like any other issue. In order to understand their effects on American society, it is necessary to pinpoint the particular problems that arise with natural disasters as well as the administrative structures designed to deal with them. This in turn helps explain how, why, and when governments become involved in disaster relief efforts. Ultimately, this background information will also help account for the success and failure of various governmental responses. In the next chapter, I begin to investigate these factors by examining the formal structure of the governmental response system for natural disasters in the United States.

Notes

1. Agenda building is sometimes called "agenda setting" in the public policy literature. Both terms represent the same process; they are used interchangeably in this study.

2. Peters (1993) identifies these four factors as the most important for an issue in the agenda-building process.

3. Downs (1972) showed how public attitudes toward the environment during the 1960s and 1970s went through an issue attention cycle. Subsequently, Peters and Hogwood (1985) traced the rise and fall of a number of other policy issues through this same cycle.

4. This is sometimes referred to as the "social construction" of problems (Best 1989; Northcott 1992; Berger and Luckmann 1967; Schneider and Ingraham 1993), "issue framing" (Iyengar 1991; Schon and Rein 1994), or "heresthetical political manipulation" (Riker 1986).

5. The political repercussions of failing to deal successfully with a crisis have been documented in other, man-made situations as well. For example, Apple (1992), Mathews (1992), and Pear (1992) provide discussions of the political fallout from the Los Angeles riots of 1991.

6. The word "disaster" is so powerful that it can be (and is) used to identify a situation that does not technically meet the strict definition of a crisis or an emergency. When a situation is described as a disaster, it is viewed with more urgency and significance.

7. For more complete accounts of disaster-relief legislation during this time period, see Bourgin (1983) and Popkin (1990).

8. There have been serious discussions, however, about the focus and impact of the government's disaster-relief policy. See, for example, the reports of the National Academy of Public Administration (1993) and the U.S. General Accounting Office (1993b).

3

The Governmental Response System

Every year, hundreds of natural disasters occur in the United States. Governmental institutions are called on to respond in virtually every case. The vast majority of these emergencies are handled at the local level, with only minimal involvement from state or federal governments. At times, however, higher levels of government play a prominent role in the disaster-assistance process. And there are some rare situations in which the federal government alone seems to be the focal point for all response and recovery activities. Thus the scope and nature of governmental activity vary greatly from one disaster to the next. Nevertheless, all governmental disaster-relief policies are supposedly guided by a single, overarching structure. This chapter examines the basic components and underlying assumptions of the emergency response system in the United States. A detailed understanding of this system is necessary before we can try to account for governmental efforts in specific disaster situations.

How the System Is Supposed to Work

The United States has an ongoing system intended to guide the governmental response to all natural disasters. The process works from the "bottom up." It begins at the local level and follows a series of prespecified steps up through the state and ultimately to the national government. Local, state, and national governments are supposed to share their emergency management responsibilities (May and Williams 1986). The higher levels of government are not intended to supersede or replace the activities of the lower levels. All three levels of government are supposed to develop coordinated, integrated emergency management procedures, and they should all participate in the process of implementing disaster-relief policies.

The Formal Structure of the Governmental Response

Municipal and county governments are the first link in the chain of the formal structure of the governmental response.[1] Their job is to deal with emergencies that occur within their jurisdictions. The basic assumption is that disaster response will be handled primarily by local law enforcement agencies and related organizations (e.g., ambulance services or civil defense coordinators). But natural disasters place exceptionally large burdens on these local officials; they are usually forced to look elsewhere for guidance and assistance with their response procedures.

In most instances, this outside assistance comes from the state and federal governments, which can provide disaster preparedness funds to local units. In doing so, most states require (or at least encourage) towns, cities, and counties to establish and support local emergency preparedness agencies (Mushkatel and Weschler 1985). This requirement is intended to impose some degree of regularity and structure on the first line of defense against natural disasters.

Emergency preparedness agencies are supposed to make sure that local communities are ready for disaster situations. Their most tangible product is a plan identifying the duties and responsibilities of all local officials during emergency situations. These plans are prepared by local officials to meet the needs, conditions, and situations of particular areas, but they also usually conform to certain guidelines imposed by the state and federal governments. After all, higher governmental levels often provide money and technical advice to help local officials prepare and maintain their emergency management plans (Rubin, Saperstein, and Barbee 1985; Rossi, Wright, and Weber-Burdin 1982). In return, they expect local governments to establish basic emergency preparedness and response procedures. Consequently, most local-level plans describe how citizens will be alerted to or warned about potential hazards, and they include procedures for evacuating or relocating the local populations in the event of an actual disaster. In addition, local plans usually specify how emergency rescue and response activities will be conducted by and coordinated across local organizations, as well as how local governments will obtain assistance from higher authorities if events exceed their capacity.

A fundamental assumption of the overall system is that many, if not most, disasters can be handled entirely by the local response organizations. Higher governmental levels are not supposed to become involved unless local-level resources are exhausted. When that occurs, the response process moves upward through one level of government at a time.

Generally speaking, the states mobilize extra resources and larger-scale organizations to deal with situations that local officials cannot handle on their own. The official responsibilities and obligations of the state government are usually set forth in a state emergency preparedness and response plan (Mushkatel and Weschler 1985). These plans vary somewhat from one state to the next, but they tend to have a number of common elements. Most state plans provide a framework to guide the deployment of statewide resources and support for local disaster-relief operations. In addition, they identify the responsibilities of various state officials (e.g., emergency preparedness personnel and law enforcement officials) in disaster situations. Related to this, the plans generally grant the governor unusually expansive powers for the duration of an emergency situation. Similarly, they identify the conditions under which the state's National Guard can be mobilized, and they specify how important resources (e.g., utility-repair services, power generators, water supplies) can be reallocated to affected areas of the state. The overall objective of the state's response plan is to ensure that there is an effective system for coordinating and supporting all emergency relief efforts within that state.

Each state is supposed to tailor its plan so that it can address its own specific priorities and needs. The response mechanisms that seem to be most effective for dealing with hurricanes are not necessarily those best suited for earthquakes, volcanic eruptions, or blizzards. Thus the state plans introduce a degree of flexibility into the respective response systems. This is absolutely necessary in order to deal with the diverse kinds of disasters that occur throughout the United States.

Each state is responsible for its own separate plan. The federal government, however, imposes some conditions that are uniform across the states. Although these requirements are not strictly enforced, they are preconditions with which a state must comply in order to receive federal financial assistance. Therefore, all states follow these guidelines in organizing their disaster-response systems (Rossi, Wright, and Weber-Burdin 1982).

The most prominent federal requirement on the states is intended to maximize the efficiency of the system. Within each state, a single agency must be placed in charge of emergency preparedness and relief. This state agency is responsible for coordinating all state-level activities. It also serves as the main liaison between local and federal relief efforts. Hence it occupies a vital, central position in the disaster-response process. The federal government uses this same requirement in other policy areas—for example, a single agency must be responsible for administering the Medicaid program at the state level. This gives the federal government one point of contact within each state, and it clarifies the intergovernmental structure of program development and implementation.

State and local officials are also required to attend training sessions conducted by the federal government. The professional backgrounds and previous experiences of state and local officials vary widely. So the federal training sessions provide at least a minimal level of uniform instruction in appropriate emergency management procedures.

The last step in the process is direct involvement by the federal government. The conditions under which the federal government can intervene are specified by the Disaster Relief Act of 1974 (PL 93-288) as amended by the Robert T. Stafford Disaster Relief and Emergency Assistance Act of 1988 (PL 100-707). These statutes specify that the national government cannot step into a natural disaster situation on its own. Instead the federal government can become involved only when a state or territorial (e.g., Puerto Rico, Guam) governor makes a formal request for assistance. When this occurs, all subsequent steps are delineated by the previously mentioned statutes.

A governor's request is first reviewed and evaluated by the Federal Emergency Management Agency (FEMA). Based on their reading of the situation, FEMA officials prepare a recommendation for the president. The president must officially decide whether the magnitude of a crisis really is beyond the capacity of state and local governments. If so, he issues a formal disaster declaration (U.S. General Accounting Office 1989).

A presidential disaster declaration has far-reaching consequences because it opens the door to all other federal assistance. The declaration specifies the geographic boundaries of the disaster area; thus it delineates exactly who is eligible for relief in the first place. The presidential declaration also contains an initial statement about the kinds of assistance that will be provided to the stricken areas. This is extremely important because it determines whether disaster victims will receive direct cash grants, housing supplements, emergency medical care, or all these things.

The presidential declaration is also vitally important to the directly affected population. It legitimizes their situation, and it is a necessary first step for obtaining federal aid. To the general public (i.e., those not directly affected by the disaster), the president's declaration is a significant piece of information. At a rather basic level, it signifies that a major event has occurred, requiring the resources of the federal government. The content of the presidential declaration structures popular perceptions about the nature and scope of the natural disaster.

Beyond its immediate effects, the president's disaster declaration also has a profound impact on the nature of subsequent relief efforts. Once a major disaster has been declared, the Federal Emergency Management Agency must appoint a Federal Coordinating Officer (FCO) to serve as the federal government's representative to the stricken area. In general, the

FCO is responsible for coordinating all subsequent response and recovery efforts. The FCO's position is delineated in federal statutes and regulations, but the specific responsibilities of the post are never explained in any detail. Consequently, this individual has a great deal of discretion over the nature and scope of governmental actions in a particular disaster situation. For example, the FCO can extend the boundaries of disaster areas beyond those originally defined by the president; alter and/or extend specific assistance requests to meet situations as they arise; and direct resources into particular parts of the disaster area to meet the needs of the affected population in the best possible manner. In sum, the FCO has a broad, open-ended grant of authority.

Of course the FCO does not act alone in organizing, directing, and implementing relief activities. Instead, he or she provides general direction to the activities of emergency management officials at the federal, state, and local levels. And the FCO works very closely with other personnel in the Federal Emergency Management Agency to mobilize all necessary and available resources. These federal officials start their work by signing an agreement with the governor of the affected state (Giuffrida 1985; McLoughlin 1985). This agreement covers several important topics. First, it includes a plan that delineates federal, state, and local responsibilities in the recovery effort. Second, it identifies the exact nature of the federal assistance that will be provided. And third, it specifies various ways that federal resources can be employed.

At this stage of the process, FEMA works directly with the state's emergency management officials. Here there are two key contacts: the state's emergency management agency and the State Coordinating Officer. Recall that each state is required by federal guidelines to establish and maintain a single agency for emergency management. This preexisting agency serves as one of the two major focal points for federal relief and assistance. The state's emergency management agency is expected to have the mechanisms in place that will enable it to channel all available resources to the disaster-stricken areas. The second state-level contact, the State Coordinating Officer, is also specified in federal regulations. Once a major disaster is declared, the governor of the affected state must appoint a State Coordinating Officer to serve as the state's counterpart to the Federal Coordinating Officer. This individual is responsible for organizing and mobilizing state and local relief efforts and for coordinating these efforts with those of the federal government. In theory, these two contacts should facilitate communications and interactions between state and federal officials as well as the overall implementation of disaster relief through the intergovernmental system.

In addition to coordinating efforts across governmental levels, FEMA serves as a clearinghouse for other federal assistance programs. Many ongoing national policies take on special relevance during disaster situations. Therefore, FEMA tries to link disaster victims with federal agencies that may be able to provide them with needed assistance. For example, it helps local businesses obtain loans from the Small Business Administration so that they can repair or replace damaged facilities. Similarly, it helps farmers and ranchers obtain emergency loans from the Farmers Home Administration. And FEMA can encourage the Internal Revenue Service to give disaster victims special consideration in filing their income tax returns. There are many other examples of this kind of activity. In every case, FEMA does not *control* the assistance that other federal agencies provide, but it does serve as a central point of contact. In this way, the disaster-relief system tries to make the most efficient use of previously existing governmental institutions and programs.

Along with its responsibilities for coordinating other agencies, FEMA administers several programs on its own. The agency can make temporary housing provisions, such as tents, mobile homes, or rent money, for people whose homes have been damaged or destroyed. It can distribute cash grants to individuals and families who are in need but are ineligible for other forms of aid. It can also make funds available to government agencies and private companies in order to restore or replace public facilities and property. Thus, FEMA acts as a direct source for certain kinds of assistance.

Finally, FEMA plays a key role in physically getting federal aid to disaster-stricken areas. One way it does so is by bringing in relief workers. FEMA maintains a nationwide registry of part-time, reserve personnel. When a major disaster occurs, it calls up these reservists and moves them into the affected area. But even with these reservists, FEMA does not have enough employees on its own; therefore, it asks state and local officials for their assistance in carrying out the federal effort. This assistance is assumed to be different from, but complementary with, the efforts that subnational governments make on their own behalf.

FEMA also provides important transportation facilities during the period following a natural disaster. The victimized population is often sorely in need of reconstruction and habitation materials, such as plywood, plastic sheeting, and safe drinking water. While these goods are often available elsewhere, major problems arise in their delivery to affected areas. FEMA has the major responsibility for obtaining and coordinating the necessary transport facilities. FEMA does not possess its own fleet of trucks, railroad cars, and so on. The agency is simply too small to justify maintaining such facilities on a day-to-day basis because they would go unused most of the time. Instead, FEMA calls on the federal and state agencies that have these resources readily available. These tend to be the U.S. Army, state National Guard units, and the federal Department of Transportation.

Another aspect of FEMA's responsibility involves public relations (Federal Emergency Management Agency 1993). Most victims simply do not know where to turn for help during the confusion that follows a major disaster. So FEMA sets up one or more Disaster Application Centers where the affected public can apply directly for aid. But disaster victims must know that these centers exist before they can use them. Therefore, FEMA uses the mass media: the agency runs commercials on television and radio stations, takes out advertisements in local newspapers, and disseminates informational pamphlets and brochures. Agency officials also try to make face-to-face contact with disaster victims. This is particularly important in rural areas where lines of communication are tenuous even in the best of times. In such instances, media-based efforts would simply miss the neediest victims. So case workers go into the stricken areas to locate and inform people who would otherwise be ignorant of relief procedures and opportunities.

FEMA is also an essential information source for state and local officials who are anxious to make aid applications for their own governmental units. Federal requirements for institutional relief and recovery are very difficult, lengthy, and confusing. Local officials who are already under a great deal of pressure are often overwhelmed with the paperwork required for federal assistance. FEMA personnel are specifically designated to assist them with this aspect of the relief effort. A major portion of their responsibilities is to explain the federal requirements and to help state and local officials collect the voluminous amount of documentation (primarily damage assessments) that is a precondition for federal aid. Thus, FEMA provides vital information to governmental officials as well as to the general public.

To summarize, the disaster-response system involves three different layers, corresponding to the local, state, and federal governments. As shown in Figure 3.1, each level is supposed to make a unique contribution to the overall system. Municipal, township, and county governments provide the first response to a disaster. If the state and national levels become involved, these local governments continue to identify and communicate the needs of stricken areas. The state supplies some aid in the form of money, manpower, and training, but its most important contribution is the development and execution of a comprehensive preparedness and response plan. This is intended to mobilize and coordinate activities across the entire state. Finally, the federal government can provide massive financial assistance, along with other essential resources. This last step is taken only when it is necessary to organize and implement large-scale relief efforts.

Figure 3.1. **Basic Structure of Intergovernmental Response System**

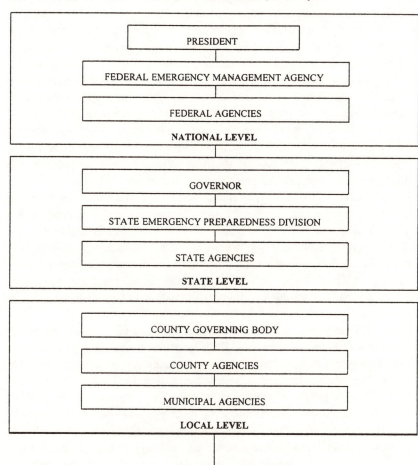

Notes: Figure 3.1 shows the major lines of communication. Others may develop in a disaster.
The size of the boxes does not represent the size of the agencies.

Basic Assumptions of the System

The description given in the preceding section shows that the governmental response system for natural disasters involves a very complicated, widespread structure. The viability of this structure is based on several crucial assumptions about the nature of disaster situations and the responsibilities of governmental institutions.

The first and most fundamental assumption is that natural disasters will occur in relatively limited geographic areas. Along with this, there is a belief that disaster preparation and response are best handled at the local level (Drabek 1984). Officials in city and county governments are most capable of anticipating and meeting the particular needs of their constituents; they should look elsewhere only when disaster-related events exceed their capabilities. Based on this reasoning, most natural disasters should be handled entirely at the local level. Of course it is anticipated that a few situations will require involvement by state governments. An even smaller proportion will exceed their capacities and require the resources of the federal government. It is assumed that this rolling, bottom-up process will be sufficient to handle any disaster situation that arises.

Second, local, state, and national governments are supposed to share emergency management responsibilities (Mushkatel and Weschler 1985; May and Williams 1986). No single level of government is to dominate or control the entire process. Even when the state and national governments become involved in a disaster situation, they are not to supersede or overpower the actions of lower levels. All three levels of government are supposed to continue working together to provide relief to disaster-stricken citizens.

Third, it is assumed that all governmental units take their emergency management obligations seriously. Each level of government must possess the administrative and technical resources necessary to perform its own disaster-relief responsibilities. Local, state, and federal officials must set aside funds for disaster-relief purposes; they must hire appropriate staff to develop and administer plans; and they must possess the requisite equipment and technical expertise to handle emergency situations. Lower levels of government can usually obtain some assistance from higher levels. Each level of government, however, still maintains a great deal of responsibility on its own.

A fourth crucial assumption (closely related to the third) is that the public officials directly involved in the process understand the structure and operation of the entire governmental response system. For example, local emergency management officials must know that they are to provide the first response to a disaster and that they are to guide any involvement by higher levels of government. At the same time, officials at the state and federal levels must understand that their role is supplementary in nature. They are to mobilize and coordinate the delivery of extra resources. In short, all relief officials must be knowledgeable about their own roles and responsibilities. They must also be aware of how their actions relate to those of others involved in the emergency management process.

Fifth, the Federal Emergency Management Agency can hold the state and local governments responsible for their actions during the relief process. FEMA is a relatively small administrative unit, so it is forced to rely heavily on the personnel and resources of state and local governments. In effect, FEMA views a disaster-stricken state government as the grantee for federal funds. The state is actually responsible for determining emergency relief eligibility and for distributing resources to those who qualify. But FEMA holds the state accountable for its actions, and it also determines how much the state and local governments must contribute to offset the nonfederal share. For these reasons, FEMA must try to obtain the cooperation and participation of relevant state and local governments (Schneider 1990).

Finally, it is assumed that people outside the immediate relief system—political leaders, private individuals, and other governmental officials—understand how the disaster-response system operates. Emergency management officials are primarily responsible for organizing, coordinating, and mobilizing the governmental response. But they cannot possibly perform all disaster-relief activities themselves. Other governmental agencies, private organizations, and individual citizens, therefore, must be involved in the process. Serious problems invariably arise when non-emergency management personnel do not understand the preestablished framework, when they consciously ignore it, or when they deliberately take steps to circumvent standard operating procedures. An effective disaster response can be mounted only when everyone abides by the overall framework of the multilevel emergency preparedness system (McLoughlin 1985).

How the System Really Works

The previously described system depicts how the governmental response is *supposed* to work. Ideally, there exists a well-coordinated, integrated management system that will automatically handle each and every emergency, no matter when or where it occurs. In reality, the process operates quite differently. Overall, the existing governmental response system is more accurately described as disconnected, uncoordinated, underfunded, and discredited. There are several reasons for this negative characterization.

First, different perspectives often develop across different governmental levels. Local, state, and national officials tend to view the process strictly from their own vantage points in the system. Local and state officials feel that their responsibilities have ended once they pass the response up to the federal government (Riley 1989). But federal officials view the system as a team effort in which the three units of government have separate but clearly interdependent and continuous obligations (Hall 1989). These differing role perceptions affect the way the entire governmental response process operates. When all three governments share the same view of the process, the whole governmental response system operates very smoothly and effectively. When perceptions differ across governmental levels, there are likely to be complications, confusion, and even breakdowns in the disaster-response effort.

Second, emergency management officials are often unable to coordinate the actions of other participants in the process (U.S. General Accounting Office 1991). Theoretically, they are supposed to mobilize and organize available resources within their respective jurisdictions. But they simply cannot control the actions of other public officials, political leaders, and private citizens. For example, a county civil defense director has little influence over the chief of the local police force. Similarly, the head of the state emergency preparedness agency cannot make the director of the state social service agency respond to the health and welfare needs of disaster victims. And the head of FEMA cannot direct the operations of other federal agencies, such as the Department of Agriculture or the Department of Transportation. There are simply too many agencies and officials involved in disaster-relief operations. Each has its own set of rules, regulations, and policies. As a result, emergency management officials find it difficult, and sometimes even impossible, to coordinate all this governmental activity.

Third, disaster-relief operations are severely underfunded throughout the entire intergovernmental system (Mushkatel and Weschler 1985; Cigler 1988; Rubin and Popkin 1990; Waugh 1990). At the local level, many emergency management agencies operate on limited budgets, with part-time personnel. The situation is not much better at higher governmental levels. In most states, the emergency preparedness division is usually the last agency to receive any funding or resources. Similarly, FEMA has a staff of only several thousand trained reservists who can be deployed to any given disaster situation and a relatively small operating budget to cover all of its day-to-day, natural disaster–related activities (Federal Emergency Management Agency 1993; U.S. General Accounting Office 1993b). Moreover, the funds available to FEMA for major emergencies—contained in the Disaster Relief Fund—are usually kept so low that Congress must appropriate additional money before FEMA can mobilize an adequate response (Federal Emergency Management Agency 1993). Emergency management for natural disasters is simply not considered a top priority at any level of government.

Finally, emergency management operations have little respect or credibility within the overall governmental system. The general impression is that the officials who work in this area are untrained and unprepared for their duties (Cook 1989). There have been repeated complaints that emergency management agencies are nothing more than dumping grounds for old military personnel or political hacks who cannot find other employment (Bandy 1989a; Miller 1992; Wamsley 1993). Instead of recruiting individuals who could provide leadership and direction during times of crises, emergency management agencies seem to attract personnel who are lackadaisical, lazy, and uncaring (Democratic Study Group 1989). This leads to the overall impression of an inept, ineffective emergency management system.

On paper, there is a well-organized, efficient system to guide governmental activity during natural disasters. In reality, this system is neither clearly articulated, completely supported, nor fully developed. This creates problems for those involved in the response process even before a disaster occurs. These problems are exacerbated by the pressures and strains that almost always arise in a natural disaster situation. The causes and consequences of this tension are examined in the next chapter.

Note

1. There is no single statute, regulation, or document that describes the structure of the entire intergovernmental disaster-response system. Instead, each level of government has policies and procedures that identify its roles and responsibilities in the process, as well its relationships with other governmental entities. I constructed the organizational framework presented in this analysis to show how all three levels of government are supposed to interact with one another. This structural arrangement matches the representations found in the academic literature (May and Williams 1986; Stratton 1989; Popkin 1990) and coincides with the descriptions provided by emergency management personnel (Bourgin 1983; McAda 1989; Peterson 1992).

4

Human Behavior and Governmental Activity in Disasters: Two Sets of Norms

This chapter examines the various norms, expectations, and values that guide human behavior during disaster situations. In everyday life, people rely heavily on norms to help determine their own activities and their interactions with others. Norms delineate a set of stable and comprehensive expectations for human behavior. They help individuals differentiate between acceptable and unacceptable conduct on a regular, day-to-day basis. Norms also serve as fundamental building blocks or frameworks for organizational and institutional life (Simon 1976, 100). They give meaning, direction, and significance to individual participation in group activities. As a result, norms are key mechanisms for societal integration and cohesion. By delineating the guiding principles for both individual and group behavior, norms provide continuity, order, and stability within a society (Durkheim 1895, 1912; Sherif 1936; Smelser 1964).

But during natural disasters, the regular, routine modes of human behavior are severely disrupted. In such situations, people often question the legitimacy and viability of established principles, and they may develop new norms and behavior patterns to guide their actions. The problem is that these newly emergent norms often conflict with existing governmental policies and procedures. When this kind of conflict arises, it has a direct impact on the disaster-response process. Let us look more closely at the two dominant sets of norms that exist in natural disasters.

Bureaucratic Norms: The Governmental Response Process

As we have seen, the governmental response system is a complicated amalgam of various organizations, plans, regulations, and individuals. Taken together, the components of the system define the role of public institutions in natural disaster situations. More specifically, the system identifies the nature and scope of governmental intervention; it delineates a basic framework for intergovernmental and intragovernmental cooperation; and it provides direction for all subsequent governmental activity. If we look at this system as a whole, it clearly possesses the same basic characteristics as most other governmental institutions and organizations. Stated simply, the disaster-response system is a bureaucracy, and it is dominated by the same norms commonly found in that type of structure.

The Characteristics of Bureaucracy

The term "bureaucracy" is often used in a derogatory, negative manner. To many Americans, it represents a complicated maze of rules, procedures, and/or organizations that are unnecessary, duplicative, and wasteful (Niskanen 1971; Goodsell 1985). Bureaucracy is synonymous with rigidity, red tape, confusion, and indifference. It is often publicly identified as a main cause of governmental inefficiency, waste, and unresponsiveness (Hill 1992).

But the term "bureaucracy" also has a more technical meaning. It represents a general way of organizing human activity so that complex tasks can be carried out in a coordinated, routine manner (Weber 1958; Downs 1967; Wilson 1989). Bureaucracy enables people to combine their efforts and achieve social objectives that would otherwise be unattainable. Consequently, bureaucratic organizations exist in all contemporary societies, and they are integral components of all modern governmental systems (Peters 1989).

In order to be considered a bureaucracy, an administrative structure must exhibit several basic characteristics.[1] The exact nature of these characteristics varies from one analyst to the next (Weber 1958; Downs 1967; Simon 1976; Rourke 1984; Wilson 1989; Meier 1993). Nevertheless, four of the most commonly identified bureaucratic properties are (1) clearly defined objectives, (2) a division of labor, (3) a formal structure underlying the process and tying together the various component organizations, and (4) set policies and procedures guiding organizational activity. Let us consider each of these characteristics in turn.

First, bureaucratic organizations are established to address specific problems and achieve clearly articulated goals. Of course, all organizations, regardless of size and substantive focus, have similar general purposes: They are created to reach collective objectives, which cannot be attained through the actions of individuals working on their own (Hill 1992). A bureaucracy, however, is different in that it represents a highly rationalized organizational form (Weber 1958). There must be a clear justification for the existence of a bureaucracy, and there must be explicitly stated purposes to direct bureaucratic operations. In short, the goals of bureaucratic activity must be known and clearly defined.

Second, bureaucratic organizations possess a clear division of labor. A bureaucracy brings together a large number of individuals in order to accomplish its prespecified goals and objectives. But each person who works in the bureaucracy cannot possibly perform all the organization's tasks. If someone attempted to do so, the result would be wasteful and redundant allocations of resources. Instead, each bureaucratic employee is assigned to a particular operation or function. This enables employees to concentrate their efforts and develop high levels of expertise in their respective spheres of activity. This in turn allows the bureaucracy to carry out relatively complex tasks in a rational, efficient manner.

A bureaucracy must, however, find some way of coordinating its employees' activities. If it fails to do so, the bureaucracy cannot achieve its organizational mission. This potential problem is addressed by the third characteristic—a formal structure that guides bureaucratic activity. Several different types of bureaucratic structures have been identified. At the one extreme, there is the centralized, hierarchical pattern that Weber (1958) and others (Taylor 1911; Gulick and Urwick 1937) identify as the hallmark of the classical bureaucracy. Here a definite chain of command exists throughout the entire organization: Decisions are made at the top, and they are implemented by lower-level officials. This results in a rigid, vertical bureaucratic structure. At the other extreme, there are bureaucracies that possess a decentralized structural form. Power, control, and responsibility are dispersed and spread throughout the organizational framework. Top-level officials are still leaders, but they coordinate rather than direct organizational activity. Lower-level bureaucrats do not simply follow orders; instead, they are directly involved in agency decision making (Kaufman 1969; Barzelay 1992). This creates a relatively flexible, horizontal bureaucratic structure. Of course, an infinite variety of structures fall somewhere in between these two extremes.[2] Even though there are many different kinds of bureaucratic structures, they all possess a common characteristic: an identifiable framework that links together all the specialized units and activities within the organization.

Finally, a bureaucracy operates on the basis of established policies and clearly designated procedures (Rourke 1984). The rules and guidelines necessary for achieving bureaucratic objectives are codified into a set of standard operating procedures. This expedites bureaucratic activities by reducing uncertainty about what is to be done in any given situation. Standard operating procedures also enhance communication within the organization. Bureaucratic employees can identify their respective superiors and subordinates; they know exactly to whom they report and to whom they give instructions. Standard operating procedures also facilitate the coordination of tasks. By clearly assigning responsibilities to administrative units and personnel, they reduce redundancy and minimize the duplication of efforts. Standard operating procedures allow organizations to treat similar cases in a uniform, expedient manner. This enhances bureaucratic effectiveness by reducing favoritism and inequitable treatment across different situations. Bureaucratic employees are expected to be familiar with the standard operating procedures related to their respective positions. When a situation arises, they are expected to use the rules, find the appropriate procedure, and apply it in a relatively straightforward, unambiguous fashion; improvisation is strongly discouraged. In summary, the formalization and institutionalization of rules is a critical bureaucratic attribute (Rourke 1984). It is intended to provide consistent, speedy, and effective policy implementation.[3]

The preceding four characteristics define an ideal bureaucracy. In reality, no organization fully conforms to this description. Instead, Anthony Downs (1967) describes "bureaucratization" as a continuum. The larger the number of bureaucratic traits manifested by an organization, the more closely it comes to becoming a complete bureaucracy. There are many organizational structures that possess most or all of these characteristics, and they clearly do adhere to a common set of norms. These norms provide guidance for individual and organizational activity. Moreover, they produce a certain style of administrative behavior that is quite distinctive. For obvious reasons, this style is called bureaucratic behavior. It is really this behavior or conduct that sets bureaucratic institutions and systems apart from all others.

Bureaucratic Norms in the Governmental Disaster-Response System

At least on paper, the governmental system for responding to natural disasters conforms precisely to the formal characteristics of a bureaucratic organization. First, the government's disaster-response process has four explicit objectives: (1) mitigating a disaster or preventing one from occurring in the first place, (2) preparing areas for potential emergency situations, (3) providing immediate relief after a disaster strikes, and (4) helping individuals and communities recover from the effects of natural disasters (McLoughlin 1985). These objectives were first advocated by the National Governors' Association in the late 1970s. Since that time, the federal government has become the strongest proponent of these principles (Giuffrida 1983; May 1985a; May and Williams 1986); it has encouraged all those involved in the process—particularly state and local governmental institutions—to adopt these objectives. As a result, most public agencies engaged in emergency management espouse these principles as their overall objectives.

Second, the disaster-response system definitely possesses a formal structure, composed of separate emergency management agencies at the local, state, and federal levels (Comfort 1988). The exact makeup and composition of these agencies does vary. The lead agency for the national government, the Federal Emergency Management Agency (FEMA), uses a core of full-time professionals on an everyday basis. During disaster situations, however, it calls on a larger group of "reservists" to augment its operations. At the state level, most emergency management agencies have extremely small staffs: they often "borrow" employees from other state agencies (e.g., highway construction personnel and social service workers) to perform important activities. Finally, many local jurisdictions cannot afford to have a permanent emergency management staff (Mushkatel and Weschler 1985; Cigler 1988). They use officials who are already serving in other capacities (e.g., firefighters and emergency rescue squads), or they temporarily activate private citizens as their emergency management personnel. Regardless of the specific composition of their staffs, these organizations coordinate governmental efforts within their respective jurisdictions. They also link the activities of one government level to those of the others. Essentially, emergency management agencies tie the entire response system together, providing structure and stability to governmental emergency relief operations. Thus the disaster-response system clearly falls near the bureaucratized pole of Downs's organizational continuum.

Third, there is an easily discernible division of labor within the disaster-response system. Each level of government has specific roles and responsibilities. As explained in the previous chapter, the overall framework works "from the bottom up" (Schneider 1990). Local governments are the first point of mobilization: they initiate governmental activity, and they provide a critical, ongoing link between private citizens and governmental resources (Rossi, Wright, and Weber-Burdin 1982; Rubin, Saperstein, and Barbee 1985). State governments are supposed to coordinate and support all emergency relief activities within their respective states. They also act as the primary intermediaries between local governments and federal agencies (Mushkatel and Weschler 1985). In addition, the federal government's role is to provide technical and financial aid to lower governmental units. Federal agencies are *not* supposed to step in and take over a situation. Their role is to stay in the background, providing general guidance, financial support, technical assistance, and coordination across governmental units (Federal Emergency Management Agency 1989b). This division of labor between the local, state, and national governments is intended to provide the most efficient utilization of public resources. Each level of government makes a unique contribution, and each must perform its functions in order to make the entire system work effectively.

Fourth, the disaster-response activities of public organizations are based on a set of formal policies and procedures. Some of these are derived from legislative statutes. For example, state and federal laws identify the conditions that have to exist in order for a response to move upward from the local level to the state and finally to the national level. At each step in the process, officials from the lower levels of government must formally request assistance from the next higher level. The laws also specify that the scope of the disaster must exceed the capacities of lower governmental units before requests for additional assistance can be made (U.S. Congress 1988). Of course, there is a degree of flexibility built into the process: administrators have some discretion in how they carry out their responsibilities. If they stray too far from their designated responsibilities, however, the institutionalized response process breaks down. As a result, there is considerable pressure to abide by standard routines.

Other operating procedures have been developed by the disaster-relief organizations themselves. For example, FEMA requires written damage assessments before it will disburse any relief refunds. It also requires verification of losses from individuals and groups seeking aid. While these are not statutory requirements, they have become permanent operating procedures mandated by official FEMA regulations (see the Federal Register 44CFR Part 206). The practice of combining statutory and administrative regulations is typical of all governmental operations in the United States. Legislative bodies set the broad parameters of public policies, while the public organizations involved in the actual implementation of services specify more precise guidelines (Lowi 1969; Rourke 1984).

Thus the governmental disaster-response system possesses the basic properties of a bureaucracy. It has a set of clearly defined objectives and principles. It has a formal structure that organizes organizational activity. It has a division of labor between national, state, and local governmental actors. And it uses a set of formal rules, procedures, and policies to guide its actions. These properties give order and stability to the governmental response process. Without them, the government would have serious difficulties responding to any disaster situation in a consistent or equitable manner.

Bureaucratic Pathologies

Despite their benefits and advantages, bureaucratic attributes can also constrain, or even completely thwart, organizational activity. When such problems arise, they are called "bureaucratic pathologies" (Rockman 1992). One such pathology is an overemphasis on organizational survival. After a bureaucracy has been in existence for some time, its focus and objectives may change. It can become more concerned with maintaining its own survival and less concerned with performing its initial functions. This is often depicted as a natural by-product or consequence of bureaucratic growth (Downs 1967).

Other bureaucratic pathologies are tied more directly to the structure of the organizational system (Thompson 1961). Bureaucracies with hierarchical frameworks are often unable to respond quickly or effectively because it takes too much time for information to flow up through the system and for instructions to flow back down. Such hierarchical systems are particularly cumbersome and slow when dealing with new or different kinds of problems. Bureaucracies with less hierarchical, more decentralized structures can react more adeptly to a variety of situations, but they experience serious difficulty trying to coordinate all their activities. In both instances, the result is delay and reduced effectiveness in meeting the bureaucratic organization's responsibilities.

There is also an inherent tension between the structure of a bureaucracy and its division of labor. Over time, bureaucratic units tend to develop higher levels of expertise in their preassigned areas of specialization (Peters 1981). But this tendency makes it more difficult to coordinate and control organizational activities. Employees focus more on the minutiae of their separate responsibilities and lose sight of the "big picture." This problem is compounded if there is any confusion whatsoever about how the system is structured or how responsibilities are assigned. In some cases, conflicts develop over which unit is responsible for a particular situation. In other instances, different units could be addressing the same problem simultaneously without any awareness of one another's activities (Downs 1967).

Finally, the formalization and institutionalization of procedures can also constrain bureaucratic behavior. Bureaucratic employees must abide by standard operating procedures. But they can get so caught up in following the rules that they fail to address the problems that are the organization's main responsibility. This leads to some of the most common complaints about bureaucratic behavior—overattention to detail, apparently needless paperwork, excessive rigidity, and indifference to the specific needs of their clientele groups (Barzelay 1992). Overly strict adherence to rules and procedures is often identified as the primary cause of bureaucratic nonresponsiveness.

Bureaucratic Pathologies and the Disaster-Response System

Like any other bureaucratic structure, the disaster-response system in the United States is susceptible to the effect of bureaucratic pathologies. First, survival considerations clearly dominate the thinking and activities of disaster-response officials. This is perhaps clearest at the federal level. The Federal Emergency Management Agency was initially created to deal with all kinds of catastrophic situations. Both nuclear attack and natural disaster–related activities were specifically placed under FEMA's jurisdiction because this seemed to be the most practical and efficient way of combining similar emergency-type operations (May and Williams 1986, 57). Over the years, however, FEMA began to focus much more attention on preparing the civilian population for nuclear war (National Academy of Public Administration 1993). This shift reflected the policy and funding priorities of the national leadership in the 1980s. Unfortunately, this severely reduced administrative attention and responsiveness to other disaster situations, natural or man-made. By the 1990s, it had produced an emergency management system that was overly attuned to nuclear-attack activities, even though the need for such activities was apparently waning.

A different problem occurred at the state and local levels. Since disasters occur infrequently, response personnel are forced to consolidate their offices with other governmental agencies. For example, local emergency preparedness offices are often combined with law enforcement or fire prevention agencies (Quarantelli 1988; Waugh 1990, 1994; Petak 1985). Similarly, state emergency preparedness departments are often responsible for general public safety programs. This guarantees the administrative survival of disaster-response personnel, but it broadens their responsibilities considerably (Mushkatel and Weschler 1985; Cigler 1988). They often have to scramble and hurriedly return to their original mission when a natural disaster actually does strike.

Response speed and coordination is a chronic problem for emergency management operations. Communications within the response structure are often unclear and disjointed as personnel try to address the most pressing problems. The difficulties are exacerbated by the fact that activities often have to be coordinated across a variety of distinct organizational units. External conditions are usually chaotic and highly stressful (Perry and Mushkatel 1984; Toulmin, Givans, and Steel 1989). All of this leads to organizational delay and confusion; in short, it slows down the disaster-response effort.

The disaster-relief system experiences division-of-labor problems because those involved often do not know exactly what their responsibilities are supposed to be. Moreover, they do not have a clear picture of how their actions fit into the entire process (Rubin, Saperstein, and Barbee 1985; U.S. General Accounting Office 1991). The net result is that any formal division of labor simply breaks down. Instead of a coordinated and efficient allocation of skills and responsibilities, the net result is a disorganized, incomplete, and redundant plethora of individual actions. This clearly reduces the effectiveness of the overall response.

Finally, bureaucratic indifference and red tape probably constitute the most frequently lodged complaints against the governmental response system (Applebome 1989; Branigin 1989a, 1989b; Kilborn 1993). Disaster victims are often distraught, impatient, and eager to restore their own life situations (Mydans 1994a; Fritsch 1994). They find it difficult, therefore, to understand the necessity of governmental reporting requirements and detailed bureaucratic procedures. This leads to mutual suspicion and even outright hostility among the parties at a disaster scene. Victims believe that bureaucrats are unfeeling and insensitive to their problems; emergency management personnel tend to view some of the victims as selfish and overly impatient (McAda 1989). As a result, FEMA—an organization that is explicitly designed to provide relief—is perceived as just another indifferent governmental entity (Morganthau and Springen 1992; Andrews 1992; Walden 1992).

Both the advantages and disadvantages of bureaucratic behavior must be kept in mind when considering the governmental response to natural disasters. On the one hand, bureaucratic characteristics have a positive impact. They provide order, consistency, and predictability to governmental operations. This allows emergency response organizations at the local, state, and national levels to respond to disasters in a relatively uniform manner, no matter when or where they occur. On the other hand, bureaucratic characteristics can bring about serious negative consequences. This kind of behavior can produce rigidity, duplication, and confusion in the delivery of governmental services. Relief agencies may be unable to respond quickly, effectively, or efficiently to some disaster situations.

When will bureaucratic behavior lead to positive results, and when will it produce negative results? Before we can answer this question, we must first examine several important aspects of disaster situations. Natural catastrophes often create problems that are extremely difficult to handle. Any administrative system would have trouble responding to such events. But bureaucratic institutions face a special challenge. Natural disasters can produce behavior patterns within the affected population that are almost directly antithetical to those found in bureaucratic systems.

Emergent Norms: Human Behavior
in Natural Disaster Situations

On a day-to-day basis, people naturally develop beliefs and expectations about their own lives and about their interactions with others. These expectations help guide and coordinate patterns of activity during normal, routine situations (Merton 1957). For example, a person goes to the end of the grocery store checkout line to purchase food, drinks, and other items. This behavior facilitates service and provides coordination to an activity that invariably involves several people pursuing individual goals. Similarly, drivers learn to comply with traffic signals because they impose order on vehicular activity, they lead to reliable predictions about other drivers' behaviors, and they are legal requirements.

The mere existence of a dominant set of social norms does not imply that individuals always agree with their merit and usefulness. Nor does it mean that people will always obey the accepted rules (Turner and Killian 1972, 1987). There may be times when individuals cut into a checkout line ahead of others because they are in a particular hurry or simply believe there are no serious sanctions against doing so. Similarly, there may be occasions when a driver runs through a stoplight. Other traffic may be nonexistent, rendering the stop unnecessary in the first place, or there may not be a police officer in the vicinity to observe the violation. But these are easily recognizable exceptions to more general patterns of behavior. Most people abide by traditional norms and values because they accept them as beneficial and useful for facilitating interactions with others. Thus, traditional norms, values, and expectations generate a sense of continuity and regularity for members of society. They also provide stability and order for the larger social and political systems.

The Effects of Unanticipated Events

Human interactions are usually guided by the existing social norms. Standard forms of interaction, however, are upset when an unanticipated event occurs. Many different situations and conditions technically can qualify as unanticipated events. The sudden death of a relative, for example, can transform a family's everyday world into one of shock, confusion, and pain. Similarly, a dramatic change in a colleague's personality might leave a co-worker confused or unsure about how to react to this person. What is important is that the people who are immediately affected by such events did not expect them to occur; they have no standardized way of dealing with them. But events like those just mentioned are relatively limited in scope. They do not lead to fundamental transformations in ongoing social norms. Such personal disruptions are usually handled by individuals or small groups who maintain (as much as possible) their adherence to traditional norms in their interactions with others (such as nonfamily members or other co-workers in the two examples mentioned here).

Other unanticipated events are so severe that universally understood and accepted values no longer appear to be relevant. The people most directly affected are confronted with previously unimaginable and often incomprehensible conditions. The natural response is for people to try to figure out what has happened to them. Some individuals may wander around aimlessly in search of explanation and guidance. Others may resort to unusual behavior, such as screaming or hysterical crying. And a few people may engage in extremely unconventional or even illegal acts, such as looting and rioting, because they feel it is no longer necessary or useful to conform to traditional behavioral standards. Human behavior during such large-scale situations may appear to be abnormal and chaotic. It is not, however, completely random. To predict *precisely* how individuals will react to unanticipated events is impossible. But there does appear to be a relatively invariant sequence of behaviors that occurs in nearly every such disruptive situation. This phenomenon is known as *collective behavior.*

Collective behavior is defined as noninstitutionalized interactions and behavior patterns (Blumer 1957; Smelser 1964; Turner and Killian 1972, 1987; Weller and Quarantelli 1973).[4] It can occur anytime there is a disruption in everyday, ordinary life. Collective behavior, however, is most likely to arise when the disruptions are large enough to intrude on interpersonal interactions and broader social activities. In such instances, the irrelevance of traditional social guidelines easily facilitates the emergence of new norms and values—that is, the collective behavior itself.

Natural disasters are certainly some of the most obvious, sudden, and significant environmental disruptions that can occur (Fritz 1961; Barton 1969; Kreps 1986; Drabek 1986). They differ from such unexpected events as automobile accidents in that they can affect large numbers of people in a relatively short period of time. Natural disasters also differ from other collective behavior situations that allow people to decide if and how they will respond (e.g., an individual's decision to participate in and subsequent actions during a riot); of course, disasters do not give participants a choice about their involvement. Disasters cause large-scale disruptions to everyday activities and social life, forcing many people to deal with them. Thus, natural disasters are exactly the kinds of events that make people question the relevance of existing norms and values. This in turn facilitates the emergence of collective behavior.

According to some of the prominent analysts in the field (Quarantelli and Dynes 1977; Harvey and Bahr 1980; Perry and Mushkatel 1984; Stallings and Quarantelli 1985; Turner and Killian 1972, 1987), there are four basic components to human interaction during a collective behavior situation: milling, rumor circulation, keynoting, and emergent norms.[5] These four components tend to occur sequentially, in the previously mentioned order. But during some disaster situations, these activities can overlap to some extent, or they may even occur almost simultaneously. Each of these activities plays a distinct and extremely important role in the development of collective behavior. Therefore, it is useful to consider each of the four components separately.

Milling

As the immediate disaster recedes, people are confronted with situations and problems that lie outside the bounds of normal, everyday existence. Damaged houses, blocked roads, contaminated water supplies, and power outages all contribute to this unprecedented environment. The natural and immediate reaction that most individuals experience is, "How do we deal with this?" This leads to the first stage of collective behavior, called "the milling process" (Turner and Killian 1972, 1987).

Milling is defined as the widespread search for meaning and appropriate standards of behavior among the affected population. Of course, the individuals who actually engage in this activity probably do not recognize that they are doing so. Nevertheless, numerous case studies of collective behavior situations demonstrate that the milling process definitely occurs (Fritz 1957; Dynes and Quarantelli 1968; Drabek 1968; Perry and Mushkatel 1984).

Milling is most pronounced when existing organizations and institutional procedures are inadequate or inappropriate for the situation at hand. It is further exacerbated by breakdowns in communication and transportation systems. The latter prevent authorities from establishing and maintaining social order and from reaffirming the relevance of traditional (predisaster) behavioral norms. In summary, the milling process represents a situation in which people do not know how to act because their usual sources of guidance are unavailable, are irrelevant to current conditions, or both.

Rumors

During the milling process, new forms of interaction and communication develop among the population affected by the disaster (Quarantelli 1983). People emerge from their homes and shelters and begin talking to one another. They want some kind of explanation for their situation. If they do not receive an appropriate or believable account from traditional authorities, they look elsewhere. They place more reliance on informal and unconventional channels of communication. This facilitates the development of rumors.

Rumors may appear to be random and sometimes malicious accounts of ongoing situations. Yet they serve an extremely important function. Rumors are a means of transmitting critical information about the nature of the disaster situation within the affected population. This information may be simplistic, incomplete, and even incorrect. Nevertheless, it gives disaster victims some guidance and structure in a highly unusual, uncertain situation.

Keynoting

At any given point in the milling process, there will probably be many rumors in circulation. As the situation evolves, some rumors are discarded (i.e., people stop reporting them), while others become distorted and change into new rumors. Over time, certain ideas and features come to be repeated more frequently and hence are emphasized by the participants in the rumor process. The selection of specific ideas, and the concurrent elimination of others, is called "keynoting" (Smelser 1963; Turner and Killian 1972, 1987; Wright 1978). In some situations, keynoting occurs rather quickly. The nature of the event and/or the preexisting attitudes of the affected population give some images a definite advantage. For example, the observable occurrence of widespread looting would help legitimize rumors about the breakdown of public authority; obviously, it would also negate rumors about the reestablishment of the existing social order. Similarly, isolated rural residents could easily interpret the slow pace of response efforts as evidence of society's indifference and hostility to their plight.

In other situations, the keynoted image develops more slowly, as it takes people more time to sort through all possible explanations for their current predicaments. Ironically, this tends to occur in areas where some communications are available and citizens have at least partially prepared for the disaster. In such cases, people simply have more information, knowledge, and understanding of what has happened. Nevertheless, it is still difficult for the affected population to settle on a single, consensual explanation of the situation. The severity and complexities of disaster situations mitigate against shared perceptions or beliefs. For example, consider the attitudes and reactions of people who live along an unstable geological fault line. Such individuals are generally aware of their precarious situation, and they are usually at least somewhat prepared for the occurrence of seismic events. Yet their lives are still severely disrupted and unhinged when an earthquake actually occurs. At the same time, it is also easy to imagine that many previously unanticipated problems would slow down and inhibit the effectiveness of relief efforts. For example, victims might find that evacuation routes are blocked or that emergency supplies have been rendered unusable.

In cases like these, general, comprehensive explanations of the disaster situation would not be clear or immediately forthcoming.

Regardless of the speed with which it occurs, keynoting is extremely important. The keynoting information identifies the specific themes and symbols that will eventually give meaning to the disruptive situation. Keynoting provides potential direction for individual and group activity. In time, it is the keynoted, or shared, image of the situation that enables the affected population to "end" the milling process.[6]

Emergent Norms

The dominant symbols and ideas that emerge from keynoting activity serve as a new set of norms for guiding behavior. These emergent norms help disaster-stricken individuals understand what has happened to them. Newly developed norms give people the reassurance they need to cope with their conditions and circumstances, and they indicate the appropriate courses of action for disaster victims to pursue. As the situation stabilizes, and predisaster conditions are restored, traditional norms come back into play, and the emergent norms are discarded. In summary, they function as acceptable, albeit fairly temporary, guides for human interaction during a disaster situation (Drabek 1970).

Collective behavior and the attendant development of emergent norms is a perfectly natural phenomenon. As Quarantelli (1983) and others (Dynes 1970; Drabek 1984; Sugiman and Misumi 1988) have written, it reflects an innate human desire to understand and "resolve" disruptive, disorienting conditions. Essentially, people want to comprehend their own environment. So they search for explanations that give "meaning" to their current situations (Stallings and Quarantelli 1985). Moreover, individuals engage in new forms of activity and behavior in order to facilitate the development of reasonable explanations for their predicaments. When these innovative behavior patterns stabilize, they tend to become institutionalized as emergent norms. The latter facilitate a return to "normal" life.

The human response to disasters centers on the development of emergent norms. These norms are the direct consequence of the larger, ongoing collective behavior process. Natural disasters are triggering events: they set the entire process into motion. Milling usually begins immediately after a disaster strikes—as soon as it is clear that traditional norms and institutions are irrelevant to the current situation. The duration of the milling process varies, depending on several factors, such as the scope of the disaster, the degree of interpersonal interaction among the affected population, and the specific content of rumor communication. Within the constraints imposed by the disaster, the milling process is completed as quickly as possible.

People engage in rumor collection and keynoting, and the net result is the development of newly emergent norms.

The exact content of emergent norms is situation-specific and highly variable, so it cannot usually be predicted on a priori grounds. In some disasters, the norms and cues that develop among the affected populations are close to those that guide everyday activities. Here the emergent norms coincide with accepted behavior patterns, such as orderly evacuations and voluntary relief efforts. In other situations, emergent norms are almost completely at odds with traditional modes of activity and behavior. This conflict may take many different forms, from vocal public dissatisfaction to violence and social unrest. What is predictable, however, is that emergent norms will develop as natural, automatic by-products of all disaster situations.

Notes

1. There is a wealth of literature on bureaucracy, and it would be impossible to provide references for all the studies that have focused on some aspect of bureaucratic organizations. Hill (1992) provides an excellent account of the major studies in this area from the 1940s through the 1980s. These works include Merton (1940), Selznick (1943), von Mises (1944), Bendix (1947), Hyneman (1950), Marvick (1954), Blau (1955), Thompson (1961), Woll (1963), Crozier (1964), Alford (1969), Gawthrop (1969), Bennis (1970), Niskanen (1971), Warwick (1973), Suleiman (1974), Benveniste (1977), Aberbach, Putnam, and Rockman (1981), Yates (1982), Burke (1986), Stillman (1987), and Gormley (1989).

2. The structure of organizational activity is perhaps one of the most frequently examined topics in the field of public administration. There is a wealth of literature that focuses on the best way to organize the internal operations of individual agencies, as well as on how to arrange entire administrative systems across governmental jurisdictions. See, for example, Gulick and Urwick (1937), Waldo (1961), Thompson (1961), Crozier (1964), Katz and Kahn (1978), and March and Olsen (1989).

3. For an excellent account of the advantages and disadvantages of standard operating procedures in administrative policymaking, see Lowi (1969, 1979) and Rourke (1984).

4. I do not attempt to present a comprehensive account of collective behavior in this study. Instead, I touch only on those aspects of the phenomenon that are the most relevant for the discussion. For a comprehensive account of the origins, development, and current controversies surrounding the general concept of collective behavior, see McPhail (1991).

5. These four components constitute what some scholars refer to simply as the "emergent norm perspective of collective phenomena" (McPhail 1991). As in any field of inquiry, there have been fairly heated discussions about the viability and usefulness of this interpretation of the collective behavior process. For alternative views, see Couch (1968, 1970), Miller, Hintz, and Couch (1975), Berk (1974), Tilly (1978), Tierney (1980), and Lofland (1981, 1985). Nevertheless, the emergent norm perspective is used in this analysis because it provides the most appropriate explanation for the kind of collective action that occurs following a disaster situation. As McPhail writes, the emergent norm perspective fits those situations in which people confront a mutual problem, "engage in some temporary gatherings," and then construct "an ad hoc solution to the problem" through their "interactions with one another" (1991, 103).

6. For a slightly different account of keynoting, see Mead (1936), Lofland (1981), Bruner (1983), Reicher (1984), and McPhail (1991).

5

The Gap between Bureaucratic and Emergent Norms

From the discussion in the last chapter, we can see that two distinct sets of norms operate together during a disaster situation. On the one hand, bureaucratic norms provide the foundation for the governmental response system. These norms facilitate the mobilization, organization, and implementation of disaster relief by public institutions. On the other hand, emergent norms serve to structure human behavior within the affected population. These norms provide guidance and meaning to the victims of natural catastrophes so that they can cope with the disorientation, disruption, and chaos that surround them. Both sets of norms perform extremely important functions during natural disasters. Without them, governmental institutions and the affected public would be unable to handle disaster situations. The problem is that these two sets of norms might not be consistent with each other. If this is the case, it can have serious consequences for the entire relief effort.

The Nature and Significance of "the Gap"

The sources of bureaucratic and emergent norms are largely independent of each other. The two sets of norms emanate for different reasons, within different groups of people, and even at different points in time. Bureaucratic norms develop slowly and methodically inside public organizations; they set the parameters for acceptable governmental activity. Emergent norms originate instantaneously and spontaneously within a disaster-stricken population, providing a framework for individual and social behavior. Given the contrast in their sources and nature, there will inevitably be some discord or disagreement between bureaucratic and emergent norms.

Each type of norm will naturally change or evolve over time. Organizations can become more or less bureaucratic in their orientation. Some agencies develop a strict, unshakable adherence to established rules and procedures, and they tend to frown on any deviations from standard operating policies. Other organizations acquire a more flexible, fluid approach to their operations; they rely less on routinized procedures and more on creative, problem-solving behavior and adaptable organizational solutions (Downs 1967). Similarly, emergent norms can also develop in a variety of ways. In some rare situations, the values and expectations guiding human behavior in disasters take a dramatic turn: individuals become so frustrated and confused that they engage in unconventional, previously incomprehensible behavior, such as looting and rioting. In other disasters, people are momentarily disoriented and confused, but they quickly regain their composure and their footing. They revert back to adherence with more traditional, acceptable behavior guidelines (Turner and Killian 1972, 1987; McPhail 1991). So the evolution of norms is not, by itself, a cause for concern.

The problem is that the two sets of norms may evolve in very different directions. When this occurs, there is a noticeable difference or *gap*[1] between governmental plans and the needs of the affected population. There is always some discrepancy of this type in every natural disaster. But the *size* of the gap has important consequences for the quality and effectiveness of the relief effort.

In some situations, the gap remains relatively small: governmental operations seem to coincide fairly well with the needs of disaster-stricken victims. In other instances, the gap is extremely wide: governmental plans and procedures are completely at odds with the expectations and behavior of the affected population. So the size of the gap captures the degree of harmony or discord that exists between bureaucratic and emergent norms in any given disaster situation. As such, it gives us a useful indicator of the match/mismatch between governmental activity and citizens' expectations. More important, the size of the gap can be used to explain the variability of relief efforts across several different disasters. It accounts for the overall performance of the governmental emergency management process.

Factors Affecting the Size of the Gap

Three variables affect the size of the gap: (1) the magnitude of the disaster, (2) the degree of governmental preparedness, and (3) the prevailing orientations of the affected population. Each factor influences the degree of congruence between the behavior of the disaster-stricken population and the activities of the public emergency management agencies. This congruence is important because it is the major determinant of the success or failure of the overall governmental disaster-response effort.

The Magnitude of the Disaster

The severity of the disaster is clearly a major contributing factor to the size of the gap. Obviously, large-scale, catastrophic events are more difficult to handle than smaller, less-disruptive disasters (Barton 1969; Drabek 1986). Neither the public nor government officials like to think or talk about the possibility of a major natural catastrophe occurring. Such events are simply unpleasant to contemplate. They are also extremely difficult to predict. They can occur suddenly and unpredictably, even in locales considered to be hazard-prone, high-risk areas. Moreover, they can produce large-scale disruptions in the physical environment, leading to major changes in the accompanying social structure. This in turn can set off a wide variety of collective behavior within the affected population. In such instances, human activities are very likely to take on a variety of forms and patterns. The only commonality among these activities is that they are unanticipated in preexisting emergency preparedness plans. For example, people who are impatient with delays in governmental distribution procedures may simply break into stores and businesses to obtain food, tools, and reconstruction supplies. At the same time, outsiders may view disasters as economic opportunities. They bring in desperately needed supplies and then gouge the disaster victims by selling these materials at highly inflated prices. These kinds of activities are perhaps understandable, but they are certainly not consistent with the normal patterns of citizen behavior, as they are assumed to exist in emergency preparedness plans. Therefore, public officials must deal with this kind of conduct by diverting resources that could be channeled into other, presumably more constructive aspects of the response process.

Major cataclysmic events can also create severe problems for governmental agencies no matter how well prepared or equipped they are to handle more routine natural disasters (Petak 1985). In theory, the disaster-response system in the United States is extremely general in focus; it is designed to handle any emergency that may occur, in any area of the country. In reality, emergency response personnel focus much more heavily on the kinds of events that are likely to arise in their own regions. As a result, they are simply less capable of dealing with the disasters that occur more infrequently in their locales, such as an earthquake that hits in an hurricane-prone area of the East Coast or a freak snowstorm that paralyzes communities in the South, which are more accustomed to severe heat and drought.

At the same time, catastrophic disasters almost inevitably place extremely heavy demands on emergency management agencies. Under such conditions, response organizations will naturally have greater difficulty putting preexisting plans and contingencies into effect. Their task becomes almost impossible if they lack the proper personnel and resources. Unfortunately, this is often the case with the perennially understaffed, underfunded emergency response organizations.

In summary, very-large-scale natural disasters produce exactly the kinds of situations in which emergent norms are likely to be completely at odds with the prevailing bureaucratic norms. Highly unusual events lead people to behave in ways that deviate markedly from their normal, everyday routines. Similarly, extreme situations cause governmental agencies to depart from their standard operating procedures. Both tendencies magnify the disparity between the behavior of the affected population and that of emergency response personnel.

Degree of Governmental Preparedness

Second, the size of the gap is affected by the degree of prior governmental planning and preparation. The entire disaster-response system in the United States rests on one fundamental premise: *the government can and should plan for natural disasters* (McLoughlin 1985; Petak 1985). This belief, along with the prevailing bureaucratic norms, assumes that public officials have anticipated and prepared for all possible contingencies; standard operating procedures have been designed accordingly. The viability of the entire response process, however, depends on several additional assumptions: All the participants directly involved in emergency relief must know and understand their respective roles; they must be willing to carry out their responsibilities; and they must possess the necessary resources to perform their preassigned tasks (Rubin and Barbee 1985). It is also assumed that standard communication channels will be open and working properly (Perry and Mushkatel 1984; Perry and Nigg 1985). This enables the government to coordinate its own internal operations and facilitates the delivery of emergency assistance to citizens in need. Moreover, it is believed that other public officials and private organizations will be on hand to maintain order and assist in the relief effort. Emergency management personnel can coordinate response and recovery efforts, but they cannot possibly supply all forms of disaster aid. Accordingly, other public and private agencies must be assigned important functions in governmental emergency management plans (McLoughlin 1985). Finally, it is assumed that any disruptions or conflicts in the system will be temporary and manageable in nature

(Giuffrida 1985). This last assumption fits the historical record of governmental responses to natural disaster situations, most of which have been handled routinely and calmly. It also conforms to general public expectations that the government should be able to handle any kind of crisis that may arise.

The problem is that these assumptions frequently do not conform to the realities of disaster situations. Actual governmental capacities for handling natural disasters are highly variable and inconsistent across the nation. For one thing, state and local governments differ widely in their degrees of disaster planning, coordination, and readiness (Mushkatel and Weschler 1985; Quarantelli 1988; Waugh 1990, 1994). Some subnational governments take disaster relief very seriously. They have developed comprehensive emergency management plans, and they have devoted many resources and a great deal of time to hazard mitigation activities. For example, some coastal communities establish and publicize evacuation routes, to be used when hurricanes threaten. Similarly, communities located along geological fault lines conduct earthquake simulations, training exercises, and drills. In such cases, local officials are relatively well prepared to deal with the kinds of emergencies that they can be expected to face. Accordingly, disaster-relief efforts tend to operate smoothly in these communities. In contrast, other state and local governments have shown little interest in any aspect of disaster planning. Their emergency management plans, if developed at all, are unrealistic and incomplete. They do not bother to prepare or train their officials in disaster-response procedures, and they make virtually no effort to inform the general public about the dangers and hazards of emergency situations. This lackadaisical orientation to emergency management is understandable, given all the other functions that state and local officials are now expected to perform, often in the face of dwindling resource levels. Unfortunately this laxity in preparation even occurs in some of the most disaster-prone areas of the United States (Mittler 1988; U.S. General Accounting Office 1991).

At the national level, the issues are somewhat different but just as severe. Here the problem centers on ambiguity in the very role that the federal government is supposed to play. As explained in Chapter 3, the governmental response process moves upward from the lowest levels of public authority. The federal government is called in only as a last resort. It is definitely not supposed to have first-response capacity. This works well for routine or normal disaster situations, such as floods, tornadoes, or blizzards. In these cases, local and state officials have little difficulty in assessing the situation and calling on national authorities and resources for supplementary assistance. But this orderly system can break down in the face of large-scale catastrophes, such as massive hurricanes, severe droughts, or volcanic eruptions. In these latter situations, local and state governments are likely to be overwhelmed or even totally incapacitated. When this happens, the national government *must* take the initiative (Riley 1989). Federal officials are frequently expected to take over the responsibilities normally left to lower-level authorities, as well as to perform their own designated activities. Federal officials, however, are unwilling to do this: they may be afraid of "overstepping" their preassigned tasks, or they may be reluctant to stray from institutionalized norms and behavior patterns (Peterson 1989). Others may be willing but generally unprepared to take on added responsibilities. After all, they are not trained in many areas of local administration, they do not have the legal authority to take over state and local responsibilities, and they are often unfamiliar with the details of local conditions (Zensinger 1992). In any event, this circumstance—the lack of federal initiative—will almost inevitably increase the size of the gap between bureaucratic plans and actual disaster conditions.

The government's bureaucratically derived response system is predicated on the assumption that the different actors and components of the system will be able to communicate with one another. Furthermore, it assumes that relevant public officials (law enforcement officers, National Guard unit commanders, and so on) and private organizations (such as the American Red Cross and the Salvation Army) are all on the scene and capable of directing their respective responsibilities. Things often do not work out this way. Communication channels almost always break down, at least temporarily, in natural disasters (Perry and Nigg 1985). Attempts to adhere to bureaucratic policies and operations in such circumstances will only exacerbate the problems that already exist. Public officials cannot receive and follow directions from their superiors or give instructions to their subordinates if it is impossible to speak to or otherwise communicate with them. When this happens, response personnel are usually not completely immobilized, but they must develop new mechanisms and guidelines to handle the situations they confront. This, of course, requires time. Unfortunately, it also produces greater delays and confusion in the governmental response, which in turn has a negative impact on the attitudes and expectations of those directly affected by the disaster. It magnifies feelings of uneasiness, uncertainty, and hopelessness, thereby further contributing to the rise of emergent norms.

In summary, delays in governmental responses are likely to occur in disaster situations. This is inevitable because, contrary to their good intentions, public officials cannot anticipate and plan for all possible contingencies during a natural disaster. When response slowdowns occur, however, they magnify the discrepancy between preexisting governmental plans and the needs of disaster-stricken citizens.

The Orientations of Disaster Victims

The prevailing values and previous experiences of the affected population are also important (Quarantelli 1983; Perry and Greene 1983; Drabek 1986). Close-knit communities with long traditions of cooperative interaction are more likely to provide mutual support and reinforcement for their members when a disaster strikes. This helps maintain social order during the disruptive situation and facilitates a relatively prompt return to "normal," predisaster lifestyles. For example, the Cajun communities in rural Louisiana usually experience very little disaster-related disruption, even during major floods and hurricanes that would incapacitate most other areas. Similarly, the close interpersonal ties that exist in many midwestern agricultural communities help farmers cope with adverse conditions such as droughts and crop failures. In contrast, other communities have little internal cohesion. The population may be composed of temporary residents, and there may be an extremely high level of mobility among the inhabitants. For example, hurricane-ravaged communities in Florida are often populated by resettled northerners. Similarly, an earthquake that strikes an urban area in California may affect thousands of commuters; these people generally live elsewhere, and they have no immediate connection with one another. In either event, social norms may not be well known or clearly articulated. At the same time, people in these latter situations are less likely to turn to those around them for support during disruptive situations. This clearly encourages the breakdown of any preestablished norms that may have existed before a disruptive event. It also leaves an "empty slate" for the establishment of new forms of interaction, thereby facilitating the onset of collective behavior and widening the deviation from governmental disaster-relief policy.

Another factor affecting the population's orientation is its experience with previous disasters. Floods, tornadoes, hurricanes, and blizzards occur frequently in some communities. The people who live in these areas learn how to cope with disasters that occur on a somewhat regular basis. They use their past experiences to guide their reactions to subsequent disruptive events. Victims have a basic understanding of what has happened to them, and they have a general sense of what actions they should take to alleviate their situation (Barton 1969; Dynes 1970). Thus, people in riverfront towns begin their cleanup efforts immediately after floodwaters recede. The residents of "tornado alley"—an area in the Midwest frequently hit by tornadoes—start repairing damaged buildings as soon as they know a storm system has passed. And citizens in northern regions quickly clear roadways and reestablish transportation facilities after major blizzards subside.

In stark contrast, consider a situation in which the victims of a disaster have never before experienced, or perhaps even considered, their current predicament. For example, imagine the reactions of people whose town has just been unexpectedly ravaged by a tornado or those of inland residents who have just gone through a major hurricane for the first time. In such instances, the affected population has trouble comprehending what has happened. They also have a great deal of difficulty trying to determine exactly how they can or should respond to the situation. They have no precedents on which to base their behavior. The nature of the public response is uncertain and volatile, and this can lead to patterns of interaction that are totally unanticipated by the governmental response system. Public officials have no established procedures or specific contingencies for dealing with these new and different forms of citizen conduct. When this kind of inconsistency occurs, there is a wide discrepancy between governmental planning and human behavior.

To summarize, the three factors mentioned earlier—the magnitude of the disaster, the degree of governmental preparedness, and the orientations of disaster victims—influence the way governmental institutions and the affected population respond to a particular disaster situation. Any one of these agents, by itself, can increase the gap between governmental activity and human behavior. And the larger the number of these factors that exists in any given situation, the greater the probability of a mismatch between governmental plans and public expectations. The gap between bureaucratic and emergent norms is likely to be extremely wide when large-scale, catastrophic events occur in completely unanticipated circumstances; for example, communities that have not previously experienced such disasters or contexts in which governmental preparation is inadequate or inappropriate.

Immediate Consequences and Inevitability of the Gap

Discrepancies between emergent norms and bureaucratic norms have a direct impact on the operations of the public institutions involved in emergency relief. The gap affects local governments' efforts to mobilize a first response, identify the most critical problems of disaster-stricken areas, and communicate these needs to higher authorities. As we have seen, local emergency relief agencies are usually understaffed, underfunded, and overburdened (Cigler 1988). Therefore, in order to operate effectively, they must depend on the immediate compliance and orderly behavior of the disaster-stricken population. But this is exactly what breaks down in the presence of emergent norms. The resultant collective behavior, in turn, has a negative impact on the effectiveness of local relief operations. For example, it is impossible to make accurate property damage and personal injury assessments if public officials are busy preventing looting and restoring order within the community.

The gap also affects the actions of state governments in several ways. First, local-level problems have immediate consequences for the state's ability to coordinate and channel additional resources to the affected areas. State officials simply cannot perform this function if they fail to receive the necessary firsthand information from local authorities. Second, local governments themselves often deviate from preexisting plans, thereby creating further problems for state governments. For one thing, local communities often believe that they are in competition with one another for state emergency relief resources, so they tend to exaggerate the severity of their problems. At the same time, local officials sometimes bypass state governments and appeal directly to federal authorities in the hope that this will expedite relief efforts. And state emergency preparedness agencies, like their local counterparts, are often unprepared for realistic disaster conditions. They do not have sufficient resources and personnel to implement their emergency management plans, especially when they are confronted with major catastrophic events. Consequently, they are also incapable of adjusting their operations to meet the new demands that arise from unanticipated forms of human behavior—emergent norms. Thus, several factors related to the gap have a detrimental impact on state governments.

Finally, the gap compromises the effectiveness of the federal government's disaster-relief efforts. A great deal of the problem stems from the breakdowns that have already occurred at the lower levels. When local and state governments fail to carry out their responsibilities, it is impossible to conceive of national authorities' "supplementing" their efforts. Instead, federal officials often have to step in and perform "first-response" operations. But, once again, this is not supposed to be the national government's primary responsibility within the current and ongoing disaster-response system. When federal officials are forced to carry out first-response activities, their attention is deflected away from their own preassigned duties. This in turn decreases the effectiveness of the overall relief effort.

In summary, the nature and size of the gap between emergent norms and bureaucratic norms have profound negative consequences for the implementation of disaster-assistance efforts. This being the case, it seems reasonable to assert that everyone involved should try to minimize the size of the gap or prevent its existence in the first place. But it is usually impossible to do so. The emergence of the gap is an inevitable consequence of a natural disaster situation. Discrepancies between prior planning and existing conditions—that is, the gap—are not particularly surprising given the general difficulties of public policy development in an intergovernmental framework, along with the unusual dilemmas that arise during natural disasters.

The previous literature on intergovernmental relations and program implementation shows that problems are inevitable when all three levels of government are simultaneously involved in policy development (Pressman and Wildavsky 1984).[2] The federal, state, and local governments have widely varying resources, capabilities, and support systems. In addition, each layer of government has its own perspective on policy implementation. These differences across the three levels of government have created serious difficulties and controversies in a number of important substantive policy areas. For example, consider the problems that have surfaced in American social policy development. All levels of government have important responsibilities in the process: the national government sets the general parameters for many social programs; state governments determine specific program requirements; and local governments direct the actual day-to-day administration of the programs. Although there may appear to be a clear division of labor on paper, it does not work out that way in practice. Over the years there have been continuous struggles across the three levels of government. Disagreements have occurred over who actually determines the funding of, and makes decisions within, social programs. The net result is a very fragmented and disjointed social welfare system (Skocpol and Amenta 1986; Cottingham and Ellwood 1989; Katz 1989). Nobody seems to be in charge of providing services, and nobody seems to be able to control the system's development. Intergovernmental relations issues are widely believed to be the root cause of most problems in American social welfare programs (Browning 1986; Peterson and Rom 1990).

These problems closely parallel those that exist within the governmental disaster-response system. On paper, there is a fully articulated structure to guide policy implementation. In practice, the lines of authority and responsibility are unclear. And, as we have seen, this causes problems for specific disaster-relief efforts.

The previous research on disaster relief emphasizes that disasters, by their very nature, constitute unpredictable, difficult, and diverse events. They can create situations and conditions that are impossible to anticipate, no matter how detailed or comprehensive the governmental plans developed to deal with them. Moreover, they occur in a variety of different forms— hailstorms, volcanic eruptions, tidal waves, and so on. Even if a community is prepared for one kind of event, it may not be expecting a different type of disaster. Natural disasters also strike in widely varying locations, thereby involving many different and highly diverse public institutions. Some of these organizations are reasonably well equipped to handle natural disasters; others are totally unprepared. Thus the sheer variability of each crisis situation contributes to even greater uncertainty about the consistency of the governmental response. It makes it even more likely that disaster relief will not be implemented exactly the same way in all disaster situations.

Three Implementation Patterns for Disaster Relief

The gap between emergent and bureaucratic norms is a critical idea for understanding the governmental response to natural disasters. The size of the gap determines the nature of policy implementation in emergency relief efforts. Specifically, there are three different implementation patterns for disaster assistance in the United States: the "bottom-up," "confusion," and "top-down" approaches.[3] These three patterns represent different intergovernmental dynamics and tensions within emergency management and recovery efforts. But which pattern accurately describes the relief effort in any given disaster situation? The answer to this question depends on the degree of agreement or disagreement between the beliefs and expectations of disaster-stricken populations on the one hand and the actions of governmental officials on the other. In short, the size of the gap between emergent and bureaucratic norms determines the nature of policy implementation in governmental disaster-relief efforts.

The Bottom-Up Approach

The first implementation pattern for disaster relief is one in which the intergovernmental process operates from the bottom up (Sabatier 1986). The relief effort begins at the local level. City and county officials provide direct emergency services and assess the scope of damages. If the magnitude of the disaster extends across several local jurisdictions, then the state government becomes involved to mobilize and coordinate activities. It also provides additional resources for local governments to deal with disruptive conditions and the problems of the affected populations. When a disaster is large enough to exceed the state's relief capabilities, then the state officials can appeal to the federal government for further assistance. The federal government supplies a vast array of additional resources that simply do not exist at the state level. Similarly, it can provide financial assistance on a scale that would be impossible if state treasuries were the only sources of funding.

The bottom-up process conforms precisely to the established governmental response system described in detail in Chapter 3. For present purposes, it is merely important to emphasize that the different levels of government initiate response activities sequentially rather than simultaneously. As higher levels of government become involved, they work *through* the lower levels; they do not *take over* the entire response and recovery operation.

Other analysts (May and Williams 1986) have called this system the "shared governance approach" to policy implementation. This seems to imply that the three levels of government have overlapping responsibilities and that they tend to concentrate on the same functions. The term "bottom up," however, provides a more accurate and graphic description for this pattern of policy implementation. Instead of sharing responsibilities, there is a clear division of labor, with each level of government focusing on distinct duties and activities. Furthermore, the officials who are actually involved in disaster relief use the terms "up" and "down" to describe their own perceptions about the intergovernmental structure of policy implementation (McAda 1989). They clearly believe that when the system works as it is intended, the needs of the affected population will be communicated upward and appropriate assistance will be channeled back down. Of course, the terms "up" and "down" refer to a path that leads from the local governments through the states and ultimately to the federal government, and vice versa. This system makes the most effective use of public officials' expertise and knowledge of local conditions. It also provides the most efficient allocation of intergovernmental resources.

The bottom-up implementation pattern can occur only when the gap between bureaucratic norms and the emergent norms that follow a natural disaster is quite small. This small gap develops when two conditions are met simultaneously. First, public officials must carry out their duties in a manner that is consistent with preexisting emergency management plans. They are attentive to their own duties and do not encroach on the responsibilities of other officials and agencies. This first condition is contingent on a second provision: the behavior of the affected population conforms to prior expectations. In other words, emergent norms do not deviate very sharply from the standard, predisaster guidelines (formal and informal) for social interactions that previously existed within the affected communities.

This kind of outcome characterizes the majority of disaster situations that arise in the United States. Severe floods in the Tennessee River valley can cause major disruptions in the social systems of that region. Both the government and the public, however, usually react to these situations in a relatively routine manner. Consequently, these major disasters can be handled and resolved with very little public attention beyond those citizens and public agencies immediately involved. The rest of the country may not even be aware that a natural catastrophe has occurred. This lack of widespread popular concern is one of the hallmarks of a successful relief effort.

The Confusion Pattern

As its name implies, the confusion pattern of policy implementation is difficult to describe succinctly. Many different kinds of disaster-related situations fall under this general heading. For example, the confusion can arise very quickly. This occurs when public officials fail to mobilize a response in the immediate aftermath of a natural disaster. Local governments may be unprepared either because the disaster itself was unexpected or because officials received inadequate training. Alternatively, they may be unwilling to act or incapable of acting because local capacities are overwhelmed by the magnitude or severity of the disaster. Similarly, the state and national governments may hesitate because they are waiting for the lower levels to take the first initiative. Regardless of the exact reason, the confusion pattern can develop quickly when government fails to establish a clear presence in the affected area and does not make itself visible to the stricken population.

The confusion implementation pattern can also develop more slowly. This occurs when governments initiate responses but fail to control their own activities very closely. Public officials may take the initiative, and, in so doing, they depart from their assigned tasks. For example, a local leader may request federal assistance without going through appropriate channels at the state or national levels. At the same time, there may be little coordination between individual actors, public agencies, and governmental levels. When these conditions exist, there does seem to be a great deal of governmental activity; however, there is no overall framework or general order to guide the emergency response effort. As a result, specific response activities may be isolated and ineffective, or redundant and wasteful. The only appropriate term to describe such conditions is "confusion."

The confusion implementation pattern is likely to occur when there is a moderately sized gap between bureaucratic and emergent norms. In most instances, relief efforts are already under way, and disaster victims are trying to deal with their own problems. But the process develops in such a way that the two sets of actors tend to "work past each other" rather than in coordinated ways that effectively resolve the disaster conditions.

The confusion pattern can stem from the actions of emergency management officials, the behavior of disaster victims, or both. Simultaneously, public officials do act, but they fail to abide by standard operating procedures. At the same time, disaster victims behave in ways that may be rational, reasonable responses to existing conditions; they are simply unanticipated in the government's emergency response plans. For example, citizens may refuse to evacuate a threatened area or may insist on returning to their communities before the latter are deemed safe. Similarly, people may rebuff governmental offers of assistance, such as tents and mobile homes, or they may demand forms of relief that are not readily available, such as restoration of utility services or reconstruction supplies.

In any event, the confusion pattern does not signal a *complete* breakdown of the social order or the governmental response system. Instead, everyone involved is taking steps perceived to be reasonable reactions to the existing situation (Anton 1989). These actions simply do not conform to prior expectations or plans. And as a result, they have an unintentionally detrimental affect on the governmental relief effort.

As an example of this confusion implementation pattern, consider a major volcano that becomes active in a region that has little recent history of geological activity—Mount St. Helens. Emergency preparedness officials in the United States have little previous experience with volcanoes, so there is great uncertainty about what needs to be done. They try to respond to the situation but do so only in a confused, makeshift manner. Similarly, the public has had no prior contact with volcanic activity; hence, people do not know what to do to prepare for or protect themselves from a major eruption. In this kind of situation, there is little to tie together bureaucratic procedures and patterns of human behavior. So the gap between the two widens. The response appears slow, misguided, and confused, and there are frequent charges of governmental nonresponsiveness and ineffectiveness. In the end, the government receives mixed reviews for its relief and assistance efforts (May 1985b). Its motives are not really at issue, but its specific actions, operations, and ability to deliver needed services are seriously questioned.

The Top-Down Approach

Finally, disaster relief can be implemented from the "top down" (Sabatier 1986). This pattern can be described very simply: The federal government takes over all emergency management activities. U.S. military personnel stabilize the situation, restore order within affected communities, and open up lines of transportation/communication to the external environment. At the same time, officials from the Federal Emergency Management Agency assume the responsibilities and administrative functions that are normally left to state and local governments. The national government is clearly the focal point of the relief effort.

The top-down implementation pattern is totally antithetical to the basic, ongoing governmental response system, which is based on the bottom-up approach to disaster assistance. In the top-down pattern there is no rolling process of intergovernmental activity, starting at the local level, moving up through the states and beyond. Instead, the federal government provides the first response, completely bypassing the lower levels. At the same time, there is no sharing of responsibilities across the three levels of government. Instead, the national governmental assumes nearly complete control over the entire situation. Local and state authorities may be required to provide assistance, but their participation is limited and subordinate in nature. The national government retains final responsibility for virtually all emergency relief and recovery activities.

The top-down pattern is likely to occur when there is an extremely wide gap between bureaucratic procedures and the behavior of disaster victims. Radical inconsistencies of this type develop when two conditions arise simultaneously. First, subnational governments cease to exist as meaningful entities. Public officials may be disaster victims themselves; as such, they are incapable of addressing other people's problems no matter how serious they may be. Or governmental authorities may be out of contact with their constituents and therefore incapable of directing the relief efforts.

The second condition that causes an extremely wide gap is closely related to the lack of governmental authority. Emergent norms encourage forms of human behavior that would be considered deviant or illegal under normal circumstances. People may resort to violence against others in order to protect themselves against perceived threats to their own lives or personal properties. They may also engage in looting behavior to obtain supplies or simply to take material advantage of the confusion that exists in the aftermath of a disaster. And people may simply refuse to obey instructions from authorities if they perceive the latter to be ineffective or nonresponsive to their problems. In any event, the demands of the disaster situation completely outstrip the capacities of local and state governmental institutions. The federal government has no choice but to step in and take over the entire response effort.

Superficially, the top-down implementation pattern may seem like a particularly effective way of dealing with natural disasters.[4] It involves only a single level of government, and the latter is precisely the one with the greatest amount of resources and the broadest scope of authority. In practice, however, top-down responses have not operated very quickly or smoothly. For one thing, the federal response is overseen by FEMA, and this agency often has trouble obtaining cooperation from other arms of the federal government. FEMA is the *coordinator* of federal emergency response operations, but it does not have the ability or the authority to *force* other federal agencies to follow its directives. At the same time, FEMA personnel are simply not equipped to carry out the responsibilities of such local officials as mayors, county administrators, and law enforcement officials. They do not have the legal authority to step in and take over the operations of lower-level governmental jurisdictions. In addition, they are usually unfamiliar with the details and particulars of local conditions and situations. This situation is exacerbated by the fact that FEMA administrators often do not want to exercise these functions and are accordingly very hesitant to do so. They are trained to follow a basic set of policies and guidelines that stress the federal government's *supplementary* role in emergency management. For all these reasons, the top-down pattern has not resulted in effective governmental responses to natural disaster situations.

In situations such as this, the government faces a serious dilemma. No matter what the government tries to do, its actions will probably be intensely criticized. Most private citizens cannot be expected to comprehend fully the difficulties and complexities involved in any recovery effort: They depend on the government for guidance and assistance. At the same time, disaster-stricken individuals are naturally absorbed with their own personal problems caused by the disaster. So the public is likely to be dissatisfied with anything short of immediate, direct, and comprehensive help. This leads to widespread criticism of governmental activities, and, in the end, it produces the impression that the governmental response is a failure.

Fortunately, the extreme catastrophes that tend to produce the top-down response pattern have been relatively rare. One example would be the 1955 flooding that occurred throughout the New England region.[5] Conditions were so severe that local and state authorities were immediately overburdened by the demands placed on them. In what was a pathbreaking effort at the time, the federal government stepped in to provide flood insurance, loan contracts, and reinsurance for the affected population. These actions set an important precedent that future disaster victims would automatically be eligible for similar kinds of federal assistance (May 1985b, 32). In short, the top-down governmental response seemed to be required by the magnitude of the 1955 disaster situation. This action, however, did not preclude the development of broader criticisms of the entire governmental effort. There was a widespread belief that the government failed to alleviate the adverse conditions caused by the floods. In the end, the federal government's efforts were still judged to be inadequate; this popular perception caused both short-term problems for flood victims and longer-term problems for public expectations about disaster relief.

The Broader Impact of the Gap

In summary, the gap between bureaucratic norms and emergent norms is a critical component of the disaster-response process. It determines which of three policy implementation patterns will be put into effect in any given disaster situation. This in turn has a direct bearing on the nature and effectiveness of the entire governmental response process. It affects the allocation of scarce governmental resources during times when demands on these resources are particularly vocal and strident. It determines the speed and efficiency with which disaster victims are able to obtain needed assistance. It also affects broader perceptions about the government's ability to cope with natural disasters. Stated simply, the size of the gap ultimately determines whether the public perceives the government's disaster-relief efforts to be successes or failures.

From a more objective perspective, virtually all governmental relief efforts could easily be labeled "successes." Over the past ten years, the federal government has assisted hundreds of thousands of citizens across the nation to recover from dozens of natural disasters, with costs running in the billions of dollars (Federal Emergency Management Agency 1993). Moreover, the governmental response system has successfully restored many disaster-stricken areas to their earlier, predisaster conditions (U.S. General Accounting Office 1989). In fact, some analysts have argued that the government's disaster-relief funds have enabled some communities to improve their conditions markedly (Wolensky and Wolensky 1991); ironically, they end up better off as a result of the natural disaster. For example, disaster-assistance funds are used to construct newer, stronger private homes and businesses. Similarly, disaster relief is often used to redesign and rebuild public works such as bridges, dams, and roadways.

But, objective indicators of governmental efforts are often outweighed by subjective assessments of disaster situations. Stated simply, the acknowledged success or failure of the governmental response is almost entirely a matter of public perception. These perceptions are often strongly influenced by images from the disaster situation itself (Scanlon, Alldred, Farrell, and Prawzick 1985; Walters, Wilkins, and Walters 1989; Goldman and Reilly 1992). For example, television news reports about orderly evacuations and efficient distribution of supplies suggest a successful response. On the other hand, news stories about the waste, fraud, and mismanagement in the allocation of relief funds convey the image of governmental incompetence. And vivid radio reports of looting, martial law, and acute scarcities of vital supplies suggest the complete breakdown of governmental authority. But, again, all these conditions are simply manifestations of the size of the gap.

Thus it is no exaggeration to say that the gap between bureaucratic norms and emergent norms provides an accurate mechanism for identifying and explaining the success or failure of governmental disaster-relief efforts.

Notes

1. "The gap" is used in this analysis because that same term was used spontaneously and independently by several officials directly involved in the disaster-relief efforts examined in this study. In addition, this particular term seems to capture the precise phenomenon of interest—the discrepancy between bureaucratic principles and public expectations.

2. For more information on the problems of implementing public policies in the American federal system, see Van Meter and Van Horn (1976), Lipsky (1978), Nakamura and Smallwood (1980), Williams (1980), Bardach (1977), Mazmanian and Sabatier (1983), Ripley and Franklin (1991), and Goggin, Bowman, Lester, and O'Toole (1990).

3. The three implementation patterns described in this study are most similar to the intergovernmental policy models presented by Sabatier (1986) and Anton (1989). There are, however, some basic differences: for example, Anton calls the confusion model a "diffusion" pattern; Sabatier concentrates almost entirely on the top-down and bottom-up approaches, giving little attention to anything in between the two extremes. For some different views on the framework of intergovernmental policymaking, see Grodzins (1966), Elazar (1962), Sundquist (1969), Peterson (1981), Chubb (1985), and Wright (1988).

4. In fact, several prominent recommendations to change the current governmental response system contain some version of the "top-down" approach to policy implementation. These suggestions are discussed in greater detail in the last chapter of the book.

5. Another, more recent example of the "top-down" pattern is examined in Chapter 7—the governmental response to Hurricane Hugo in the Caribbean Islands.

Part Two

Case Studies of
Natural Disasters

September 1989. Hurricane Hugo toppled and destroyed thousands of homes in the Caribbean Islands. *Photo by BD Communications and Publishing, Inc.*

September 1989. Disaster victims posted warning signs to deter looters who tried to take advantage of Hurricane Hugo's destruction in the Virgin Islands. *Photo by BD Communications and Publishing, Inc.*

6

A General Framework for Examining the Success or Failure of the Governmental Response to Natural Disasters

Up to this point, the discussion has been couched in fairly abstract terms and there has been virtually no coverage given to specific events that occurred in actual natural disasters. For present purposes, this general orientation is preferable to a more detailed, particularistic approach precisely because it does focus attention on the common patterns of human behavior that occur during and after natural disasters. Otherwise, it is all too easy to think of specific disasters as unique events. After all, many different phenomena fall under the general heading of "disaster": severe floods, tropical storms, volcanic eruptions, earthquakes, and so on. Moreover, these cataclysmic events occur in a wide variety of settings: river valleys, ocean coastlines, midwestern plains, mountainous areas, and so on. The apparent uniqueness of these events is further emphasized by the mass media, which link each natural disaster with their own set of potent, nearly unforgettable images: devastated forests marking the destructive swath of a hurricane, homes toppling down cliffs during mudslides, automobiles disappearing into a gap torn into a roadway by an earthquake, and dejected farmers paddling boats through water that covers normally dry fields.

If natural disasters truly are unique events, then it would be impossible to prepare effectively for them or to deal systematically with their destruction and disruption. But, across the nation, communities *do* have plans for dealing with disasters, from the evacuation routes that exist along the southeastern seaboard, through the tornado drills carried out in midwestern schools and businesses, to the earthquake simulations held by officials along the West Coast. At the same time, communities and people *do* recover from disasters. In most instances, the physical destruction caused by hurricanes, tornadoes, and floods is repaired very quickly. In other situations, the physical evidence of the disaster may be longer lasting: collapsed overpasses in the California freeway system following major earthquakes, the deforestation of productive timberlands following East Coast hurricanes, and the major beach erosion that results from the pounding of coastal storms. But even in these extreme cases, most people adjust to the situation and get on with their lives (Wright, Rossi, Wright, and Weber-Burdin 1979; Friesema, Caporaso, Goldstein, Lineberry, and McCleary 1979; Wright and Rossi 1981; Petak and Atkisson 1982; May 1985b; U.S. General Accounting Office 1991). The historical record shows that the American public can deal with natural disasters.[1] Nevertheless, it is certainly better to do so in a comprehensive manner rather than view each disaster as an isolated incident. This, in turn, requires a general framework for understanding disaster-related behavior regardless of the specific nature or details of the disaster situations themselves.

It is important to emphasize that the governmental response system is itself based on a comprehensive view. An unstated but nevertheless central assumption of FEMA's standard operating procedures is that all disasters (man-made as well as natural) can be handled in exactly the same way. This allows emergency management personnel to develop generic policies and procedures that cover any contingency, no matter when or where it occurs. But this also imposes a high degree of rigidity on the system. Public officials often cannot adjust their activities to meet the unique needs of a specific disaster situation. As a result, the comprehensive nature of disaster-response planning itself has a detrimental impact on the response and recovery process. What is needed is a more effective, flexible framework—one that integrates the common elements of emergency management and response and the unique behavioral components of particular disaster situations.

The concept of the gap between bureaucratic norms and emergent norms can be used as exactly this kind of framework. It provides a parsimonious means of subsuming many specific activities carried out by a wide array of different actors—primarily governmental emergency management personnel and disaster victims within the affected population. The notion of the gap serves as a skeletal structure. It can be "fleshed out" with details of the many different natural disasters that have hit portions of the United States in the past. The gap also provides an ongoing mechanism for viewing and understanding the future disasters that will inevitably occur. The overall objective in the following chapters is to show how this can be done.

Part Two covers the governmental responses to a series of recent natural disasters: Hurricane Hugo in the Caribbean, South Carolina, and North Carolina; the Loma Prieta earthquake in California; major flooding that recently occurred in the state of South Carolina; and Hurricane Andrew in southern Florida and southern Louisiana. Note that for the purposes of this study, each of the hurricanes actually constitutes several distinct disaster situations: three in the case of Hugo and two in the case of Andrew. Although there was only a single storm in each case, the relief and recovery operations varied dramatically across different political jurisdictions. At the same time, the affected populations within each state (and U.S. territories in the case of Hugo) reacted quite differently to the respective hurricanes. For these reasons, it is more appropriate to treat the various responses to Hugo and Andrew as separate incidents.

These particular events have been selected as case studies for two basic reasons. First, the six situations share some common characteristics. One obvious similarity is their severity: they all qualify as unambiguously *major* natural disasters. This is important because each of these situations placed unusually difficult burdens on governmental institutions and processes. In addition, all six disasters occurred within the relatively short time period from September 1989 to August 1992. Thus, the first and last events to be analyzed (Hugo in the Caribbean and Andrew in southern Louisiana) took place within less than three years of each other. This is important because it means that the same basic governmental response structure was used to handle all the situations. As we see, the nature of the response process varies widely across the six disasters. But since the governmental structure is effectively "held constant," this variability is more likely to stem from differences in human behavior than from formal changes in governmental institutions and practices.

The second reason for selecting these disasters is that they clearly illustrate the wide variability in the perceived effectiveness of the governmental response. At one extreme, there is the complete collapse of the governmental response system in the Caribbean Islands following Hurricane Hugo. At the other end of the continuum, there is the calm, successful resolution of problems during the 1990 South Carolina floods. The other four cases fall at intermediate points along the success/failure dimension. The governmental responses to Hurricane Andrew in Florida and Hurricane Hugo in South Carolina are located closer to the failure pole. The Loma Prieta earthquake is positioned almost exactly midway between the two extremes. And the relief efforts in North Carolina after Hurricane Hugo, along with those in Louisiana after Hurricane Andrew, are closer to the success side. Thus, the disasters examined here truly illustrate the full range of perceived success

Figure 6.1. **Continuum Showing Relative Successes and Failures of Selected Governmental Responses to Natural Disasters**

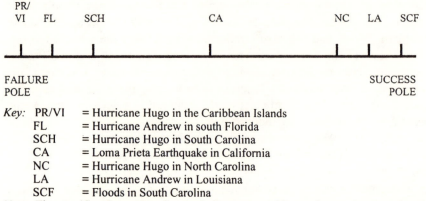

PR/
VI   FL   SCH   CA   NC   LA   SCF

FAILURE   SUCCESS
POLE   POLE

Key: PR/VI   = Hurricane Hugo in the Caribbean Islands
     FL   = Hurricane Andrew in south Florida
     SCH   = Hurricane Hugo in South Carolina
     CA   = Loma Prieta Earthquake in California
     NC   = Hurricane Hugo in North Carolina
     LA   = Hurricane Andrew in Louisiana
     SCF   = Floods in South Carolina
Note: The specific placement of natural disasters on this continuum is approximate; however, the ordering conforms to the analysis presented in this study.

and failure in governmental disaster responses. The approximate placement of each of the case studies on the success/failure continuum is shown in Figure 6.1.

The six disasters are not covered in their chronological sequence. Instead, they are presented according to the size of the gap that developed in each case, from largest to smallest. First, the Caribbean Islands following Hurricane Hugo represent a situation in which the gap between bureaucratic norms and emergent norms was extremely wide. In the next three disasters— south Florida's experience with Hurricane Andrew, South Carolina during Hurricane Hugo, and the Loma Prieta earthquake in California—a noticeable gap emerged during some phase of the relief effort and had a detrimental impact on some aspect of the response. Then, Hurricane Hugo in North Carolina and Hurricane Andrew in southern Louisiana pose situations in which a gap developed but did not seriously impede the recovery process. Finally, South Carolina's experience with severe flooding in 1990 provides a "normal" disaster scenario, in which there is virtually no gap between governmental actions and the expectations of the affected population.

The case studies presented here are not intended to provide comprehensive descriptions of their respective disasters.[2] Instead, coverage focuses on the factors that contribute most directly to the effectiveness of governmental relief efforts: emergent norms; bureaucratic norms; the size of the gap between the two sets of norms; and the resultant pattern of policy implementation in the response process—top down, confusion, or bottom up. Once again, by focusing on these common features of six events that seem to be vastly different, it is possible to demonstrate that there is a general and discernible structure underlying the ways in which private citizens and public officials behave during natural disasters. This immediately contributes to the more general objective of this study: a clearer understanding of why some governmental disaster responses are believed to be successful, while others are deemed to be failures. It also provides insights into how the governmental response process can be strengthened so that public organizations can address future disasters in a more effective and efficient manner.

Notes

1. It is important to recognize that there are many different types of disaster-related consequences. These include the more obvious physical changes to the natural environment as well as the severe economic losses to families, businesses, and public entities. Disasters can also produce psychological disruptions and changes within individual disaster victims that are less visible but perhaps more profound. Clearly, some of these problems are more easily handled than others. Moreover, the recovery process may not be the same for all members of the affected population. There is evidence to suggest that low-income individuals do not recover as quickly or as completely from a disaster situation as do victims from middle- or upper-income groups (Cochrane 1975, 1990; Petak and Atkisson 1982; Rossi, Wright, Weber-Burdin, and Pereira 1983; May 1985b). Further support for the differential impact of disasters across various population groups is also provided in several of the case studies described in this book.

2. The specific events associated with these six disaster situations have been described in detail in many newspapers and news magazines. For more information, see the *New York Times,* the *Washington Post, Time,* or *Newsweek* during the time periods in which the disasters occurred—for example, September and October 1989 for Hurricane Hugo and August and September 1992 for Hurricane Andrew.

7

Hurricane Hugo in the Caribbean Islands

Hurricane Hugo began as a band of thunderstorms off the coast of Africa. It was upgraded to a tropical storm on September 11, 1989, and given hurricane status a few days later. It first touched American territory in the Caribbean. On September 18, Hugo slammed into the U.S. Virgin Islands. On the following day, it struck Puerto Rico. After assaulting the northeast portion of Puerto Rico with 125-mile-per-hour winds and 10 to 20 inches of rain, the huge storm headed back out into the Atlantic Ocean. But Hurricane Hugo had already transformed the Caribbean Islands from a tropical paradise into a tropical nightmare.

Parts of buildings, pieces of furniture, and articles of clothing were thrown everywhere. Trees were stripped of their leaves and uprooted. Roofs were torn from homes and businesses. Entire neighborhoods were leveled. Electrical power was knocked out. Water and sewer systems were disrupted. In its wake, Hugo left at least eighteen people dead, thousands more homeless, and over $1 billion in physical destruction. On the island of St. Croix alone, 95 percent of the buildings were damaged, and nine out of ten citizens experienced storm-related damages (U.S. General Accounting Office 1991).[1] (See photo at top of page 74.)

The destruction caused by Hugo in the Virgin Islands and Puerto Rico was so massive that it could not be handled by individual citizens or private organizations. Clearly, governmental resources were needed, yet conditions on the islands made it extremely difficult for any governmental entity to initiate a relief effort. A sizable gap developed between the norms that guided the behavior of disaster-stricken victims and the government's preexisting plans and policies. Thus, emergency management agencies had to circumvent standard operating procedures and design a top-down method of implementing disaster relief. Eventually, the governmental response system was able to provide critical assistance to disaster-stricken areas. But the public perception was (and is) that the government's response to Hurricane Hugo in the Caribbean Islands "failed."

The Development of Emergent Norms: Deviant Behavior

In the Caribbean Islands, the milling process began immediately after the hurricane. Hugo destroyed virtually all transportation and communication systems on the islands. This made it difficult for individuals to contact others affected by the storm. "Thousands of . . . citizens wandered dazed through the streets . . . amid almost unbelievable wreckage" (Harrison 1989). Moreover, the damage was so severe that local inhabitants could not communicate with the outside world. In the words of one disaster victim, "as far as we knew, the rest of the world had disappeared" (Branigin 1989a).

Reports from survivors indicated a general feeling of helplessness and alienation. An officer in the Virgin Islands National Guard remarked: "In all my military experience, I had never seen anything like it" (Branigin 1989a). But the severity of the situation is perhaps best summed up in the statement of one local resident: "It looked and felt like the day after a nuclear holocaust" (*Hugo* n.d.).

Local and territorial leaders were similarly disoriented and paralyzed. They were unprepared and ill equipped to provide guidance or assistance to their own citizens, particularly in the face of such a cataclysmic event. During the first twenty-four hours of the crisis, most local police and territorial emergency management personnel could not even be located by their superiors, let alone be called on to respond to the situation (Branigin 1989a). Consequently, island authorities were unable to alleviate the most pressing conditions and to maintain social order within the disaster-stricken areas. This created a truly noninstitutionalized situation in which traditional norms and values did not apply at all.

Local residents engaged in activities they would not even consider during normal circumstances. Widespread looting and domestic violence erupted on the islands of St. Thomas, San Juan, Guadeloupe, and St. Croix (York 1989). In the words of an American tourist who was vacationing on the island of St. Croix, "There was no control. There was anarchy in town" (Harrison 1989). Others described the situation as carnival-like, punctuated by periods of rampant hysteria and looting frenzies (Branigin 1989a). There were reports that gangs of citizens, armed with rifles, roamed the streets of Christiansted in the U.S. Virgin Islands, ransacking local stores and businesses. Virtually everything worth taking was stolen. These chaotic, near-anarchic conditions existed for several days in some of the disaster-stricken areas that were hardest hit. (See photo at bottom of page 74.)

Keynoting behavior took place when acts of social deviance went unpunished. Territorial leaders were unable to stop the looting and pilfering; consequently, they implicitly encouraged more such acts. In addition, local officials may have even played a more direct role in this process: there were numerous reports that some local police, National Guardsmen, and political leaders were actual participants, not just innocent bystanders, in the looting frenzy (Branigin 1989a; Christian 1992). Nonetheless, deviant behavior emerged as the norm. It is important to emphasize that this deviant behavior was not the result of criminal activity within one segment of society. Instead, it represented the actions of a broad cross-section of normal citizens. Literally thousands of island residents from all age groups and all social strata engaged in looting. Small children and old women alike were spotted among the mobs, grabbing merchandise from local stores (Harrison 1989); poor residents from public housing projects, as well as some of the most prominent island citizens, were charged with offenses ranging from grand larceny to possession of stolen goods (Branigin 1989a). Amazingly, there were very few incidents of personal violence or malicious acts of terrorism. Most participants simply got "caught up" in undisciplined, unsupervised conduct. According to one analyst, "They had the opportunity and they took it" (York 1989). Most of the looting and pilfering appeared to be primarily motivated by panic and hysteria. The vast majority of residents who engaged in unorthodox behavior were simply trying to obtain the basic necessities of life, which were in extremely short supply.

Bureaucratic Norms and the Governmental Response

All these conditions made it extremely difficult for the government to administer disaster assistance using routine procedures and processes. To start with, territorial officials on the islands could not even ask for help from the national government. By law, only the governor of a territory or state can request federal assistance, and the federal government has been unwilling to bend this rule no matter how severe the situation.

Yet the governor of the Virgin Islands, Alexander Farrelly, could not be contacted. He was on the island of St. Thomas with no means of communicating with the other side of the city, let alone with the U.S. mainland. Fortunately, he had access to a ham radio. When federal officials discovered this, they set up a special high-frequency radio communication channel. This makeshift device enabled Governor Farrelly to submit a verbal request for federal aid. Two hours later, President George Bush declared the

Virgin Islands a "major disaster." Almost immediately after this, the federal government received another verbal request for federal assistance—this time from Governor Rafael Hernández Colón of Puerto Rico. Within a matter of hours, President Bush declared another emergency, this time in Puerto Rico (Peterson 1989). Now the federal government could officially initiate a full-scale response.

The national government had to deal with three immediate problems in the Caribbean (Peterson 1989). First, it had to address the general breakdown in civil order. Public officials had to stop the looting and vandalism and counter the development of additional chaotic acts. Second, the government had to resolve life-threatening issues. Island water supplies had been contaminated, food reserves destroyed, and shelters demolished. The third problem was air traffic control. Even in normal times, the islands depend entirely on outside assistance. But all U.S. air traffic in the Caribbean is controlled from Puerto Rico, and Hugo had knocked out these facilities. Thus there were severe difficulties in reaching the islands.

Agencies from the government, particularly at the federal level, worked fairly quickly to address these problems (McAda 1989). The Federal Emergency Management Agency established a temporary mechanism for directing air traffic in the Caribbean. Then the agency authorized an airlift of millions of pounds of water, food, and plastic sheeting (for makeshift covers) for the islands. FEMA also had electrical generators, utility equipment, and medical supplies flown in from the mainland to restore essential services as quickly as possible. Finally, President Bush dispatched federal law enforcement officials and military police to the islands in order to restore social stability and public order.

Once the most immediate problems had been alleviated, national governmental organizations could begin to administer the basic package of disaster-assistance programs. FEMA was the main coordinating force, overseeing the delivery of supplies and equipment to the Virgin Islands and Puerto Rico. First, the agency established field headquarters on the islands as well as a number of Disaster Assistance Centers (DACs) at a number of locations in the Virgin Islands and Puerto Rico. Then it began the process of accepting and verifying claims and dispensing checks for the needy. FEMA also constructed thousands of makeshift housing facilities and airlifted tons of debris out of the islands.[2]

Emergency relief was not, however, dispensed quickly or efficiently throughout all the disaster-stricken areas in the Caribbean. On the island of Puerto Rico, several thousand displaced residents were still living in makeshift shelters six weeks after the storm (Branigin 1989b). And it took several months for some hurricane victims in the Virgin Islands to receive safe drinking water and appropriate medical supplies (Christian 1992). Electrical power and communication systems were not repaired in some areas for almost a year (U.S. General Accounting Office 1991).

In the end, FEMA did play a critical role in facilitating recovery efforts in the Virgin Islands and Puerto Rico. It distributed massive amounts of financial aid to private businesses and governmental institutions. And the agency helped over 200,000 victims obtain essential disaster assistance (McAda 1989).

The Gap between Emergent Norms and Bureaucratic Norms

The plight of the Caribbean Islands in the aftermath of Hurricane Hugo illustrates an extremely wide gap between emergent norms and bureaucratic norms. The norms that developed following Hurricane Hugo centered on acts that would be considered socially deviant by normal standards. At the same time, the government was virtually powerless to do anything about the situation. Although the Caribbean Islands are a frequent target of tropical storms and hurricanes, the local response bureaucracy never anticipated a situation of this nature and magnitude. The system was designed to deal with "normal" disasters, in which communication and transportation networks could be easily restored and in which local officials could provide a first response. By almost any standard, Hurricane Hugo's devastation of the Caribbean was not a "normal" disaster; consequently, existing bureaucratic institutions were incapable of dealing with the situation. From this perspective, it is hardly surprising that the institutionalized governmental response process broke down entirely.

Top-Down Implementation Pattern

The experience in the Caribbean clearly illustrates an approach to policy implementation that is almost the exact opposite of the intended bottom-up pattern. In this situation, the federal government stepped in almost immediately and took control over virtually the entire effort. Disaster relief was initiated, directed, and actually implemented from the top down.

There are three main reasons why this top-down pattern occurred. First, the scope and severity of the disaster were a factor. Even before Hurricane Hugo struck the Caribbean islands, it was clear to all that this was an abnormally massive, extremely violent storm. It was highly likely that it would create a *major* natural disaster situation, thereby requiring the resources of the federal government. Normally, it takes almost two weeks after an event occurs for a governor to request federal aid and then another ten days for the president of the United States to reach a decision (U.S. General Accounting Office 1989). In the case of the Virgin Islands and Puerto Rico, standard procedures were accelerated greatly. Federal officials played a critical role in expediting this process. They located and established contact with appropriate territorial authorities, instructed them on how to ask for federal assistance, obtained their requests over makeshift telephone devices, and hand-carried the requests to the White House.

Second, local and territorial governments were unprepared and ill equipped to handle the massive destruction. They had not developed adequate emergency alert, recovery, and response plans. And they were unable to perform even the basic functions of government, such as maintaining law and order. Local situations deteriorated to such an extent that the federal government could not wait to supplement local and territorial efforts (U.S. General Accounting Office 1991). Consequently, the federal government stepped in and took control of virtually all activities. U.S. troops were sent in to stop the looting and pilfering. This was an extremely unusual scenario. It marked the first time since the 1960s that federal law enforcement officials had been used to curtail an outbreak of domestic unrest on U.S. soil (Christian 1992). The ineffectiveness of local and territorial organizations prompted this action. More specifically, the collapse of subnational institutions made it necessary for the governmental response to begin at the federal level.

Third, preexisting economic and demographic factors created difficulties. Hurricane Hugo hit some of the most densely populated, economically depressed, geographically dispersed, and racially tense areas of the Caribbean islands (York 1989). For example, St. Croix (in the U.S. Virgin Islands) has the highest population density of any of the fifty states. Similarly, almost one-third of the residents of Puerto Rico live below the federal poverty level. Even under the best scenario, it would be difficult to provide relief to disaster-stricken locales such as these. In the wake of one of the most violent hurricanes of the century, the utter absence of local and territorial support made it impossible to administer government assistance to these areas using the normal implementation procedures.

Perception of the Governmental Response: Failure

By almost all accounts, the government's response to Hurricane Hugo in the Caribbean was extraordinary. Standard operating procedures and processes quickly proved to be unworkable in the face of complete confusion and chaos. So the federal government stepped in and took charge of the situation. The top-down implementation pattern allowed the government to address some of the most pressing concerns on the islands. Order was restored; water and food were distributed to those in need; temporary housing was provided to thousands of victims; debris was cleared and removed; electrical systems were reconnected; and communication and transportation systems were rebuilt. FEMA's estimated expenditures for Puerto Rico and the Virgin Islands, as of January 1993, amounted to over $1 billion (Federal Emergency Management Agency 1993). And this does not include the funds that have, and will be, distributed by other federal agencies (e.g., the Small Business Administration and the departments of Agriculture, Education, and Transportation) or by territorial and local institutions. Unquestionably, the government has helped thousands of individuals, families, and businesses recover from the disaster.

But these efforts are overshadowed by other images. Most reports focused on the outbreaks of civil disobedience (such as the looting and domestic violence), the total failures of communication linkages with the U.S. mainland, and the massive breakdown in electrical power systems on the islands. In addition, there are serious issues surrounding the government's handling of this crisis (York 1989; Branigin 1989a; Piacente 1989). Why were local and territorial governments so ineffective? Why was the federal government caught off guard? Why did it take so long to provide assistance to some disaster-stricken citizens? And why was it necessary to bypass normal policies and procedures and create a top-down implementation pattern for emergency relief? In sum, the government seemed to be almost totally unprepared for this disaster situation (U.S. General Accounting Office 1991). Thus the public perception of the governmental response to Hurricane Hugo in the Caribbean Islands is clearly one of failure.

Notes

1. Much of the information for this case study was collected directly from the *Briefing Books* and *Mission Assignment Statements*, maintained by the Federal Emergency Management Agency in Washington, DC.

2. For additional information on the governmental response to Hurricane Hugo in the Caribbean, see the *Interagency Hazard Mitigation Team Reports*, prepared by the Region II Interagency Hazard Mitigation Team, Federal Emergency Management Agency.

8

Hurricane Andrew in South Florida

On August 14, 1992, a low-pressure weather system materialized off the coast of Africa. At first, there was nothing to distinguish this atmospheric ripple from the dozens of others that form every summer in this region of the world. But this one was different. Instead of dying out, this weather system slowly gained strength. By August 16, 1992, it had grown into a tropical depression. And the following day it was upgraded to a tropical storm and given the name "Andrew."

Over the next week, Andrew meandered nonchalantly across the South Atlantic. Then it suddenly picked up strength, gathered momentum, and developed into a Category IV hurricane. On August 24, Hurricane Andrew struck its first blow. It hit the Bahamas with 120-mile-per-hour winds, leaving at least four people dead and thousands more homeless. After ravaging the islands, this powerful storm moved back out into the Atlantic Ocean, where it proceeded to move along in a northwesterly direction.[1]

Early on August 24, Hurricane Andrew smacked into the U.S. coastline just thirty-five miles south of Miami, Florida. For several hours, Andrew pummeled the areas of Homestead, Cutler Ridge, and South Dade with 145- to 160-mile-per-hour winds and torrential rains. Andrew moved at about eighteen miles per hour across the tip of southern Florida. Everything in the storm's path was either leveled or severely disrupted. Gradually the storm moved back over open water in the Gulf of Mexico. Yet Andrew had changed the face of south Florida, perhaps forever (*The Big One* 1992, 8). At least thirty people died, over 175,000 were left homeless, and about 1.5 million residents lost electrical power. Several communities were severely damaged: for example, 65 to 75 percent of all the buildings in Homestead were obliterated. Overall, the storm caused $20 billion in property damages in south Florida, making it

August 1992. One of many trailer parks near Homestead, Florida, that was severely damaged by Hurricane Andrew.
Photo by Al Diaz, Miami Herald.

one of the most costly natural disasters ever to hit the United States (EQE International 1992).

The government's responsibility in the recovery process seemed perfectly clear: it should mobilize, organize, and channel all available resources to address the conditions in south Florida. Once again, however, the system was ill equipped to handle a disaster of this magnitude. Many public organizations were simply unable to respond, or they reacted slowly and ineffectively. And, to make matters worse, there seemed to be little or no coordination to any of the relief efforts.

Almost immediately, disaster victims began to feel that "they were on their own." They did not think that they could count on the government for assistance. As a result, a sizable gap developed between the attitudes of disaster victims and the policies of the government's emergency response organizations. In an attempt to deal with this situation, the government tried to alter many of its standard operating procedures. Unfortunately, these changes did more harm than good. They produced a disorderly, confusing system of policy implementation, and they led to even greater criticism of the government's efforts. As a result, the governmental response to Hurricane Andrew in south Florida is widely believed to have been an abysmal failure.

Milling Process: An Immediate Beginning

Hurricane Andrew left south Florida in a "collective mess" (*Andrew: Savagery from the Sea* 1992, 14). The storm caused extensive property damage across an 1,100-mile radius. Entire electrical systems were knocked out of commission because everything from wooden utility poles to oil-powered transformers was destroyed. Roads, highways, and airports were blocked by so much debris that normal transportation systems were virtually paralyzed. "A drive that would normally take less than an hour was a day-long obstacle course of downed trees, limp power lines, wrecked vehicles" (Manegold 1992b, A1). In addition, communication channels were disrupted, and in some cases totally destroyed, making it extremely difficult to place telephone calls into or out of the area (Federal Emergency Management Agency 1992a). All these factors created an eerie, desolate situation. Many disaster-stricken communities were isolated, their residents' fates unknown (Manegold 1992b).

Because of these conditions, the milling process began almost immediately. Hurricane victims stumbled around the rubble looking for food, water, and shelter. But the entire environment seemed to be transformed (Booth 1992a). Everyday surroundings appeared strange and unfamiliar.

Nothing looked the same; nothing sounded the same; nothing smelled the same; nothing *was* the same (*Andrew: Savagery from the Sea* 1992, 15).

First, people asked: why? Then, they wondered: where do we go from here, and how? The situation was simply too severe for individuals and families to handle on their own. One factor that made matters worse was that many of the disaster victims were relatively new to Florida and had never before experienced a serious hurricane, certainly not one the magnitude of Andrew. Some residents had been attracted to south Florida because of the climate. Others had moved into the area because of the military base or because of employment opportunities (Manegold 1992a, A9). As a result, they probably had greater difficulty grasping the scope and severity of their predicament. So their natural reaction was to begin searching for some direction and assistance.

Local officials tried to help. But they themselves were disaster victims (*Andrew: Savagery from the Sea* 1992, 24). Their own homes had been damaged or destroyed. And their families, friends, and neighbors were experiencing the same problems as everyone else. As a result, local officials were able to respond only to the most serious requests. It was simply impossible for them to address the vast majority of emergency calls (Peterson 1992). This in turn led to a situation in which chaos and confusion reigned. Or, as one bystander described the situation: one zone of society came unglued (Treaster 1992b).

Law and order became a major problem. Frightened and frustrated disaster victims stole supplies from neighborhood stores where they had once shopped. People simply took whatever food, water, and clothing they could find (Booth 1992a). Normal citizens became thieves and looters. "In malls, record shops, liquor stores, groceries, and electrical stores from Coral Gables to Florida City, it was like an insane party as laughing thieves helped themselves" (*Andrew: Savagery from the Sea* 1992, 40). Then, to make matters worse, greedy store owners sold the supplies that were available at outrageous prices; such gouging was widespread throughout the affected areas (Booth and Jordan 1992; Jordan 1992a; Treaster 1992a).

Local police and National Guardsmen were dispatched in order to stabilize the situation. But these forces were relatively small in number and were dispersed throughout the disaster-stricken areas, so they were no match for the miniarmies of looters and price-gouging citizens. Law enforcement officials were unable to stop the disorderly and unlawful behavior (Gore 1993). Local residents felt they had to take matters into their own hands. Homeowners walked the streets with pistols, rifles, and shotguns to protect what little remained of their dwellings and possessions. Business owners hired private security guards to prevent further looting and theft (Jordan 1992a).

Disaster victims were engaged in behavior that previously (before Andrew) was universally deemed unacceptable. Now, however, they believed that such actions were necessary for their own survival. Erratic, deviant behavior became the norm. One storm victim was caught taking food from a convenience store and rationalized the deviant behavior by explaining: "I need food. I need milk for my cousin's baby. We have nothing. You don't understand. What can I do?" (*Andrew: Savagery from the Sea* 1992, 40, 42). This truly chaotic situation continued for several days following the hurricane.

Governmental Response: Slow and Misguided

For many years, experts had been issuing warnings about exactly this kind of disaster: a monster storm hitting a major urban area. And Andrew was also the type of event that the government had been expecting. Several months earlier, in April 1992, the federal government presented a set of policies and procedures to guide public and private actions during a major disaster situation (Federal Emergency Management Agency 1992b; Lippman 1992a). The fundamental assumptions, structure, and workings of this system were outlined in a document called the Federal Response Plan. This plan was to provide the basic "architecture for a systematic, coordinated, and effective federal response" (Federal Emergency Management Agency 1992b, 1). Signed by twenty-seven federal agencies, the plan had already been "field proven" for implementation during a large-scale natural disaster (Peterson 1992). This was the basic plan that would guide governmental activity before, during, and after Hurricane Andrew.

Several days before Andrew hit the U.S. mainland, hurricane watches were issued for south Florida from Titusville to the Keys. And the entire intergovernmental emergency response system was activated (Rohter 1992a). Local emergency preparedness personnel were put on alert. City and county officials issued warnings to citizens who lived in the low-lying, coastal communities. Florida's emergency management and civil defense personnel were placed on "stand-by" status. The Federal Emergency Management Agency alerted its own personnel and sent an advance team into Florida to assist state and local operations (Peterson 1992).

Then, on Sunday, August 23, the National Weather Service issued a hurricane warning for south Florida. It was now clear that Andrew would strike somewhere between Vero Beach and the Florida Keys. Florida's Governor Lawton Chiles declared a state of emergency. He ordered the mandatory evacuation of about a million people who lived on the barrier islands, and he strongly encouraged other residents living along the coast to leave their homes. The governor opened emergency shelters for those who could not or would not leave the area. By midafternoon, the evacuation was in full swing, and the highways heading out of south Florida were almost completely jammed with evacuees. Later that evening, just about the time that Andrew reached the Bahamas, major airports in the area were shut down and Miami Beach was closed. FEMA personnel, who were already prepositioned in the area, set up their own Emergency Operations Center and convened a Catastrophic Disaster Response Group with other federal agencies. The FEMA officials who were working in Governor Chiles's office in Tallahassee immediately began preparing the necessary paperwork for a presidential declaration of a major disaster (Federal Emergency Management Agency 1992a).

Within hours of Andrew's onslaught, emergency management personnel began assessing the damages in south Florida, and it was obvious that extraordinary measures were needed. Governor Chiles called in the National Guard to help local law enforcement officials, and he formally requested that President Bush declare south Florida a federal disaster area. Within hours, the president approved Governor Chiles's request, thereby authorizing the federal government's intervention in this particular disaster. Later that same day, Bush flew to the area to inspect the damages firsthand (Federal Emergency Management Agency 1992a). It appeared as though the government would mobilize all its powers and resources to address this catastrophe. And it would use the new Federal Response Plan to coordinate and guide the entire effort. But it would take time to "prime the pump" of the giant governmental response system (Peterson 1992). Until that occurred, the disaster-stricken communities in south Florida would be on their own.

For the first few days after Andrew, local emergency management personnel tried to respond to the disaster. County officials opened shelters for citizens who had lost their homes, and they provided free public transportation for local residents; however, these measures were woefully inadequate for the situation at hand (*Governor's Disaster Planning and Response Review Committee* 1993). For example, in Dade County, the police force (a team of 1,500 officers) could respond only to "life-threatening emergencies and crimes actually in progress." They simply could not answer or handle any other calls or requests for assistance. Dade County's emergency officials were like "children battling a forest fire with squirt guns" (*The Big One: Hurricane Andrew* 1992, 17).

State officials tried to supplement local-level actions. Florida's emergency operations center was activated for twenty-four-hour operations, and all available personnel were sent to the disaster-stricken areas to augment local efforts. Governor Chiles had already called up five battalions of National Guard troops to augment local efforts. These troops were primarily used to maintain law and order. They patroled devastated neighborhoods and business areas with rifles in order to stop the stealing and looting. And they set up checkpoints and roadblocks along major thoroughfares in order to turn back sightseers and those who would take advantage of the situation. When conditions in the disaster-stricken areas did not improve, the governor sent in additional troops of National Guardsmen (*Governor's Disaster Planning and Response Review Committee* 1993).

Meanwhile, the Federal Emergency Management Agency concentrated on implementing the Federal Response Plan. It deployed a mobile Emergency Response Support unit to Orlando, sent additional personnel into the disaster areas, and established a disaster field office at the Miami International Airport. Basically, FEMA focused its initial efforts on getting itself into position so that it would be ready to respond (Federal Emergency Management Agency 1992a). It was waiting for the state of Florida to submit specific requests for aid. This was precisely what FEMA was supposed to do, according to the policies and procedures of the intergovernmental response system.

Unfortunately, this did not bring relief to the disaster-stricken victims of south Florida. In fact, it actually exacerbated their problems. Local officials were completely overwhelmed and unable to respond. The state of Florida erroneously believed that it could handle the situation without direct federal intervention (Zensinger 1992). And FEMA would not circumvent standard operating policies to initiate actions on its own. The entire intergovernmental response system was paralyzed.

Emergent Norms: "Where the Hell Is the Cavalry?"

Private donations poured into south Florida from all over the country, and volunteers flocked to the area to provide assistance. But many roads and highways remained blocked because of hurricane-related debris and traffic jams. As a result, it was virtually impossible to get supplies and equipment to those in need (Hamilton and Johnson 1992). Four days after the hurricane, 250,000 people lacked food and water and about 50,000 were homeless. Over a million residents were still without electrical service (Federal Emergency Management Agency 1992a).

Theft, looting, and price gouging continued to be major problems. "Many residents struggled with deep fear for their own safety" (Treaster 1992b, A8). In general, people were becoming more frustrated, more impatient, and more irritable. Disaster victims had to stand in long lines to

August 1992. Residents of South Dade County, Florida, found new and unusual ways to express their feelings about the response efforts following Hurricane Andrew. *Photo by Chuck Fadely, Miami Herald.*

obtain even such basic necessities as food and water (Barron 1992a, A14). The relief effort seemed to be almost totally uncoordinated. No one appeared to be in charge.

Stories and rumors proliferated (Booth 1992b). There were accusations that the government agencies responsible for the relief effort were actually conducting a massive cover-up. Some residents believed that the government was not reporting the "real" death toll. Others even claimed that public authorities were themselves removing dead bodies and burying them in massive secret grave sites (Rohter 1992d). Most public attention, however, focused directly on the federal government's emergency response activities. The day after Andrew hit, President Bush had promised storm victims that "help was on the way." But local and state officials claimed that the federal government was not responding (Rohter 1992b). Governor Chiles complained that urgent requests for federal assistance had been delayed or hopelessly lost because of bureaucratic red tape and confusion (Jordan 1992b). Kate Hale, director of Dade County's Emergency Office, stated: "We have appealed through the state to the federal government. We've had a lot of people down here for press conferences. But [in the end] it is Dade County on its own. . . . Where the hell is the cavalry on this one?" (*Andrew: Savagery from the Sea* 1992, 28). This question captured the overall sense of frustration and helplessness that disaster victims felt. Moreover, it characterized the public's general impression of the government's efforts—particularly those of the federal government. The image of an uncaring, unresponsive, and inept federal government became the emergent norm in south Florida.

In order to change this image, the government tried to modify its own policies and procedures (U.S. General Accounting Office 1993b; Federal Emergency Management Agency 1992a, 1993). Two days after the storm, President Bush appointed Andrew Card, the secretary of transportation, to lead a Task Force on Hurricane Andrew Recovery (Peterson 1992). Secretary Card went to south Florida as the president's personal representative to the disaster. His major objective was to "cut through the bureaucratic mess" (Mathews et al. 1992, 27). Secretary Card monitored the entire relief effort, and he became involved in the actual implementation of disaster assistance. For example, he encouraged FEMA personnel to distribute money directly to storm victims without going through the lengthy assessment and verification processes. Basically, he wanted relief workers to provide assistance quickly and expeditiously, regardless of standard operating procedures (Federal Emergency Management Agency 1992b). Unfortunately, this only created more problems and delays for the governmental response system. Normal procedures were circumvented, but there were no new policies or measures to replace them. Thousands of disaster victims were still without food, water, electricity, and shelter (Treaster 1992b).

In order to address this situation, President Bush decided to take additional steps. He ordered federal troops to south Florida. The first U.S. Army and Marine forces arrived in south Florida on Saturday, August 29—five days after the storm. Almost immediately, they airlifted in supplies and began distributing food, water, and generators (Peterson 1992). They set up field kitchens to feed storm victims and relief workers. They also constructed tent cities to shelter the homeless, and they started clearing roads and airport runways of debris so that transportation systems could reopen (Rohter 1992b, A1). In addition, military forces were sent to stabilize conditions in the most devastated areas: They were to help state and local law enforcement officials stop the looting, pilfering, and price gouging (Treaster 1992b, A1, A8).[2]

The federal government now seemed to be aware of the problems in south Florida, and it was pouring personnel, materials, and supplies into the storm-hit area (Wines 1992). In fact, federal agencies were channeling an extraordinary array of resources to this disaster situation. In order to view the relief effort firsthand, President Bush flew back to south Florida. During this second visit, the president expanded the scope of federal disaster assistance even further. He promised that Homestead Air Force Base would be completely rebuilt and that the federal government would shoulder the entire financial burden for such cleanup projects as debris removal, sewer maintenance, and school reconstruction (Rohter 1992c). At this time, there was no way to estimate the cost of all this federal aid. Yet President Bush indicated that such actions were necessary because of the extraordinary magnitude of this disaster.

Clearly, however, there were also strong political pressures to bring additional federal resources to bear on this situation. Hurricane Andrew struck Florida in the summer of a presidential election year. And Florida was considered by many analysts to be a vital state in determining the outcome of the election (Davis 1992b; Rohter 1992e). As one campaign official remarked, "It wouldn't be so bad if Andrew blew on up to Kentucky and the rust-belt states" where Bush was behind in the polls (Mathews et al. 1992, 27). Overall, the politics of disaster relief are easy to follow: "Show up, express concern, promise money—and you will be rewarded with votes" (Mathews et al. 1992, 27).

The Gap between Emergent Norms and Bureaucratic Procedures

In south Florida, a wide gap developed between the public's expectations and the government's actions. The general public felt that the federal government should be responsible for a disaster of this magnitude. Clearly, the situation in south Florida was beyond the capability of state and local authorities. But the federal government did not step in and take charge of the relief effort. Instead, it dealt with this situation as it had dealt with hundreds of other disasters by trying to get itself into a position from which it could supplement state and local actions. During the interim, however, conditions in south Florida deteriorated even further. Thousands of storm victims still lacked even the most basic life-support services—food, water, ice, electricity, and shelter. Frustrated, irritable, and disenchanted citizens took matters into their own hands in order to obtain essential supplies for themselves and their families. Looting and security were major problems (Peterson 1992).

The federal government did modify its standard operating policies and procedures to address these unusually severe conditions. Unfortunately, this did not change the way people viewed the relief effort. In fact, it actually raised more questions and concerns about the federal government's role in a major natural catastrophe.[3] After all, why did disaster-stricken communities have to ask for federal assistance? Why did the federal government respond so slowly? Why wasn't the military called in sooner? Why was it necessary to appoint a presidential representative to lead the relief effort? And where was FEMA? To paraphrase the quote presented earlier from Kate Hale, director of Dade County's Emergency Office, "Who the hell was the cavalry, and why didn't they charge in and address the problems?"

Mass Confusion Implementation Pattern

The governmental response to Hurricane Andrew in south Florida conforms, once again, to the confusion pattern of policy implementation. Clearly, the process did *not* move smoothly and methodically from the local level to the state and ultimately to the national government—as it should have done, according to the bottom-up pattern. Nor did it resemble a top-down approach in which the national government stepped in and took over the process. Instead, different actors at each level of government tried to respond to the situation without any real coordination or synchronization to guide these efforts. As a result, there was both intergovernmental and intragovernmental confusion in the implementation of emergency relief.

First, there was almost complete chaos at the local level. As previously mentioned, local emergency management officials were themselves victims of the storm. Their natural concerns were about their own situations. This made it extremely difficult for local relief workers to focus on all the other problems that existed in what was left of their communities. Even if this had not been the case, local officials still would not have been able to mobilize an effective "first" response to an event such as Andrew. They simply did not have the resources, manpower, or authority to handle a disaster of this magnitude. In addition, they were ill equipped to perform their preassigned responsibilities once the relief effort was initiated (*Governor's Disaster Planning and Response Review Committee* 1993). Exactly *what* should they request from higher levels of government? It seemed as though everything was in short supply. *Whom* should they ask for help? Several federal agencies were on the scene, but none of them seemed to be in charge. *How* should they request assistance? They were unable to communicate with their own personnel, let alone with higher governmental units. In sum, local officials were completely overwhelmed by the severity of this disaster.

There were also serious problems at the state level. In the intergovernmental response system, state governments play an important intermediary role. They are to direct all their resources to situations that are clearly beyond the scope of local authorities. And they must request and then coordinate the federal government's intervention during major disasters. If these functions are not performed, the intergovernmental process collapses. Unfortunately, this is exactly what happened in south Florida following Hurricane Andrew.

The state of Florida appeared to be totally unprepared for this kind of emergency. A major hurricane had not hit Florida in a number of years. And some state officials may simply have believed that they did not really need to worry about disaster preparedness or response. This attitude even seems to have been prevalent within the state's emergency management system. Officials from the Florida Department of Community Affairs had not attended regional meetings on disaster preparedness for quite some time. In sum, they seemed to have adopted a "don't bother us" approach (McKay 1992). Clearly, emergency preparedness was not a high priority in the everyday agenda of Florida's state government.

Florida officials also may have seriously underestimated the severity of this particular situation (*Governor's Disaster Planning and Response Review Committee* 1993). Governor Chiles did submit a request to President Bush for federal aid almost immediately following the hurricane. But state officials did not have any clear idea about the extent of the damages in south Florida (Mathews et al. 1992, 24). As a result, they did not ask for certain critical resources. For example, the governor apparently thought that the Florida National Guard could handle the situation. So he did not initially request federal military support (Peterson 1992). But state and local law enforcement officials were quickly overwhelmed. They were unable to deal with the problems—looting, pilfering, price gouging—that emerged almost immediately within the disaster-stricken areas. Eventually, federal military troops were called in to stabilize conditions. Nevertheless, serious questions have been raised about why the state did not request federal law enforcement assistance earlier.

Overall, Florida did not perform its intermediary role in the emergency response process (Zensinger 1992). The state did not effectively channel local requests upward to the federal government, nor did it direct federal assistance back downward to the areas most in need. As a result, Florida was a "nonplayer" in the intergovernmental response system. At times, it almost disappeared from the scene altogether.

Unquestionably, however, the largest degree of confusion occurred at the national level. The federal government did not respond quickly to the situation in south Florida. And when it did respond, it did not act in a unified or coordinated fashion. Instead of one focus (or central organization) for the federal effort, there were actually three: FEMA, Transportation Secretary Card, and the U.S. military. All three of these "leaders" played an important role in channeling federal assistance to the storm-damaged areas of south Florida. Unfortunately, each one usually acted independently of the other two. This led to miscommunication and duplication among federal agencies, and it created massive confusion within the entire intergovernmental response system.

As always, the Federal Emergency Management Agency was supposed to be the official leader of the national-level governmental response. The agency did try to mobilize and coordinate the relief effort. Before Hurricane Andrew struck the U.S. mainland, FEMA officials were in south Florida helping the state prepare the necessary paperwork required to request federal assistance. Immediately after President Bush declared the area a major disaster, FEMA sent in additional personnel and established field operations in the storm-damaged communities. FEMA set up Disaster Assistance Centers (DACs) within the affected areas so that storm victims could apply for emergency relief. It also used a national teleregistration system (actually located in Denton, Texas), which enabled the agency to double its processing capacity for disaster-assistance requests. By the end of 1992 (three and one-half months after Andrew), FEMA had approved approximately 44,000 applications for temporary housing and over 48,000 requests for individual and family grants. It had already distributed hundreds of millions of dollars in aid, and it was projecting total expenditures to run in the billions (Federal Emergency Management Agency 1993). Thus, FEMA played a major role in helping the south Florida disaster victims recover from Hurricane Andrew.

Despite these accomplishments, FEMA did not react to this disaster in a timely or efficient manner. The agency did not step in immediately to provide emergency assistance to storm victims, and it did not coordinate the actions of other public or private disaster-assistance organizations. In sum, it did not mobilize, coordinate, or lead the governmental response.

Because of FEMA's inability to handle the disaster, President Bush appointed a presidential task force, called the "Hurricane Andrew Relief Effort," to cut through the bureaucratic red tape and "to make the response happen" (Mathews et al. 1992, 26). Transportation Secretary Card was placed in charge of the task force, thereby creating a second leader for the federal government's operations. Secretary Card took charge of the federal command system and issued a series of directives to "jump-start" the entire response process. For example, he ordered relief workers to make immediate eligibility determinations for individual assistance, without waiting for the normal inspection of damages. And he doubled the maximum amount of money that storm victims could receive for making repairs to their homes. Although these measures helped expedite the delivery of governmental assistance, they also bypassed existing policies and processes. In the end, they were disruptive, confusing, and expensive.

When the military was sent in to bring order to the affected areas, the federal government placed a third leader on the scene. The Department of Defense effectively used army and marine troops to assess the seriousness of the situation and develop appropriate strategies for dealing with the most pressing problems. The military airlifted in tons of food, supplies, and equipment; it cleared debris from the streets and airports; it used mobile field kitchens to serve meals to hungry citizens and relief workers; it erected tent cities to house the homeless; and it operated clinic facilities that provided emergency medical care to local residents (Federal Emergency Management Agency 1992a). In addition, army and marine troops were used to stabilize conditions in the disaster-stricken areas. They were sent in to reassure citizens that relief was on its way and to remind them not to engage in unorthodox behavior. The military played a critical role in the government's relief efforts in south Florida. Yet it often acted independently of other organizations and agencies. More specifically, the military bypassed the official disaster-response structure as well as the "unofficial," presidential emergency operation (U.S. General Accounting Office 1993a).

Thus there were three parallel relief systems all trying to administer disaster assistance. Consequently, it is really not surprising that there were delays, disorder, and at times even complete chaos at the federal level. Moreover, this "three-headed" leadership of the federal government's operations undoubtedly created more confusion throughout the entire intergovernmental response system: state and local governments may simply not have known whom to contact to receive appropriate assistance. Once again, no one appeared to be in charge of the relief effort. In the end, the government reacted in a sluggish, haphazard, and disjointed fashion.

Public Perception: Abysmal Failure

The government was eventually able to mobilize a massive relief operation to help the storm victims in south Florida. In so doing, the federal government provided an unprecedented amount of assistance to the Hurricane Andrew victims. Despite these efforts, however, the public's perception of the governmental effort was primarily negative (Walden 1992). The government did not react quickly, and it did not respond immediately to this disaster situation, even though thousands of storm victims lacked critical life-sustaining supplies. Local citizens were forced to take matters into their own hands because the government did not provide effective guidance or support. Even when the government did respond, it did not act in a coordinated or unified manner. This created further delays in the administration of disaster assistance.

The national government is widely believed to be primarily responsible for the apparently poor performance of the disaster-relief system. Local and state governments were completely overwhelmed; only the federal government had the resources and the authority to handle a disaster of this magnitude. But, to paraphrase the aforementioned quote from a local emergency management director, where the hell was the cavalry? More specifically, where was FEMA? Unfortunately, FEMA was both unable and unwilling to respond quickly and effectively to this disaster. Once again—just as in South Carolina following Hugo, FEMA, not the hurricane, was considered to be the real disaster (Lippman 1992b).[4] The entire governmental response was regarded as a complete failure.

Notes

1. Most of the material on the origin and movement of Hurricane Andrew was obtained from the National Oceanic and Atmospheric Administration (U.S. Department of Commerce 1993).

2. For a more complete description of the military's role during the Hurricane Andrew relief efforts in south Florida, see the U.S. General Accounting Office Report (1993a) *Disaster Assistance: DOD's Support for Hurricanes Andrew and Iniki and Typhoon Omar*. As the title implies, this report also contains information on the military's efforts in several other disaster situations.

3. There are several excellent newspaper articles on the inability of the federal government's relief agencies, particularly FEMA, to respond quickly and effectively to the situation in south Florida. See, for example, Davis (1992a, 1992b), Lippman (1992a, 1992b), Kilborn (1992), and Claiborne (1992a, 1992b).

4. Criticism of the government's actions during this disaster led to a series of investigations into and analyses of the federal response system. See, for example, U.S. House (1993), U.S. Senate (1993b, 1993c), U.S. General Accounting Office (1993b), Federal Emergency Management Agency (1993), and the National Academy of Public Administration (1993).

9

South Carolina's Experience with Hurricane Hugo

Hurricane Hugo's path of destruction did not end in the Caribbean. Shortly after midnight on September 22, 1989, Hugo struck the U.S. mainland approximately forty miles northeast of Charleston, South Carolina. Although most hurricanes weaken when they reach land, this one did not. Instead, it pounded the coastal areas for several hours and then moved quickly and violently in a northwesterly direction up through the center of the state.

By sunrise the next morning, the storm was far to the north. But Hurricane Hugo had left an indelible mark on South Carolina. Power was out in approximately half the state; houses were torn apart, moved, or destroyed. Personal belongings were scattered everywhere. Roads, bridges, and fishing piers were demolished. Trees were twisted, toppled, and uprooted. Thousands of people were left without shelter, food, water, electricity, and sewer facilities. Overall, much of the state of South Carolina looked like a "war zone" (Schneider 1989).

Once again, it was clear that governmental resources would be needed to address this disaster situation. Emergency management personnel at all governmental levels took steps to activate the response process even before the storm hit the coast of South Carolina. But the government was simply unable to administer disaster relief using the standard bottom-up process. Problems at local, state, and federal levels produced a confusion pattern of policy implementation. This affected the speed and efficiency of the governmental response and influenced the public's perceptions of the government's effort. Similarly, it led to sharp criticisms of the actions (and inactions) of the federal government, particularly those of the Federal Emergency Management Agency. In the end, it fostered a lasting impression of governmental nonresponsiveness.

September 1989. Hurricane Hugo sheared off the tops of the vast majority of longleaf and loblolly pines in the 250,000-acre Francis Marion Forest in South Carolina. *Photo by BD Communications and Publishing, Inc.*

An Early Milling Process

The milling process began almost immediately in South Carolina. Hugo had altered, and in some cases completely changed, the entire landscape. Whole buildings were flattened, and automobiles were crushed beyond recognition. Sidewalks were pulled up from the ground, and bridges were twisted apart. Boats were resting on top of garages and lawns, having been picked up out of the water and placed ashore miles from their original locations. In addition, the storm had disrupted almost all transportation and communication systems in the affected areas. Streets and roads were impassable because of waist-deep water and mounds of debris. Airports were inoperable due to the storm's damage to planes, runways, and hangars. Telephone and television service was almost nonexistent.[1]

These conditions made it extremely difficult for the affected population to comprehend exactly what had happened to them. Many victims were now faced with problems that they had never before even contemplated, let alone experienced. They were stunned, almost shell-shocked. They felt that their world had been turned upside down. One resident described his family's reactions as they emerged from their house immediately after the

September 1989. Numerous homes on Sullivan's Island, the oldest of Charleston's resort areas, were severely damaged or completely flattened by Hurricane Hugo. *Photo by BD Communications and Publishing, Inc.*

storm: "At first when we walked outside, we couldn't figure out where we were. . . . It was desolate." Another victim remarked: "I was just numb with feelings. . . . It seemed like the day after the end of the world" (*And Hugo Was His Name* 1989, 14).

Unlike events in the Caribbean, there were no instances of social unrest or disorder in South Carolina. Disaster victims were disoriented and confused, but they did not engage in extreme forms of unconventional conduct or behavior—looting or rioting. This partly reflected the actions taken by public officials before the storm moved onto the U.S. mainland.

Governmental Response Activated, Then Stalls

The governmental response process was already well under way before Hurricane Hugo hit the South Carolina coastline. At the local level, steps were taken to prepare coastal communities for a major storm. Disaster-relief agencies alerted residents in the storm's path to take precautionary measures, and they began to activate their own emergency response plans. Mayor Joseph P. Riley of Charleston, South Carolina, used a series of radio and television announcements to urge people, especially those in low-lying areas, to move immediately to higher ground. Mayor Riley used the strongest terms to convince people that the storm was extremely dangerous and that they had to evacuate (Riley 1989).

The state's response system had also been activated. The South Carolina Emergency Preparedness Division had been tracking the storm for several days and had already alerted local disaster agencies, as well as other state officials, of the impending emergency. Based on these warnings, South Carolina Governor Carroll Campbell officially declared a "state of emergency" and recommended that residents leave the coastal areas. The governor also sent the National Guard to the coast to help state and local law enforcement officials evacuate the areas and maintain order. The governor issued a stark warning that the state would not tolerate any looting or disorder after the storm (Beckham 1989). In addition, the governor established his own communication and command center, separate from the existing state apparatus. This was done so that the governor could receive information directly from the counties and deploy the state's resources "swiftly and effectively" (Carter 1989). On September 21, 1989, Governor Campbell took the extreme step of ordering a mandatory evacuation of the coastal areas around Charleston (Sponhour 1989a; Carter 1989).

The federal government was also involved by this time. In fact, FEMA had already sent personnel (on September 20) to the three areas on the U.S. mainland most likely to be hit by Hugo—Georgia, South Carolina, and North Carolina. When it became clear that South Carolina was to bear the brunt of the storm, FEMA was able to concentrate its efforts and go to work quickly (Mosco 1989; Peterson 1989). The night before Hugo struck, top-level FEMA personnel met with Governor Campbell and his staff in Columbia, the state capital. They began to prepare the materials necessary to document a gubernatorial request for federal aid to South Carolina (Carter 1989).

Around eight o'clock the next morning (on September 22, 1989), FEMA headquarters in Washington, D.C., received Governor Campbell's official request for federal assistance. Approximately two and a half hours later, President Bush declared an emergency and initiated the federal response. Thus the South Carolina gubernatorial request and the presidential declaration both occurred less than six hours after Hugo's departure from the state (Peterson 1989). Again, the response moved quickly through local and state governments up to the federal government. Almost immediately, the federal government became the focal point for disaster assistance, and once again, FEMA was in charge of relief efforts.

To the greatest extent possible, FEMA tried to create order out of chaos (Hall 1989). FEMA determined that one of its first priorities was to restore electrical power. Electricity was needed in order to provide many other essential services. So the agency focused much of its early efforts on locating and transporting emergency generators and repairing power lines in disaster-stricken areas. Along with this, FEMA concentrated on clearing roads and on reopening bridges and ferry services so that life-sustaining supplies such as food, water, and medicine could get to affected areas. The agency also quickly authorized and financed a number of important construction and cleanup activities—such as repairs to roadways and bridges, extensive debris-removal activities, public health and safety precautionary measures, and the construction of an emergency sand dune in the Myrtle Beach area (Peterson 1989). Once these basic steps had been taken, FEMA tried to take an active role in directing federal assistance to severely damaged areas. The agency's actions added more counties to the list of federal disaster areas, beyond those originally specified in the presidential declaration. After FEMA's extensions, more than half the state (twenty-six of the forty-six counties) qualified for federal aid (Hall 1989). FEMA eventually set up more than thirty Disaster Application Centers in these counties, in order to help people obtain public and private relief.[2]

As a result of these massive efforts, most of the state of South Carolina recovered fairly quickly from the disaster. Food, water, and medical supplies were distributed to those in need. Temporary housing facilities were transported into the state, providing immediate shelter to individuals and families who had lost their homes. In many of the affected areas, power was restored, bridges and roads were repaired, and tons of debris were removed within several weeks. But this was not the situation everywhere.

Milling Process Accelerates

Many small coastal towns and cities were largely cut off from the rest of the state, and they received little outside assistance and relief. Even more severe isolation occurred among rural families located in the swampy, low-lying areas of eastern South Carolina. Many of these people had experienced the full force of the hurricane, and their needs were particularly acute. Yet the government was unable to provide relief to these victims in a timely or effective fashion. Consequently, some families lived for months without electricity, telephones, or any real contact with the outside world (Lewis 1989).

The sense of helplessness and anomie intensified among disaster victims as the recovery effort progressed in South Carolina. Many disaster victims were told that it would be weeks, even months, before they would receive emergency relief. Others still had not been informed that they could obtain assistance. When one victim was asked if he would apply to FEMA for help, he replied, "I haven't heard of them" (Lancaster 1989). The impression developed across the state that no one seemed to be helping those truly in need and that no on really appeared to be in charge of the response or recovery efforts.

Because of these conditions and sentiments, the milling process continued in South Carolina for several months. During this time, the most prominent keynoting behavior was exhibited by Charleston Mayor Joseph Riley and U.S. Senator Ernest Hollings. Both officials were highly critical of the federal government. Mayor Riley (1989) initially complained that the federal response had been slow and inadequate. He later stated that "the *national* government should assume *full* responsibility for a *national* disaster like Hugo" (Riley 1989). Senator Hollings was even more critical of the federal government's efforts, particularly the actions of the Federal Emergency Management Agency. Senator Hollings called the Federal Emergency Management Agency a "bunch of bureaucratic jackasses," and he claimed that it was more concerned with regulations, forms, assessments, and inspections than with helping those in need (Bandy 1989b).

The media provided support for these charges. There were numerous reports that FEMA's obsession with paperwork and documentation was preventing the release of critical emergency assistance to disaster victims (Miller 1989a; Livingston 1989; Lancaster 1989; Sponhour 1989b; Bandy 1990). This led to the widespread perception that FEMA was ineffective, inefficient, and unresponsive (Parker 1989; Cook 1989; Bandy 1989a). Beliefs about FEMA's incompetence became the emergent norm during the recovery process in South Carolina.

On the other side, the government departed from its standard operating procedures in several ways. First, local-level emergency management officials were largely ineffective because they were untrained and unprepared: They simply did not know what procedures to follow or how to work within the existing response system (Rubin and Popkin 1990). Consequently, they often failed to submit requests to proper authorities, or they used bureaucratic end runs to obtain relief through unofficial means (Lancaster 1989; Lewis 1989).

There was also a serious problem at the state level. Instead of one central disaster-response unit in South Carolina, there were two. The first was the South Carolina Emergency Preparedness Division, a permanent unit within the state government. The second was hastily created in the governor's office during the night before the storm hit. The result was a dual system that added to the already chaotic situation created by the hurricane (Eichel 1989; Schneider 1990; U.S. General Accounting Office 1991). This adversely affected standard operating procedures and generated confusion within the entire intergovernmental response system.

The federal response effort—particularly FEMA—had severe problems of its own. FEMA's organizational resources were simply inadequate. Immediately after Hugo, hundreds of FEMA workers were activated from around the country and sent to South Carolina (McAda 1989). Nevertheless, this large contingent was quickly overwhelmed by the demands placed on it. Furthermore, FEMA's reporting, assessment, and inspection procedures were inappropriate for the severity of the disaster and the extreme isolation of much of the affected population. FEMA officials expected Hugo's victims to come to them. There was (at least initially) no provision for the people who were out of contact with government and the rest of society (Fretwell 1989a, 1989b). Hence they were largely forgotten during the weeks immediately following the hurricane (Applebome 1989; Tuten 1989).

The Gap between Emergent Norms and Bureaucratic Procedures

In South Carolina, the gap between the public's expectations and the government's efforts was quite large. This occurred because the predominant emergent norm was overtly hostile to the governmental response process itself: the public thought the *federal* government was primarily responsible for the relief effort, even though the response system depends on *state* and *local* guidance. The gap also developed because the government's response process did not conform to prevailing conditions within the affected areas of South Carolina. Even when governmental officials followed standard operating procedures, their actions often appeared to be inappropriate for the situation at hand.

Confusion Implementation Pattern

As explained earlier, FEMA officials as well as state and local governments anticipated the hurricane before it hit the coast of South Carolina. But there was no clear-cut line of communication from counties and municipalities through the state up to the national government. Thus South Carolina is a perfect example of the "confusion" pattern of intergovernmental policymaking. The response process was initiated simultaneously at the federal, state, and local levels, but there was little coordination or integration between and across different governmental units. For example, Governor Campbell and Mayor Riley worked independently of each other to bring relief to the Charleston area. And South Carolina Senator Ernest Hollings tried to channel needed relief into the state apart from the ongoing, institutionalized efforts (Schneider 1990).

Many of the problems experienced in South Carolina stem directly from the existence of the confusion pattern. This affected the response effort in at least five different ways. First, the scope of the disaster was itself a problem. Most "normal" disasters, such as floods and tornadoes, occur in fairly limited geographic areas. In such situations, the federal response is less urgent because state and local officials can usually handle the most pressing concerns. Even most hurricanes do not require an immediate federal presence. There is usually time for state and local officials to alert the population and to prepare their own response (Peterson 1989). But Hugo caused massive destruction for hundreds of miles. Many of those who were hit the hardest lived in isolated, economically depressed, rural communities throughout the entire eastern portion of the state. It would be difficult to reach these individuals even under the best of circumstances (Sponhour 1989c). Given the scope and severity of the situation, however, it was virtually impossible to provide relief to these victims quickly or effectively. The normal response and recovery system was ill equipped to handle a catastrophe of this magnitude.

Second, the "confusion" pattern revealed several basic weaknesses in the local response system. The entire intergovernmental process is based on the assumption that federal aid will supplement state and local efforts. In order for this to work, local governments must be able to identify the needs of disaster-stricken areas and communicate them through the proper state channels to the federal government. Hugo made it clear that many local officials in South Carolina were not fully aware of their own responsibilities in a crisis or how the response system worked (Mittler 1988). They did not know that they had to determine local needs and then process them through the governor's office before the federal government could respond. Even those who understood the system were not prepared or equipped to cope with a disaster of Hugo's magnitude. They simply did not have the experience, expertise, or resources to handle such a massive emergency. They thought the federal government would step in and take charge of the situation (Schneider 1990). Stated simply, they developed unrealistic expectations about the federal government's capabilities and obligations. Hence they became extremely frustrated with and critical of the agency at the helm of the federal effort—FEMA.

Third, the existence of two emergency management units at the state level added to the already confused state of affairs in South Carolina. A basic assumption of the intergovernmental response system is that each state has a well-developed, coordinated disaster-response mechanism and that a single state agency is in charge of this process. This is absolutely essential so that requests for assistance can be channeled quickly and efficiently to appropriate sources of relief. On paper at least, South Carolina has such a system. According to state statutes and regulations, the Emergency Preparedness Division is the primary state agency responsible for disaster relief. It serves as the designated, coordinating point of contact between the state and local governments during an emergency situation (South Carolina State Regulations 58-101, D).

But the night before Hugo hit the South Carolina coast, the governor used his emergency powers to create a second emergency management command post. This allowed the governor to communicate more directly with local communities and to mobilize additional state resources (i.e., agents from the South Carolina Law Enforcement Division were utilized in relief operations). The creation of a second command post also allowed the governor to circumvent the existing state emergency management system. Perhaps there were doubts about the state's ability to handle a crisis such as Hugo using standard organizational mechanisms. After all, the South Carolina Emergency Preparedness Division had a long history of being underfunded and understaffed (Eichel 1989; U.S. General Accounting Office 1991). Moreover, the agency reportedly had internal management and leadership problems, which had led to seriously sagging morale within the agency (Miller 1992).

Although it may have seemed like a sound decision at the time, the creation of a second state emergency management system weakened the preexisting intergovernmental response framework. More specifically, it undermined the state government's ability to serve as a clearinghouse for the overall relief effort. This in turn severely hampered efforts to deploy critical resources, even though plenty were available for distribution. There is some evidence that local requests for supplies (electrical generators in particular) were directed to the wrong source or completely lost in the system (Thrift 1989). As a result, the proper authorities never received some of the requests, and appropriate relief was not provided to some needy victims.

Finally, FEMA's own policies were an obstacle. FEMA, like all bureaucratic organizations, has developed a set of policies and standard operating procedures. Many of these procedures facilitate the response process; they enable the agency to implement assistance almost automatically when a disaster strikes. Other procedures are designed to prevent unnecessary and/or inappropriate government spending. Taken together, these measures try to reconcile routine agency decision making with guarantees to ensure that only those who fit preestablished criteria and follow specific guidelines will obtain federal assistance (Hall 1989). But such regulations may also impede the responsiveness and adaptiveness of an agency such as FEMA. The resultant questions raised by disaster victims and their advocates are easily understandable: How can FEMA expect people who have lost every-thing to produce evidence documenting their losses? Why does FEMA have to assess and inspect damages before it distributes aid? And why does FEMA have to be asked (by the governor) before it responds? Bureaucratic procedures and regulations may be necessary to prevent fraud, but they are of little consolation to those with urgent disaster-related problems (Miller 1989b).

In addition, FEMA's own resources were literally stretched to the limit. In the fall of 1989, the agency had an annual operating budget of $450 million to $500 million, a staff of about 2,400 full-time employees located in offices throughout the country, and only a handful of supplies and equip-ment at its immediate disposal (McAda 1989). Moreover, FEMA's position within the federal government at this point in time was considered to be somewhat ambiguous. Like many other small federal agencies (Ingraham 1987), FEMA suffered from internal management problems. It had eight political appointees within its leadership ranks and had gone without a permanent director since June 1989 (Democratic Study Group 1989).

Furthermore, natural disasters were not considered to be FEMA's pri-mary responsibility. Instead, most of the agency's planning, resources, and activities had focused on dealing with nuclear strikes against the United States (National Academy of Public Administration 1993; Wamsley 1993). Thus the agency had to scramble to cope with even one major natural disaster. But South Carolina was FEMA's third major disaster in less than a week, following closely on the heels of those in the Virgin Islands and Puerto Rico. Because of this, FEMA personnel from across the country were called to South Carolina. Full-time employees from as far away as Seattle and Denver were reassigned. "On-call" reservists and volunteers were activated, state employees were recruited, and additional personnel (such as schoolteachers not currently employed) were hired to work in local areas. Eventually, FEMA was able to get over 3,000 people into the field in South Carolina, but doing so took several weeks (Hall 1989).

Public Perception of Governmental Response: Failure

The relief effort in South Carolina following Hurricane Hugo represents a classic example of intergovernmental confusion. Local, state, and national governments all tried to respond to the disaster, but their efforts were not integrated. Moreover, the government's own policies and procedures were simply inappropriate for the severity of the disaster and the extreme isolation of the affected population.[3] As a result, disaster assistance was implemented sluggishly and ineffectively.

These problems facilitated intense criticisms of the entire governmental response. Overall, there was a nationwide perception that the government's disaster-relief efforts—particularly those of the federal authorities—were a failure in South Carolina. But FEMA, the federal agency in charge of the response process, received most of the blame: FEMA, not Hurricane Hugo, seemed to be the real disaster (Cook 1989).

Notes

1. For more graphic accounts and illustrations of Hurricane Hugo's destruction in South Carolina, see *And Hugo Was His Name* (1989), *Hugo* (n.d.), and *Hurricane Hugo: Storm of the Century* (1990).

2. Much of the information on the governmental response to Hugo in South Carolina comes directly from the "Mission Assignments" issued by the Federal Coordinating Officer and obtained from the Federal Emergency Management Agency Disaster Field Offices in North Charleston, South Carolina, from September through December 1989.

3. FEMA accepted applications from disaster victims in South Carolina for six months following Hurricane Hugo, representing the longest application period for any major disaster situation (Heflin 1990).

10

The Loma Prieta Earthquake in California

Shortly after 5:00 P.M. on October 17, 1989, an earthquake shook the San Francisco Bay area. The quake, later called "Loma Prieta" by geologists, rocked the area for about ten seconds with a force measuring 7.1 on the Richter scale (U.S. Geological Survey 1990). Severe damage was reported within a hundred-mile radius around the quake's epicenter (located eight miles northeast of Santa Cruz); tremors were felt for several hundred miles in all directions. The quake destroyed or damaged thousands of buildings. Roads were cracked open and bridges crumbled. Natural gas and power lines snapped apart, water pipes exploded, and structural fires erupted everywhere. In all, there were more than sixty deaths, thousands of injuries, and an estimated $6.8 billion in direct damages (*The October 17, 1989, Loma Prieta Earthquake* 1990, 4).[1]

Another major disaster had occurred while the nation was still reeling from Hugo's destructive rampage through the Virgin Islands, Puerto Rico, and the Carolinas. And, to make matters worse, the earthquake was actually seen on television by millions of Americans who were preparing to watch the third game of the World Series, being held in San Francisco's Candlestick Park. The governmental response system was put into effect once again. This time, private citizens and public institutions reacted calmly and quickly. Consequently, the gap between emergent norms and bureaucratic procedures was *initially* quite small in California. Over time, however, the gap increased in size. This was the joint result of a growing sense of frustration and the local governments' departures from their preestablished role in the recovery process. The size of the gap had a direct impact on the implementation of disaster assistance. More specifically, it produced another example of the confusion pattern, or the breakdown in orderly cooperation and coordination between levels of government. Therefore, the government's disaster-response efforts received mixed reviews.

Initial Public Reaction: Calm and Orderly

The Loma Prieta earthquake certainly disrupted normal routines and behavior patterns. Yet the public's immediate reaction was largely calm and was directed toward the alleviation of the most pressing problems (Archea 1990). There were numerous reports of normal citizens engaging in heroic efforts. Rescue workers and volunteers took extraordinary steps to locate survivors and pull them away from dangerous situations (Magnuson 1989). For example, a construction worker spent two hours extricating a man trapped in his crushed car on Interstate 880, and a firefighter spent over three hours freeing a woman pinned between the beams of her crushed apartment complex ("Task of Pulling Survivors from Debris" 1989, 10A). Attention was given to rescuing those who were in life-threatening situations and to preparing for the aftershocks of the quake. Overall, the public's initial response was remarkably composed and orderly.

Initial Governmental Response: Calm and Routine

The government also seemed to respond quickly and effectively to the situation in California (Piacente 1989). Early on October 18—the morning following the earthquake—local, state, and federal officials surveyed the damages in stricken areas. It was abundantly clear to all observers that the resources and assistance of the federal government were needed. State and federal officials worked closely together to activate the emergency response process. Within hours, President Bush declared San Francisco and surrounding communities a major disaster area and authorized FEMA to mobilize and coordinate the relief effort (Hamner 1990; Bolin 1990).

The government's response to the San Francisco earthquake was different from its response to Hurricane Hugo for at least five important reasons. First, it is crucial to recognize that there are fundamental differences between earthquakes and hurricanes, which in turn affect the nature of the governmental response (Miller 1989a; Hall 1989). Earthquakes cannot be predicted, and there is no time to evacuate or even alert the population prior to the event. So the focus must be on immediate rescue efforts (Quarantelli 1990, 1991; National Research Council 1991). This is a direct contrast to the hurricane relief efforts in the Carolinas. In that case, there was ample warning, which allowed South Carolina's governor and other public officials to urge the evacuation of coastal areas long before the hurricane struck. This precautionary step clearly saved many lives (Wagar 1990).

Second, the federal government is especially prepared for earthquakes in the West Coast areas where they are likely to occur. Several years ago,

Congress mandated the development of a Comprehensive Earthquake Hazards Reduction Program. This plan identifies key emergency support responsibilities and describes how federal agencies will work together to provide assistance to quake-stricken areas (Piacente 1989, 33). A central facet of the plan is the assignment of one federal agency to take the lead in coordinating each of the prespecified emergency support functions.[2] As an extension of this program, FEMA has spent a great deal of time and money developing its earthquake-response capabilities. It has worked closely with West Coast states in order to establish efficient and fast earthquake-response mechanisms. In August 1989, just two months before the Loma Prieta earthquake, FEMA conducted a major earthquake training exercise in California. Federal and state officials simulated their response to a major earthquake. This gave them a dress rehearsal to test the implementation of their plans (Piacente 1989, 33). It also helped delineate the responsibilities assigned to the respective governmental officials and institutions (Hamner 1990). Thus, governmental officials at all levels not only knew what their responsibilities were, but they actually had some timely practice in carrying them out.

Third, the White House seemed to respond with greater urgency to the earthquake than to Hugo. The day after the quake, Vice-President J. Danforth Quayle arrived at the scene to survey the damages and explain proper procedures to state and local officials. Three days after the quake (on October 20), President Bush flew to the Bay Area to assess the situation firsthand. Other top-level officials also went to California to guide the federal effort. For example, Transportation Secretary Samuel K. Skinner was inspecting the damage caused by the collapse of Interstate 880 less than twenty-four hours after the quake. In its actions, the White House was sending a clear message: the federal government would respond quickly to the Loma Prieta disaster (Hamner 1990). This was a sharp contrast to the low presidential visibility and lack of concern during the situation in the Caribbean and the Carolinas. The president never visited the areas affected by Hugo in Puerto Rico or the Virgin Islands. And he did not survey the situation in the Carolinas until ten days after the hurricane. Moreover, no cabinet secretaries were sent to any Hugo-related disasters. In the period immediately following Hugo, Marilyn Quayle, the wife of the vice-president, was the most visible representative of the White House (Schneider 1989, 1990). The sluggish, lackadaisical response of the federal government during Hurricane Hugo did not sit well with state and local officials in the Caribbean or the Carolinas. Some political leaders complained vociferously about the incompetence of FEMA and the uncaring attitude of the Bush administration (Riley 1989; Thrift 1989). These criticisms contributed to a widespread perception (correct or incorrect) that the federal government was indifferent to the suffering of victims of Hurricane Hugo.

Fourth, FEMA acted quickly to inform Californians about its services, procedures, and responsibilities during the earthquake disaster. A toll-free hotline was immediately put into operation (in fact, this was a part of the initial presidential declaration). Within fifteen hours after the quake, top-level FEMA personnel held a nationally broadcast news conference. This was the first of many public information campaigns to explain what the agency could and could not do (Hamner 1990). On October 22, FEMA opened its first Disaster Application Center in California. Shortly thereafter, FEMA established three other major centers. FEMA also used a number of mobile units, making it easier and more convenient for people to apply for assistance (McAda 1990). FEMA even tried a unique "mass registration" technique. Instead of taking applications one at a time, several hundred people were brought into a facility, where an overhead projector was used to explain the application forms to everyone at once. FEMA also took steps to streamline other facets of the process: the agency issued temporary housing checks immediately to all those whose homes had been destroyed; its inspectors delivered checks at the same time that they assessed the extent of other damages. FEMA seemed to be doing everything it could to get the San Francisco Bay area back on its feet (Hamner 1990). By February 1990, it had processed over 77,000 applications for assistance and distributed more than $31 million to individuals and families (Federal Emergency Management Agency 1990b). By that time, it had also funded almost $600 million in repairs to roads, bridges, buildings, and other facilities. In California, FEMA's actions often appeared to be more decisive and oriented toward expediting widespread assistance to the public than they were in the East Coast disasters. There seemed to be much less emphasis on standard operating procedures and bureaucratic red tape than there had been before (Hamner 1990). Overall, this seemed to be a "new" FEMA.

Fifth, state and local governments also seemed to be better prepared to respond to the Loma Prieta earthquake. Local disaster preparedness plans went into place almost automatically. Emergency personnel knew what to do, and they took action without state or federal prompting or supervision. State officials played a major role in the emergency response operations. They were able to coordinate local efforts and serve as intermediaries between local and federal officials (U.S. General Accounting Office 1991). They possessed the resources—expertise and personnel—and the ability—preparation and organization—to perform this function. In addition, having gone through the training exercise in August, they were knowledgeable about their responsibilities and the capabilities of other governmental units.

Overall, the government's initial efforts, particularly those of state and federal officials, proceeded relatively smoothly. Nevertheless, problems soon developed.

Milling Process during Recovery

The milling process actually began in California during the recovery phase, as the population began to realize that life would not return to normal immediately. Badly disrupted traffic patterns in the Bay Area, damaged houses in outlying regions, and problematic aspects of processing insurance claims led to a mounting sense of public frustration (Piacente 1989). There were few life-threatening, dangerous situations remaining by this time; however, there was a popular belief that public institutions were not solving problems and operating the way they should (Wagar 1990; Fitzpatrick and Mileti 1990). This triggered the ongoing search for meaning, which in itself constitutes the milling process.

The keynoting behavior in California was carried out largely by the mass media (Magnuson 1989, 40; Rogers, Berndt, Harris, and Minzer 1990). The dominant message, drawn in part from the experiences in South Carolina, was that FEMA was incapable of providing disaster assistance to earthquake victims. The agency had lost a great deal of respect and credibility with the public. Many Californians had heard stories about the federal government's nonresponsiveness and inefficiency in dealing with Hurricane Hugo. They became afraid that their concerns and problems would also get lost in the government's bureaucratic jungle. As a result, thousands of Californians called the agency and hundreds more lined up at the doors before FEMA even opened the first application centers. When the agency officially began to process applications, it was immediately faced with a backlog of 10,000 requests for assistance. The impression developed that the government was not doing all it could to help disaster victims (Wagar 1990).

The Gap between Emergent Norms and Bureaucratic Norms

The emergent norm in this context was an extreme sense of disillusionment. California citizens responded well to the actual disaster, and in this phase the government operated effectively—maintaining order, dealing with life-threatening situations, and restoring essential services. But citizens felt abandoned during the later recovery period. People tended to believe that they would have to help themselves; they did not think they could depend on the government for assistance.

The sense of anomie and frustration was probably greatest among low-

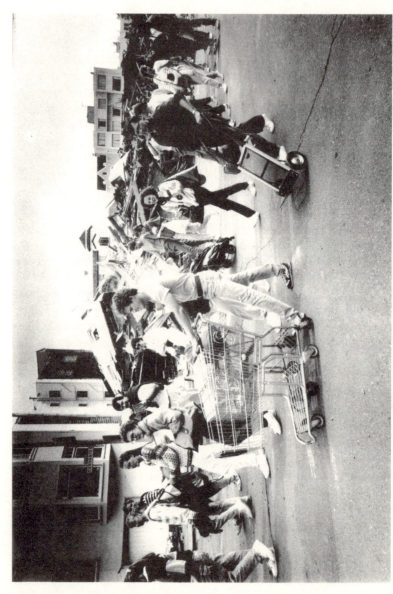

September 1989. Residents of the Marina District in San Francisco are allowed back into their homes following the Loma Prieta earthquake. As this picture shows, residents appeared to be fairly calm and collected, using shopping carts to carry out the belongings that they could find. *Photo by Fred Larson, San Francisco Chronicle.*

income population groups in and around the city of San Francisco. The governmental response system was unable to provide adequate shelter or emergency services for quake victims living in the most depressed, economically disadvantaged areas. Poverty and housing shortages made it difficult for the government to relocate people displaced by the disaster (Gross 1990). Moreover, there were serious language barriers to overcome: many government assistance workers spoke only English, and they were unable to communicate with the Spanish-speaking segments of the affected population (Panetta 1990). Consequently, some quake victims took matters into their own hands. In the city of Watsonville about 1,200 displaced people who had lost their homes during the quake constructed a tent city to protect themselves and their families from the elements. Basically, these victims formed an independent community because they did not have confidence in the governmental relief system.

Confusion Implementation Pattern

Although local officials dealt with the immediate dangers of the earthquake, they were less successful in addressing longer-term aspects of the relief effort—for example, helping residents file insurance claims, providing adequate housing, and directing supplies to appropriate areas.[3] Despite greater general preparedness, some local officials still had difficulty dealing with the disaster. As with the situation in South Carolina, local officials were often not familiar with their own responsibilities or with the role of other governmental agencies. Some disseminated inaccurate information; for example, officials in Watsonville did not realize the severity of the situation in their area and did not request help for several days (Wagar 1990, 13). A few localities did not understand that they had to assess their damages and ask for appropriate assistance. They simply expected the federal government to step in and do everything. And a very common breach of procedures occurred when local officials bypassed county personnel and tried to get help directly from state and federal agencies. Undoubtedly, such actions seemed appropriate and necessary at the time. But they disrupted the functioning of the entire intergovernmental response process (U.S. General Accounting Office 1991).

The net impact of these problems was more pronounced because local governments always serve as the main interface between the government and the affected population. As Thomas Hamner (1990), FEMA's federal coordinating officer for Loma Prieta, remarked, "Local interface was a problem." He said that local officials should have been included in the government's disaster preparedness and training exercises. This would have given them a better understanding of how the entire system works.

In addition, FEMA was working under several tremendous handicaps. The agency was now seriously understaffed and ill equipped to handle its fourth major disaster in a row (after the three Hugo-related situations that occurred one month earlier), along with several others that had developed during the same time period (primarily another hurricane in Texas and floods in the upper southern states). This placed even more severe strains on the agency's resources. In order to respond to California, all available FEMA personnel across the country were activated; staff members no longer needed in the Caribbean and the Carolinas were relocated to the area. Employees from other federal agencies (such as the Army Corps of Engineers) and from state government were also used to supplement FEMA's personnel (Peterson 1989).

In California, the state and federal governments worked fairly well together. But the intergovernmental partnership did not extend to the localities. As a result, their role in the recovery process was never defined very clearly. This ambiguity had a direct effect on the entire governmental response system. Although the recovery efforts in California differed from those in South Carolina following Hurricane Hugo, both situations conform to the confusion pattern of intergovernmental activity. The hallmark of this pattern is the breakdown of orderly cooperation between levels of government. As we have seen, this problem can occur in a variety of ways (across all three levels of government or concentrated within a single layer). But it is clear that it did occur in California as well as in South Carolina and Florida.

Perception of Governmental Effort:
Partial Success/Partial Failure

In California, the gap between emergent norms and bureaucratic norms was initially quite small. It increased in size because of the growing sense of public frustration over the slow progress and ineffective nature of recovery efforts. Another contributing factor was the local governments' departures from their preestablished role in the recovery process, which produced serious "kinks" in the response process. Thus, California represents another example of the confusion pattern of intergovernmental policy implementation.

Yet, even at its most severe, the gap between emergent norms and bureaucratic procedures remained quite narrow, especially when compared to the previous hurricane-recovery situations in the Caribbean, South Carolina, and south Florida. The government was effective in restoring normal social conditions immediately following the quake, although its efforts did not proceed smoothly or effectively during the longer-term recovery phase.

Consequently, it is probably accurate to place the governmental response to the Loma Prieta earthquake about midway between the success and failure poles.

Notes

1. Total damage estimates for the Loma Prieta earthquake have varied from $6 billion (U.S. Geological Survey 1990) to $10 billion (Fairweather 1990). Part of the variability stems from how "social costs" are determined—that is, the costs of replacing low-income houses or relocating lower-income populations (Bolin 1990).

2. For a more detailed and comprehensive account of the governmental approach to earthquakes, see the *Federal Catastrophic Earthquake Response Plan* (Federal Emergency Management Agency 1988).

3. Fitzpatrick and Mileti (1990) argue that some local officials failed to heed and respond to aftershock warnings. This suggests that local governments involved in the Loma Prieta disaster had problems carrying out their immediate emergency response functions, as well as their long-term recovery/relief responsibilities.

11

Hurricane Hugo in North Carolina

Hurricane Hugo moved out of South Carolina and into North Carolina shortly after 6:00 A.M. on September 22, 1989. At this point, nobody expected the hurricane to have much power or strength. After all, it had just barreled its way across an entire state and was now two hundred miles from the Atlantic coast. But Hurricane Hugo was still able to deliver one last, devastating blow.

The storm was in North Carolina for a relatively brief period of time, but its impact was extremely violent. One-fifth of the state suffered serious damages from heavy winds and flooding. Thousands of North Carolinians, especially residents in the Charlotte metropolitan area, lost electrical power. Overall, Hugo caused seven deaths and several billion dollars in damages to homes, businesses, and natural resources in North Carolina. And, of course, these losses came on top of the damages previously caused by the devastating storm.[1]

North Carolina's experience with Hugo was severe; however, this disaster seemed to place few additional strains on governmental resources. Emergency management personnel stayed within their standard operating procedures, and the public seemed to work with, not against, these officials. The gap between emergent norms and bureaucratic procedures was virtually nonexistent. So the response process actually flowed from the bottom up, exactly as it was supposed to: local governments responded first, then the state, and finally the federal government stepped in to help. This, of course, was a much more conducive environment for governmental operations. There was little confusion, hesitation, or fanfare concerning the governmental efforts in North Carolina. As a result, the North Carolina situation represents a much more successful response to a major natural disaster than those considered in the previous chapters.

The Milling Process: An Immediate Beginning but Quick Ending

Unlike the situations in the Caribbean and South Carolina, the milling process was short-lived in North Carolina. Nevertheless, everyday activities and routines were disrupted. Immediately after the storm, "dazed residents scrambled for food, ice, flashlights and candles, and exchanged stories of destruction" (*And Hugo Was His Name* 1989, 49). Some residents in the Charlotte area went without electrical power for several weeks. Despite these conditions, however, there was no extended period of time during which normal institutions were unable to provide guidance and direction. As Gerald Fox, the manager of Mecklenberg County, testified: "Clearing of streets to provide emergency and normal access; property security and functioning without electrical power; damage assessment; and public information were the early orders of the day" (U.S. House 1990). Hence there was no need for the affected population to engage in an ongoing search for meaning.

Instead, the public seemed to focus immediately on getting conditions back to "normal." With the help of emergency management officials, disaster victims originated a "Hugo Citizens Task Force" to help individuals and families who were "falling through the cracks" of the relief effort (Fox 1990). Public and private agencies worked together and demonstrated that the situation was manageable by restoring transportation, power, and communication systems within a very short period of time. Stated simply, life went on after a brief, albeit serious, disruption (McAda 1989).

The brevity of the milling process meant that keynoting behavior was relatively unimportant. Telephone and radio communications were available and accessible to most of the population. As a result, people looked to the usual authorities—law enforcement officials, emergency management personnel, and private insurance carriers—for assistance (Faust 1989).

A Smooth Bureaucratic Response

For its part, the government had already taken important precautionary steps before the storm hit. Anticipating the hurricane's onslaught, state and federal officials met in Raleigh, North Carolina, on September 20, 1989—two days before Hugo moved onto the U.S. mainland. They monitored the path of the storm and determined there was a very good chance that Hugo would strike a major blow to the state of North Carolina. So personnel from the Federal Emergency Management Agency worked with state officials to prepare a request for federal assistance.

Immediately after Hugo left the state, on the morning of September 22, state and local officials began assessing the storm's damage. Then, on September 24, North Carolina's governor, James Martin, officially asked President Bush for federal assistance. Within twenty-four hours, the president declared four North Carolina counties to be federal disaster areas (Peterson 1989). Once again, the federal government was almost immediately involved in a major relief effort. This time, however, the system actually operated quite smoothly—unlike earlier situations involving Hugo.

The governmental response in North Carolina functioned in a fairly routine, straightforward fashion (U.S. General Accounting Office 1991). State and local emergency management personnel stayed within their standard operating procedures. Overall, they seemed to have a better understanding of their own responsibilities—perhaps because they had been involved in several other disaster situations over the previous year. And public officials seemed to work *with,* not *against,* these emergency management personnel.[2]

The Gap between Emergent Norms and Bureaucratic Procedures

The emergent norms in this situation were entirely consistent with the ongoing social structure: there was absolutely no looting or rioting as there had been in the Caribbean. And, unlike the situation in South Carolina, there was little vocal dissatisfaction with governmental efforts. Prominent political leaders in North Carolina did not try to interfere in the process. For example, Senator Terry Sanford visited the disaster-stricken areas in North Carolina shortly after Hugo's departure. He tried to reassure North Carolinians that assistance would be forthcoming, and he explicitly refused to criticize the relief effort (Faust 1989).

Of course, problems did develop during the process. There was some confusion about getting material assistance to the areas of the state that most needed it. For example, local representatives in a heavily damaged county did not understand the proper procedures for debris removal, thereby unnecessarily delaying the cleanup efforts (U.S. General Accounting Office 1991). But these difficulties were resolved fairly quickly, and there was no serious attempt to work "outside" the basic structure.

Bottom-Up Implementation Pattern

In North Carolina, the governmental response conformed to prior expectations and planning. Local governments responded first, then the state, and finally the federal government was called in to help. Moreover, when higher levels of government became involved, they did not take over the relief effort. Instead, they worked with and through lower levels. All three levels of government continued to function closely with one another throughout the entire relief and recovery effort. Consistent with the structure of the ongoing disaster-response system, governmental activities "bubbled up" from the local level through the state and ultimately to the national government.

Several factors contributed to this bottom-up implementation pattern. First, there were better disaster preparedness plans at both state and local levels (Mosco 1989). Moreover, the state conducts an average of four training sessions every year to ensure that all relevant parties know how to implement these plans in an actual emergency situation (U.S. General Accounting Office 1991). This provided North Carolina officials with very effective, tested guidelines for carrying out their responsibilities. More important, perhaps, it enabled state and local personnel to acquire firsthand experience with the actual implementation of hazard mitigation policies (Mittler 1988).

Second, state and local personnel had more resources and manpower available to handle the recovery effort. North Carolina spends more money than South Carolina on disaster-relief activities. The state uses some of these funds to support a fairly large staff of full-time emergency management personnel. It funnels the remainder of its money to local governments so that the latter can enhance their own capabilities. In turn, this allows the state to *coordinate* rather than actively *direct* a recovery effort (U.S. General Accounting Office 1991).

Third, North Carolina used its preexisting emergency management system to coordinate disaster relief. Unlike the situation in South Carolina, there was no bifurcated communication or command structure at the state level. Consequently, all information and assistance flowed through the appropriate channels (McAda 1990).

Because of these factors, FEMA was able to maintain its designated role. It supplemented the state's resources and channeled federal assistance into the areas where North Carolina officials said it was needed. FEMA became involved in the relief effort almost immediately after the hurricane (Morrill, Williams, and York 1989). The agency quickly opened a disaster field office in North Carolina, and it began accepting applications for assistance within seven days (U.S. General Accounting Office 1991). FEMA officials eventually added twenty-five more North Carolina counties to the list of federal disaster areas. Over the next three months, FEMA processed more than 30,000 claims and provided $37 million in relief (McAda 1990). In this state, the recovery effort wound down very quickly. FEMA closed its Disaster Application Centers by December 1, 1989, precisely at the end of the normal sixty-day application period.

Public Perception of the Governmental Response: Effective

North Carolina's experience with Hurricane Hugo represented a response pattern that was close to optimal. The process unfolded more slowly, giving officials time to organize and coordinate their efforts. In addition, the norms that developed within the affected population were supportive of existing policies and procedures. Thus there was virtually no gap between emergent norms and bureaucratic procedures. As a result, the process flowed exactly as it is intended to operate, from the bottom up.

This episode shows how effective the system can be when all relevant governments work together. If public agencies perform their previously defined disaster responsibilities, there is no need to depart from standard operating procedures. This in turn reduces the level of confusion, and it produces a conducive environment for governmental operations. The government can step in, provide relief, and terminate its efforts within its pre-established time frames. Overall, there is very little fanfare, no widespread criticism of any kind, and, indeed, little public notice outside the immediately affected areas.[3] In the end, the image is one of a successful governmental response to a major natural disaster. North Carolina's experience with Hurricane Hugo fits this scenario almost perfectly.

Notes

1. For more detailed information on Hugo's impact in North Carolina, see the *Charlotte Observer*, particularly the daily issues from September 22 through October 8, 1989, and the Special Supplement to the October 11, 1989, edition, which was devoted entirely to "The Wrath of Hugo."

2. The information on the governmental response to Hurricane Hugo in North Carolina was obtained from a variety of sources, including the Federal Emergency Management Agency's Office of Public and Intergovernmental Affairs in Washington, DC, and the *Interagency Hazard Mitigation Team Report* prepared by Region IV of the Federal Emergency Management Agency, headquartered in Atlanta, Georgia.

3. In fact, the lack of media and public attention given to this disaster situation is probably one of the main reasons why the relief effort proceeded smoothly and routinely.

12

Hurricane Andrew in Louisiana

Hurricane Andrew moved into the Gulf of Mexico after its assault on south Florida. First, the huge storm swirled in a westwardly direction. Then it turned toward the northwest and moved at a steady pace across the Gulf waters. Early on the morning of August 26, 1992, Andrew hit the coast of Louisiana, about twenty-five miles southwest of Morgan City. The storm ripped its way up through the south-central portion of the state. It destroyed thousands of homes and knocked out electrical power to more than 320,000 residents. Andrew was responsible for ten more deaths and an additional $300 million in damages in Louisiana beyond those losses already incurred in the Bahamas and Florida. As Andrew moved north, it was downgraded from a hurricane to a tropical storm and then to a tropical depression. By Thursday, August 27, the storm had finally expended its last punch; it was now classified as just "severe weather" (U.S. Department of Commerce 1993).

It was clear that governmental resources would be needed to help citizens deal with and recover from this disaster. Unlike what happened in south Florida, however, the government seemed willing and able to handle the problems caused by Hurricane Andrew in Louisiana. Emergency management officials responded quickly and appropriately. Moreover, the entire process worked exactly as it was supposed to: the response moved from the bottom up.

There was also little, if any, conflict between the public's expectations and the government's preexisting plans. For its part, the affected population reacted calmly and quietly; they focused their efforts on getting their lives back to normal, not on disruptive, deviant behavior. As a result, disaster assistance was implemented smoothly, quietly, and effectively. Overall, Louisiana's experience with Hurricane Andrew is an example of a successful governmental response to a major natural disaster.

An Early and Brief Milling Process

Hurricane Andrew caused extreme havoc and destruction in southern Louisiana. The powerful storm blasted its way through the state, unleashing 140-mile-per-hour winds, heavy rain, and tornadoes. It smashed homes, toppled trees, and leveled neighborhoods. The storm knocked out electrical service to more than 150,000 residents, and it left many communities without such basic necessities as safe drinking water and food supplies. In addition, travel into and within the affected areas was a severe problem. State and local highways were washed out, and the Intracoastal Waterway was closed from the Texas-Louisiana border to Morgan City (Federal Emergency Management Agency 1992a).

The milling process began almost immediately in southern Louisiana. Local residents were naturally confused and disoriented by the severity of the situation. Their normal surroundings had been transformed. Everything seem to be disheveled and out of place. In order to deal with this situation, some citizens resorted to unusual behavior and actions. Looting occurred in several of the most devastated communities, and there were reports of price gouging across the entire hurricane-ravaged area (Sanchez 1992). Yet these instances of unconventional behavior were relatively unusual in Louisiana, especially when compared to the situation in Florida.

The entire milling process did not last long in southern Louisiana. Instead, a sense of calm and order quickly returned to the hurricane-stricken areas. There are several reasons why the milling process ended so abruptly in this particular situation (Zensinger 1992). First, Hurricane Andrew did not cause a complete breakdown of communication and transportation systems in southern Louisiana. Several major highways, railroad lines, and airports were initially closed, but they reopened within a matter of days. So travel in the disaster-stricken communities was only temporarily disrupted. Telephone service into the area was congested immediately following the hurricane, but it never completely broke down (Federal Emergency Management Agency 1992a). As a result, disaster victims in southern Louisiana were able to talk with one another about their situation. And they were able to communicate with people outside the disaster-stricken areas. In sum, they were never really "cut off" from their neighbors, friends, and relatives or from the rest of society.

Second, the local population may have been better equipped to handle a major hurricane. Louisianians saw the reports from south Florida, and they knew that Andrew was a fierce, deadly storm. Accordingly, they took the warnings for their areas seriously and began to make the necessary emergency preparations before the hurricane arrived (Marcus 1992, A12). Since many of the local residents had lived in low-lying areas all their lives, most had already experienced other large storms and floods. So they knew how to plan for and respond to such events. As one local resident remarked, "We've been running from hurricanes for years . . . it's just part of living in the bayou" (Suro 1992a).

In addition, many residents in this part of Louisiana have Cajun ethnic backgrounds. This is relevant because Cajuns have strong attachments to their families, their community, and their heritage. They also have a fairly positive outlook, no matter how severe their predicament (Sanchez 1992). As one victim remarked, "It's just us poor crawfish Cajuns here. If we don't get city water, well we're just going to go get clean in the bayou. That's what our people have always done" (Suro 1992a, A11). In times of trouble, Cajuns tend to stick together and help one another. Basically, the victims of Hurricane Andrew in southern Louisiana possessed exactly the values and attitudes that are antithetical to milling.

Finally, the government played an important role in ending the "search for meaning" (or milling) in southern Louisiana. The government's standard operating procedures seemed to "fit" this particular disaster situation very closely. Existing policies were appropriate and believable guides for citizen behavior. Under such circumstances, there was really no reason for the affected population to search for *other* standards to guide their actions. Consequently, the milling process ended abruptly, almost as soon as it began. The affected population focused its efforts on getting life back to the way it was before the storm.

Governmental Response: Orderly and Routine

The government took steps to prepare the Gulf Coast region for Hurricane Andrew immediately after the storm swept across the tip of southern Florida.[1] The National Weather Service posted hurricane warnings from Port Arthur, Texas, to Pascagoula, Mississippi. Emergency management officials in states all along the Gulf were closely monitoring the movement of the storm. Residents from Texas to Alabama were warned to take precautionary measures (Federal Emergency Management Agency 1992a; Maraniss 1992a).

The exact path of the storm was unknown. But forecasters predicted that Andrew would probably hit land again around the mouth of the Mississippi River, just west of New Orleans. Local and state officials in Louisiana accelerated their efforts to prepare for the storm. The mayor of Grand Isle, Louisiana's only inhabited barrier island, issued a mandatory evacuation order for all island residents and visitors. The New Orleans Levee Board closed the floodgates surrounding the city of New Orleans to prevent wide-spread flooding throughout the area. Mayor Sidney Barthelemy encouraged all people living in the low-lying areas around New Orleans to evacuate. Louisiana's Governor Edwin Edwards declared a state of emergency and urged all coastal residents to leave their homes before the hurricane struck (Maraniss 1992a).

The national government was also monitoring the situation in Louisiana. The Federal Emergency Management Agency activated its regional office in Denton, Texas, and it placed other regional offices on alert. FEMA deployed a package of critical resources to the area, and it sent in an advance team of emergency personnel to help state and local officials prepare for the storm (Federal Emergency Management Agency 1992a).

Almost immediately after Hurricane Andrew moved out of the state, Governor Edwards submitted a request to have the storm-damaged areas between Baton Rouge and New Orleans designated as major disaster areas. Several hours later, President Bush declared a major disaster for Louisiana, making eight parishes eligible for federal disaster assistance. Once again, the national government was involved in a major disaster situation. This time, however, the federal officials did not take control of the entire relief effort. Instead, they worked closely with state and local governments to coordinate their activities in a very effective manner (Peterson 1992).

Local parish officials assessed the extent of the storm's damages and identified their most urgent problems. Recognizing that they could not handle the situation on their own, they immediately called on the state for assistance. State officials quickly stepped in to alleviate some of the most pressing problems that existed at the local level. For example, the Louisiana National Guard was extensively involved in maintaining law and order throughout the hurricane-ravaged parishes; it also took an active role in distributing emergency supplies. But state officials had no illusions about their own capabilities in this disaster. They were more than willing to pass local requests that they could not handle on up to the federal government.

For its part, the federal government acted quickly to get supplies and personnel into Louisiana. The Federal Emergency Management Agency immediately sent 100,000 military field rations (called "Meals Ready to Eat"), 8,000 cots, and 1,000 rolls of plastic sheeting. It deployed a Mobile Emergency Response Support unit to Alexandria, to facilitate a range of emergency operations. And FEMA called up personnel from across the country to supplement its efforts. Within the first twenty-four hours, the agency had set up a temporary field office at Camp Beauregard, Louisiana, and it had identified several possible locations for Disaster Assistance Centers (DACs; Federal Emergency Management Agency 1992a).

By August 28, 1992, FEMA had established a "permanent" Disaster Field Office in Baton Rouge, Louisiana. Agency officials identified water treatment as the most pressing concern. So the agency ordered thousands of gallons of water into the area, and it sent for generators to restore electrical power to the water-treatment facilities. FEMA also issued contracts for the removal of hurricane-related debris, and it worked with private relief agencies to get the truckloads of food, supplies, and clothing to storm victims. The agency opened four Disaster Assistance Centers and added seven more parishes to the list of those eligible for federal assistance (Federal Emergency Management Agency 1992a). All this was accomplished within the first forty-eight to seventy-two hours after the storm struck Louisiana.

The Gap between Emergent Norms and Governmental Actions

Unlike what happened in south Florida, there was virtually no gap between emergent norms and bureaucratic actions in southern Louisiana. Clearly, the hurricane's impact was less severe. Hence the situation was inherently more manageable. Yet the attitudes of the affected population were extremely important.

Basically, the victims of Hurricane Andrew in Louisiana understood what had happened to them, and they knew what actions to take in order to relieve their situation (Maraniss 1992b). They did not panic. They did not behave irrationally or erratically. They did not blame others for their predicament. Instead, they concentrated on helping one another in order to get conditions back to normal. Their focused their efforts on "pulling themselves up" (Suro 1992a, A8) and rebuilding their homes, their communities, and their lives.

Governmental actions complemented those of private citizens. Emergency management personnel across all three levels of government seemed to be fairly well prepared for this disaster situation. Local and state officials in Louisiana had been emphasizing hazard mitigation and disaster planning, so they were able to perform their preassigned emergency response operations (Peterson 1992). This in turn allowed the federal government to supplement, not supplant, their efforts. Basically, emergency officials relied on existing procedures and policies, and they worked with, not against, each other to address the most pressing problems. As a result, they were able to provide credible and consistent guidance to the affected population.

Rolling, Bottom-Up Implementation Pattern

In Louisiana, local governments were the first point of mobilization. Parish officials identified the needs and problems of disaster-stricken areas. They recognized immediately that they could not address this situation on their own and quickly requested assistance from higher authorities. Local officials did not, however, disappear from the recovery effort. They continued to work closely with state and federal authorities to get aid into the hurricane-ravaged communities. They were the clearinghouse for local needs throughout the entire relief effort.

The state of Louisiana served primarily as the intermediary between local communities and the federal government; of course, this is precisely its mandated role in the general response system. State personnel mobilized available resources to support local efforts. And they channeled requests beyond their means up to the national government. These officials knew that the state simply could not handle this situation: federal assistance was essential. So state officials were willing and eager to do everything that they could to facilitate federal involvement. They took their intermediary role within the intergovernmental response system quite seriously (Federal Emergency Management Agency 1992a).

The efforts of state and local governments made it easier for the federal government to respond in this particular disaster situation. Federal authorities did not have to step in and take over the entire governmental efforts. They could actually supplement the actions of lower governmental units. This enabled the federal government to mobilize its own resources quickly and coordinate the entire intergovernmental relief effort effectively.

In sum, the response to Hurricane Andrew in Louisiana closely paralleled the ideal intergovernmental pattern. Local, state, and national governments were involved in the implementation of disaster relief, and each level of government performed its preassigned duties and responsibilities. As in any disaster situation, there were instances when local-level requests were "lost" or misdirected. But, overall, the governmental effort unfolded routinely. The entire process operated almost exactly as it was supposed to: from the bottom up.

Perception of Governmental Response: Success

In Louisiana, public expectations coincided with governmental actions. The affected population had fairly realistic notions about the government's role in a disaster situation. They did not expect the government to step in immediately and solve all their problems. Instead, they were willing to work with governmental authorities to alleviate storm-related conditions. This in turn allowed the government to address this disaster situation more slowly and carefully. Public organizations at the local, state, and national levels relied more directly on standard operating procedures, and the relief effort proceeded according to preexisting plans and processes.[2]

In the end, there was very little criticism of the governmental response to this particular disaster situation. Perhaps most of the attention and publicity remained focused on south Florida. This may have enabled Louisiana to recover from the disaster quietly and with less fanfare than might have occurred. Nevertheless, the general impression developed that the governmental response to Hurricane Andrew in Louisiana was a successful effort.

Notes

1. I collected much of the information on the governmental response to Hurricane Andrew in Louisiana from the *Briefing Books* at the Federal Emergency Management Agency, Washington, D.C., in December 1992. This information was then supplemented with material from additional government reports (e.g., the *Interagency Hazard Mitigation Team Report, Prepared by the Region VI Interagency Hazard Mitigation Team in Response to the August 26, 1992, Disaster Declaration*), as well as by phone and personal interviews with federal, state, and local public officials involved in the relief effort.

2. It is important to note that several other disasters occurred as the relief effort was under way in Louisiana. First, there was the situation in south Florida, also created by Hurricane Andrew. In addition, the territory of Guam was declared a major disaster area on August 29 as a consequence of Typhoon Omar, and a major recovery effort was initiated and mobilized by the federal government to deal with this situation. Then, on September 12, the Hawaiian Islands were declared a major disaster area after being struck by Hurricane Iniki; once again, federal resources were channeled into a hurricane-stricken area.

13

"Normal" Disasters: 1990 Floods in South Carolina

So far, this study has examined the components of the gap between bureaucratic procedures and emergent norms during *major* disasters. Hurricane Hugo, the Loma Prieta earthquake, and Hurricane Andrew were extreme events that placed unusually severe strains on the governmental response process. But it is also important to consider what happens during a more typical disaster situation. Of course, to the people who are affected, no disaster is ever really "normal." Nevertheless, events such as floods, tornadoes, blizzards, droughts, and minor hurricanes do occur with some regularity. Emergency management agencies usually respond to these situations in a straightforward, perfunctory manner; consequently, the governmental responses to these situations are usually quite successful. There are several reasons for the general effectiveness of governmental activities during the kinds of events that might be called "normal" disasters.

First, the sheer magnitude of the situation is a factor (Fritz 1957, 1961; Barton 1969). Normal disasters do not usually produce severe or prolonged disruptions in the social or physical environments. As a result, public organizations can respond to these situations cautiously and slowly. Such a response is more in line with the customary patterns and routines of public-sector activity.

A second consideration is the frequency and regularity of the event (Dynes 1970). Hundreds of natural disasters occur in this country every year. Fortunately, very few of them become major catastrophes;[1] most are fairly typical geological episodes or weather patterns. Thus the American public is relatively familiar with normal disasters because they experience them frequently and on a fairly regular basis (Perry and Mushkatel 1984). Similarly, governmental institutions are aware of and attuned to these phenomena, and they have designed a response system with exactly these situations in mind.

Third, the degree of attention given to a disaster is also important. A drought in the Southeast, a blizzard in the Northeast, or a mudslide along the West Coast may not be unusual or extraordinary. These events do not receive a great deal of public or media attention.[2] Without such close scrutiny, there is usually little vocal criticism of the governmental efforts. This gives the government the latitude to work at its own pace, using standard operating procedures.

These normal disasters can fit perfectly within the theoretical framework presented in this study. Stated simply, they represent situations in which the gap between bureaucratic and emergent norms is extremely small or even nonexistent. This normal disaster scenario can be illustrated by events that occurred in South Carolina one year after Hurricane Hugo; however, it is important to note that this scenario could be illustrated equally well by the vast majority of governmental responses to natural disasters.

Severe Floods in South Carolina

During the first week of October 1990, two tropical storms converged off the South Atlantic coast of the United States.[3] These storms sent a continuous band of heavy showers and thunderstorms across the state of South Carolina. In some locations, between twelve and fifteen inches of rain fell in a twenty-four period (Bennett 1990, 1). The heavy rains caused the water in many creeks and rivers to rise substantially above normal levels. Record flooding was reported in the central portions of the state; several areas reported water levels that exceeded the expected hundred-year flood marks (Bennett 1990, 1). A number of earthen dams failed, roads washed away, farmland and homes were destroyed, and bridges collapsed. Hundreds of people were evacuated, and nine persons died as a result of the floods (Federal Emergency Management Agency 1990a, 5).

An Immediate but Short Milling Process

The flooding in South Carolina was definitely serious enough to be characterized as a natural disaster: it was clearly more than "severe weather conditions." Twelve of the state's forty-six counties experienced heavy storm-related damages (Federal Emergency Management Agency 1990a). In these counties, the floods disrupted everyday routines and behavior patterns, and they triggered the immediate onset of the milling process.

Milling was most pronounced in areas where the local population was caught off guard. In some communities, the flooding occurred so quickly that residents did not know what they should do to protect their families, their belongings, and their homes from the rising floodwaters. They were confused and disoriented. This led to the usual search for meaning that defines the milling process. The situation stabilized very quickly, however, usually within a matter of hours and never longer than one day. Affected citizens regained their composure and began dealing more calmly with their problems and conditions.

There are several reasons for the short duration of the milling process during the South Carolina floods. First, some people simply did not accept the seriousness of the situation. They insisted on traveling into flood-prone areas and generally refused to admit that anything out of the ordinary had occurred (Smith 1990, 2B). When individuals believe that life is proceeding normally, then the milling process is irrelevant; there is just no need to conduct a search for meaning.

Second, the floods covered a wide area, but their direct impact on people was relatively sporadic and temporary. Some communities escaped the floods entirely, although they experienced the heavy rains that led to them. In other areas, the rivers crested and floodwaters receded quickly. Thus, even when serious social disruptions did occur, they did not last for a long period of time. Accordingly, the relevance of traditional norms and behavioral standards was reestablished quickly.

Third, communication and transportation systems did not break down, even in the areas hit hardest by the storm. Although some roads and railroad lines were blocked, there were almost always alternate transportation routes available for people to use. Most residents did not lose electrical power or telephone service. Therefore, channels of mass communication (radio and television) and interpersonal communication networks remained open throughout the entire period of the disaster (Federal Emergency Management Agency 1990a). With standard information sources available to flood victims, there was no need to search for further meaning or explanation, once again rendering the milling process moot.

Emergent Norms Consistent with Governmental Plans

As in any milling situation, keynoting behavior did take place. But it was carried out by officials *supposed* to provide guidance and direction—law enforcement agencies, fire departments, county rescue squads, and emergency preparedness units. The particular nature of the milling process and keynoting activity guaranteed that emergent norms were virtually nonexistent, at least insofar as they deviated from traditional, legally sanctioned norms and standards of behavior. There was never any perception that the existing institutions were inappropriate or incapable of dealing with the situation caused by the severe weather. Most residents viewed the floods as a temporary and annoying, but manageable, interruption to their everyday lives (Schneider 1992).

Government's Standard Operating Procedures

The floods in South Carolina represent exactly the kind of disaster anticipated by the standard response system. Appropriate governmental agencies at all three levels had time to assess the severity of the conditions, to identify appropriate response mechanisms, and to deploy available resources in an organized fashion. Public officials concentrated on working within, not outside, the preestablished structure (Schneider 1992). Most emergency personnel seemed to understand their roles and responsibilities in the governmental response process, and they seemed willing and able to implement disaster assistance according to the prespecified format. As a result, the process unfolded smoothly and methodically.

This does not mean that the entire process worked perfectly. There were problems and breakdowns in the system, most noticeably during the early stages of the disaster. The flooding occurred so quickly that local emergency management personnel in a few areas were not able to predict it or alert their respective communities adequately (Tuten 1990, 2B). Consequently, some citizens were not made aware of the dangerous conditions, and several drowning deaths occurred when people drove into suddenly flooded areas or washed-out roads (Federal Emergency Management Agency 1990a, 5, 6).

There were also several instances of miscommunication among governmental officials involved in the response and recovery efforts. For example, some local administrators did not coordinate the release of excess stormwater from levees, dams, and reservoirs with local personnel in neighboring areas, thereby exacerbating the flooding in these other communities (Tuten 1990, 2B). Fortunately, these problems were relatively rare, and they were quickly resolved. Overall, the government responded to this disaster in an orderly, routine, and almost perfunctory manner. In this situation, the nearly automatic procedures of the bureaucratic system worked quite well.

The Size of the Gap

The gap was virtually nonexistent following the 1990 floods in South Carolina. The postdisaster emergent norms in the population were fully consistent with the bureaucratic norms in the response agencies. Citizens usually reacted calmly and behaved rationally throughout the entire process. This created exactly the kind of situation anticipated in the disaster preparedness plans. As a result, the government followed its basic operating procedures in order to help the affected population recover from the floods.

Bottom-Up Implementation Pattern

The governmental response process worked from the bottom up, exactly as it is supposed to. Local officials dealt with the affected population, and they handled immediate problems. The fact that communication and transportation systems were not completely disrupted facilitated their access to threatened areas and people. Generally, they concentrated their efforts on evacuating residents, restricting access to flooded areas, and preventing dam failures (Federal Emergency Management Agency 1990a). In short, local emergency management personnel mobilized an effective first response.

Although the state government was peripherally involved during the early stages—issuing evacuation warnings and mobilizing the highway patrol—it became directly involved only when the storm and flood damage spanned several local jurisdictions. At that point, state personnel coordinated activities across local boundaries (e.g., warning county governments of water releases that originated in other counties and directing dam maintenance in the most serious trouble spots), and they channeled state resources (such as social services personnel and road maintenance crews) into the affected areas. State emergency management officials initially acted as coordinators and facilitators. Once the national government became involved in the response effort, state personnel served very effectively as intermediaries between local and federal organizations.

Officials from the national government were on hand from the beginning to provide technical assistance; for example, the Army Corps of Engineers made recommendations regarding water management and flood control. But the federal government did not officially step in until a request was filed through the proper channels. Ten days after the initial flooding, President Bush declared the floods to be a "major disaster." At that point, it was clear that the recovery process would require resources beyond those available in South Carolina. But it is important to emphasize the time span between the initial disaster and the presidential declaration. This apparent delay is actually typical of most disaster situations that occur in the United States. In fact, there is no real "delay" at all. Local and state officials require a certain amount of time to carry out their responsibilities as the first two levels of the standard governmental response system.

After the presidential disaster declaration, federal involvement in the response process took several forms. The initial declaration covered only nine counties. FEMA officials quickly extended coverage to three more, bringing the total to twelve counties (Federal Emergency Management Agency 1990a, 1). This enabled citizens in those counties to receive critical individual assistance grants for repairing and rebuilding their homes and property. FEMA also sent in damage-assessment teams and inspectors who evaluated the ongoing integrity of dams, levees, and other public facilities. Finally, FEMA officials oversaw a comprehensive review and evaluation of South Carolina's emergency management system. It is important to emphasize that, throughout the response process, the national government acted in a *supportive* capacity. Officials from FEMA and/or other federal entities never tried to take over the process or supplant the activities of lower-level governmental personnel. This is exactly the way the process is supposed to work.

Over the next few months, the government implemented disaster assistance in an orderly and methodical fashion. Federal and state officials worked closely with local emergency management personnel to assess the extent of the damage and channel resources into affected areas. In addition, representatives from a wide variety of different agencies (at all three levels of government) used this opportunity to make recommendations about future hazard mitigation efforts in South Carolina. Overall, governmental efforts proceeded smoothly, closely following the policies and procedures laid out in the State Emergency Preparedness Plan and in relevant federal statutes and regulations.

Perception of Governmental Response: Complete Success

There are definite advantages to the bottom-up implementation pattern. When all involved adhere to designated plans and procedures, governmental efforts proceed with little conflict or controversy. The entire governmental response system operates very effectively. The experience in South Carolina during the 1990 floods demonstrates what happens when the system works as designed. By the standards of both the disaster-stricken population and the governmental officials involved, the recovery effort was highly successful.

One of the interesting aspects of the South Carolina floods was the fact that they attracted very little attention outside the immediately affected areas. In fact, most South Carolinians were unaware that their neighbors were undergoing the disruptions caused by a major natural disaster. This apparent inattentiveness almost certainly contributed to the success of the recovery effort because it eliminated the critical and distracting public scrutiny that often accompanies FEMA's operations. The governmental response to the South Carolina floods unfolded quietly and with little fanfare. This enabled public institutions at all levels of government to dispense critical emergency assistance without having to channel resources into the more "cosmetic" components of public relations.[4]

Thus a great deal of the perception that the governmental response to the South Carolina floods was successful reflects the fact that there were few crystallized public perceptions of the disaster in the first place. It is important to point out that this is the case in the vast majority of the natural disasters that occur in the United States. When a governmental response is successful, it attracts little public attention. And this tends to occur when the disaster conforms to the assumptions underlying the ongoing governmental response system and its bottom-up implementation process.

Notes

1. There are an average of twenty-four presidentially declared "major" disaster situations every year in the United States. Technically, this means that these events are severe enough to warrant the resources and assistance of the national government. It does not mean that all these events are monumental or catastrophic phenomena. Only a handful of all the presidentially declared situations would actually qualify as true catastrophes (Peterson 1992; U.S. General Accounting Office 1993b; National Academy of Public Administration 1993).

2. For additional information on the role of the media in disaster situations, see Quarantelli and Dynes (1972), Waxman (1973), Scanlon (1977), Scanlon, Alldred, Farrell, and Prawzick (1985), Quarantelli (1988), Gitlin (1989), Guider (1989), Medsger (1989), and Rogers, Berndt, Harris, and Minzer (1990).

3. I collected much of the information for this section as a member of the hazard-mitigation team that assessed the flood damage, monitored the relief effort, and presented recommendations to improve governmental efforts.

4. Public relations is not the same as public information. Public information—issuing evacuation warnings, providing information about the availability of emergency shelter and food, publicizing how and where disaster victims can apply for disaster assistance—is a critical responsibility of emergency management agencies. Public relations activities refer to the steps taken by agencies to justify their actions or to change the public's perceptions of their roles and responsibilities.

Part Three

Summary, Implications, and Conclusions

14

The Paradox of Governmental Performance

The case studies presented in Part Two fill out the framework presented in Part One of this study. They illustrate the wide variability of the perceived governmental response to natural disasters in the United States, ranging from the nearly complete failure of the system in the Caribbean Islands during Hurricane Hugo to the successful resolution of conditions in South Carolina following the 1990 floods. The other cases fall in between these two extremes: Florida and South Carolina (during Hurricane Hugo) lie nearer to the failure pole; North Carolina and Louisiana fall closer to the success side; and California is positioned almost exactly halfway between the two poles.

Variability in the Effectiveness of Disaster Responses

The overall objective of this book has been to explain why there is variability in the effectiveness of the governmental disaster-response process. The answer that has been proposed focuses on the size of the gap that develops between bureaucratic norms and emergent norms. The former are composed of the rules, regulations, and standard operating procedures that characterize official behavior in virtually all modern large organizations. They guide governmental activity during natural disasters and the period immediately following. In contrast, emergent norms consist of the largely informal behavioral standards that develop during the uncertainty of the postdisaster period. They provide direction and meaning to the stricken population.

When the two sets of norms converge, the size of the gap is relatively small, and the disaster-response process works well. For example, the 1990 floods in South Carolina caused major disruptions in the social system, but both the government and the public reacted to these conditions in a calm, orderly manner. Consequently, this natural disaster was handled and re-solved with very little public attention beyond those immediately involved. Overall, the governmental response was regarded as a success. Similar pro-cesses develop in many other presidentially declared disaster situations.

In other instances, bureaucratic and emergent norms diverge dramati-cally. The response process falls apart because governmental agencies are either totally unprepared or are prepared for situations that do not occur. Meanwhile, public behavior follows unusual patterns that deviate from tra-ditional norms. In this kind of situation, there is nothing to tie together bureaucratic procedures and the actions of disaster victims. So the gap between the two is quite wide, and the governmental response is widely considered a failure. This is exactly what occurred in the Caribbean Islands following Hurricane Hugo.

Most disaster situations fall somewhere between these two extremes. In some instances, governmental planning seems roughly to coincide with the public's expectations. There is confusion, disarray, and disorder, but these conditions do not prevent public agencies from implementing their pre-specified emergency management plans. Disaster assistance still bubbles up through the intergovernmental system, and the relief effort proceeds fairly smoothly and effectively. Louisiana's experience with Hurricane Andrew and North Carolina's with Hurricane Hugo fit this pattern quite well.

Of course, there are other disasters in which governmental planning and human behavior are more at odds with each other, even though the system basically works as it is intended. In such cases, a response occurs, but questions arise about its effectiveness. The government reacts too slowly or inappropriately, and the public develops unrealistic expectations. This leads to widespread confusion within the intergovernmental system and intense criticism of the entire recovery effort. Florida and South Carolina during Hurricane Hugo are vivid examples of this latter scenario; California's situ-ation during the recovery phase of the Loma Prieta earthquake also fits this pattern.

Taken together, these cases show the range of governmental responses to natural disasters in the United States. But they do not constitute a *represen-tative* sampling of governmental responses—some of these activity patterns occur more frequently than others. Consider the two most extreme situa-tions examined in this study: The complete breakdown of governmental operations is, fortunately, extremely rare (Peterson 1992). Therefore, the single instance of the scenario considered here—the Caribbean Islands dur-ing Hurricane Hugo—represents an "oversampling" of this problem relative to other disaster responses. In contrast, the vast majority of governmental relief efforts are carried out smoothly and effectively (U.S. General Accounting Office 1991, 1993b). Hence the one example of this kind of response—the 1990 South Carolina floods—is greatly "undersampled" compared to the other disasters.[1] In summary, the governmental disaster-response system works well most of the time. Problematic responses are relatively infrequent, and complete failures are very rare.

But this skewed distribution of disaster-response effectiveness poses a dilemma for the public emergency management system. When the system operates smoothly, it does not receive any publicity. Public officials carry out their responsibilities in a businesslike, routine manner. Therefore, their actions are simply not very interesting to the mass media. Instead, coverage focuses on the ravages of the disaster itself and the personal burdens of the victims (Scanlon, Alldred, Farrell, and Prawzick 1985; Drabek 1986; Rogers, Berndt, Harris, and Minzer 1990; Singer 1993; Benthall 1993).[2] Most citizens are simply not aware that the governmental disaster response has been mobilized; hence they have no idea that it is operating successfully.

In a tiny minority of natural disasters, public attention focuses directly on the response process. When this occurs, that attention will almost certainly be critical in tone. The disaster-response system receives extensive media coverage only when it is "news" in itself; in other words, when it is operating in a manner that is contrary to prior expectations. To use the terms of this study, there is a large gap between governmental planning and human behavior. These are the situations where the effectiveness of the relief efforts are called into question. They are also the natural disasters that people tend to remember. As a result, large-scale disasters have long-term consequences, shaping public perceptions of the entire governmental disaster-response system.

It is tempting to assert that the success or failure of the governmental response is a direct by-product of the magnitude of the disaster. In other words, it might seem that the system can handle small disasters relatively well but that it experiences partial or complete failures during large, catastrophic events. This simple explanation does not always hold true. It is the size of the gap, rather than the size of the disaster, that determines the effectiveness of the governmental response.

There are large-scale disasters where bureaucratic and emergent norms converge, producing a small gap. For example, the Great Flood of 1993 placed tremendous strains on many Midwestern communities, as well on the nation's governmental relief system. Yet the government and the flood victims both dealt with the situation in a relatively calm and orderly fashion. Numerous stories circulated among the media and governmental officials, relating how individual citizens worked tirelessly for days to build up levees around their homes and businesses in order to ward off the rising floodwaters (U.S. Department of Commerce 1994). Similarly, there were many reports describing how emergency management personnel, including FEMA officials, went out of their way to help flood victims obtain assistance as quickly as possible (Claiborne 1993; Kilborn 1993). Overall, the response effort received high marks from the affected population, the general public, and the government itself (U.S. Senate 1993b, 1994a, 1994b).

In contrast, there are cases in which relatively small, isolated disasters have led to a large gap between bureaucratic and emergent norms. When a tornado touched down in Plainfield, Illinois, during the summer of 1990, neither the affected population nor the governmental relief system seemed to know how to handle the situation. No warnings were issued about the possibility of a tornado hazard; consequently, precautionary steps were not taken to protect residents, homes, and businesses. The twister struck suddenly but violently, killing twenty-five people and injuring several hundred more. It knocked out telephone and electrical services and made transportation into and within Plainfield virtually impossible. Local residents reacted to the situation with disbelief, despair, and fear. The governor of Illinois, James R. Thompson, sent National Guard troops into the affected areas to patrol against looters and reassure disaster victims (Schmidt 1990). By objective standards, the Plainfield tornado was a small disaster. Nevertheless, there was clearly a period when the plans and actions of governmental officials did not meet the needs of the affected population, generating a fairly wide gap between the two sets of behavioral norms. Thus the size of the gap must be considered as a factor that is distinct and separate from the size of the disaster that produces it in the first place.

Even though the size of the gap and the magnitude of the disaster are separate variables, the two are certainly related. Major natural disasters are definitely more likely to produce the conditions that facilitate the emergence of a large gap. Catastrophic events impose particularly severe strains on social and political institutions and normal patterns of human interaction (Fritz 1957; Drabek 1986; Silverstein 1992). Under such conditions, people follow courses of action that, to themselves, appear to be perfectly rational (Stallings and Quarentelli 1985). But when viewed in the broader context of the disaster situation, these actions tend to magnify the gap. This problem arises among all the major actors in any natural disaster situation. First, bureaucrats and public agencies want to maintain order so they can retain preestablished plans and standard operating procedures. The problem is that during severe disasters, administrative mechanisms are often impaired or inappropriate for the situation at hand. Second, elected officials are largely outside the normal response system, but they still have incentives for providing relief to their constituents (Abney and Hill 1966; Mayhew 1974).

Therefore, they often intervene in the emergency management operations, creating more complication and confusion when they do so. Third, the mass media covering the disaster have direct incentives to relay the most newsworthy events. Therefore, they always focus on highly dramatic or unusual stories that emphasize human suffering, the breakdown of law and order, and governmental disarray (Perry and Mushkatel 1984). But this presents an incomplete and generally misleading picture of the recovery process. Fourth, disaster victims want to comprehend their own situations and obtain immediate relief. But major catastrophes impair the normal lines of communication and supply. Therefore, the public engages in collective behavior, searching for understanding and assistance in ways that are inconsistent with traditional norms.

Thus the conditions imposed by major natural catastrophes along with the narrowly defined rational behavior of *all* relevant actors widen the gap between human behavior and governmental planning. This in turn hastens the breakdown of the response and recovery process and thereby increases the likelihood of intense criticism aimed at the entire governmental disaster-response system.

The Nature of Success and Failure

Success and failure in disaster recovery are almost entirely a matter of public perception rather than objective reality. Sometimes the success of the governmental system is signaled by the very lack of public attention to the response process. In the vast majority of the disaster situations that occur in the United States, the government steps in, provides relief, and terminates its efforts within its own preestablished time frames. There is little fanfare, no widespread criticism of any kind, and indeed little public notice outside the immediately affected areas (Federal Emergency Management Agency 1993).

On a more objective level, the governmental response system is also very effective in dealing with the most violent natural upheavals—those that tend to produce the most vocal public criticism of the response process. Breakdowns in public order and official assistance are usually temporary and short-lived. Most inhabitants do return to their homes. Most local businesses and industries do resume operations. Community infrastructures are eventually rebuilt. And, after a period of time, life simply returns to "normal"—that is, to its predisaster conditions.[3] In some situations, the rebuilding efforts following a disaster actually leave the community in better shape than it was previously.[4] Thus, if one takes a broader perspective, all governmental efforts are successful.

Individual citizens rarely view disaster relief through the long-term perspective required to appreciate the effectiveness of the system fully. Therefore, they cannot reasonably be expected to comprehend fully the difficulties and complexities involved in any recovery effort. Disaster victims are naturally absorbed with their own personal problems and situations. For obvious and perfectly understandable reasons, they tend to view anything short of immediate, direct, comprehensive help as failure. This view is often picked up by the mass media and by elected officials who use emergency management administrators as convenient scapegoats. Therefore, the negative impression of governmental activity endures.

Once again, the government has distributed massive amounts of disaster assistance during the last few years (Berry 1994). It has been able to restore virtually all affected areas to their predisaster conditions (Peterson 1992). This is an enormous accomplishment when one considers the number and magnitude of the natural catastrophes that have struck the United States over the years. Still, the disaster-response system in the United States is intensely criticized and ridiculed, and governmental relief efforts are widely viewed as failures.

It is tempting to take an optimistic view of this situation. After all, if the failure is only "perceived" and not "real," then it can be discounted as not posing a critical threat to the response system. But this seriously underestimates the true state of affairs. Public perceptions are extremely important in the American political system: they have a direct impact on the ways in which social problems gain access to the governmental agenda and on the ability of public institutions to address important public problems (Eyestone 1978; Cobb and Elder 1983a; Kingdon 1984; Baumgartner and Jones 1993). Perceptions of failure in the disaster-response system have implications that reverberate throughout the policymaking process. The media take a hostile stance, and other governmental agencies take a skeptical view of emergency management officials. Legislative oversight committees assume a critical and restrictive tone; funding levels for disaster assistance decline. And the public develops a cynical outlook toward disaster-response officials that seriously undermines their credibility and authority during the very times when the latter are most essential. Thus, *perceptions* of failure cannot be dismissed; they have a serious, long-term, detrimental effect on the governmental response system.

The importance of perception creates a paradox for public policymaking in the area of emergency management and disaster relief. Most of the time, people are completely unaware that the government is responding to a natural disaster. Yet these are precisely the situations in which the process runs smoothly, effectively, and successfully. The general public only learns about governmental relief activities when there are problems, difficulties, and/or breakdowns. These latter situations generate a lasting, negative impression among the general public. If the government wants to change this impression, it faces an interesting dilemma: In order to restore public confidence in its activities, it must fix the problems that have developed in only a very few disaster situations. At the same time, the government must retain the components of the system that seem to work so well in the vast majority of natural disaster situations, but attract little, if any, public or media attention.[5] Accomplishing these two objectives simultaneously can be highly problematic.

Notes

1. This analysis has focused on major natural disasters—that is, those that the president declares to be severe enough to require the resources of the national government. It is important to keep in mind that in addition to these situations, hundreds of other "minor" disasters occur every year in the United States, including tornadoes in the Midwest, ice storms in the Northeast, and mudslides in the West. These minor disasters are handled by individual citizens, private organizations and local emergency management agencies, and they never escalate beyond this to state or national government levels.

2. The role of the media in disasters is not restricted to natural phenomena. For more information on the media's coverage of other crisis situations—technological mishaps, riots, health care epidemics, and so on—see Wilkins (1987), Fensch (1990), Rochefort and Cobb (1994), and Brown (1990).

3. There are notable exceptions to this return to normalcy. Some disaster victims experience long-term psychological trauma as a result of their ordeal. And some homes and businesses are never rebuilt after a devastating earthquake or hurricane. But, remarkably, most disaster-stricken populations and communities do recover from their experiences. See, for example, Gross (1994), Mydans (1994a), Hamilton (1994), and Ayres (1994) for an indication of how the affected population handled the 1994 Los Angeles earthquake.

4. This has led some critics to argue that the government is too generous in providing disaster relief. The argument is made that disaster assistance may actually make people too complacent and less conscientious about taking the necessary precautions to mitigate against and prepare for natural catastrophes (Berry 1994). For more information on the long-term impacts of disasters, see Friesema, Caporaso, Goldstein, Lineberry, and McCleary (1979), Haas, Kates, and Bowden (1977), Wright, Rossi, Wright, and Weber-Burdin (1979), May (1985b), and Drabek (1986).

5. This same dilemma occurs in other public policy areas as well. For example, the public hears more about problems in the administration of public assistance—welfare fraud, corruption in the food stamp program, inefficiency in the social security system—than it does about the positive benefits of governmental aid.

15

Considering Recommendations for Change

There have been a number of recommendations presented for improving the governmental response to natural disasters in the United States. These proposals cover a wide range of possibilities. They originate from a variety of sources, including the mass media, the National Academy of Public Administration, the General Accounting Office, congressional oversight committees, and FEMA. The content varies widely, from proposals for overhauling the entire system to plans that entail only modest adjustments to existing policies and procedures. Some of these ideas are quite old, predating the current disaster-response system itself. Others are of more recent vintage. But all these recommendations are certainly receiving more attention today than ever before. Much of the reason for this stems from the recent frequency of major natural disasters, coupled with the extreme variability in the governmental responses that have been mounted. More important, however, events such as Hurricane Hugo, the Loma Prieta earthquake, and Hurricane Andrew have left a lasting impression of governmental non-responsiveness, incompetence, and failure. But, as explained in the previous chapter, the situation is not that simple. While there have indeed been significant breakdowns, there are many more unambiguous successes. Any changes to the existing disaster-response system must take this fact into account. Unfortunately, several of the most prominent recommendations fail to do so.

Theoretically, the entire existing disaster-response system could be abolished. The federal government could take charge of all disaster-response operations, or alternatively, state and local governments could assume complete responsibility for emergency management activities within their respective jurisdictions. Fortunately, such extreme suggestions are not receiving serious attention. They would involve massive reallocations of resources and new designations about lines of authority and responsibility. Furthermore, they would eliminate the successful aspects of the current process exactly as explained above. Therefore, recommendations for completely eliminating the existing system will not receive further consideration in this study.

At a more reasonable level, there are four frequently mentioned suggestions for building a more effective emergency management system in the United States: (1) place the military in charge of the system; (2) abolish FEMA and create another federal agency to lead the effort; (3) keep the current general framework, but give the federal government more responsibility for cataclysmic events; and (4) reorient and reinvigorate—or "reinvent" to use the popular term—the governmental response system. All these recommendations build on currently existing institutional arrangements. Therefore they represent viable alternatives, worthy of serious consideration.

Place the Military in Charge

One of the most popular recommendations is to strengthen the role of the military in relief operations. This idea almost always surfaces in the mass media following major catastrophic events (Lippman 1992b; Moniz 1992). During recent disaster situations, the military has often appeared to be the only governmental institution capable of responding in a timely and effective manner. Moreover, there is clearly a need to find new peacetime roles for the armed forces, which are being scaled down in the post–Cold War period. Therefore, why not give the military a larger role in the nation's disaster-response process? Why not place the military in charge of the entire system?

Superficially, military organizations seem to be well equipped to handle emergencies (U.S. General Accounting Office 1993a). They are structured in a fairly rigid, hierarchical manner, which simplifies decision making and policy implementation during crisis situations. They have experience handling a wide variety of emergencies, ranging from international terrorism to feeding the starving masses in Somalia. Individuals within their ranks are well trained and well versed in emergency management practices and procedures. They have the equipment (such as tents and electric generators) and resources to provide relief to the victims of natural catastrophes. And they have the authority to enforce their actions and support the efforts of other relief workers. Taken together, these attributes seem to make the military the perfect emergency management organization.

Recent events have demonstrated just how effective military organizations can be in actual disaster situations. For example, it was the U.S. Army, with help from the U.S. Navy, the U.S. Air Force, the Federal Bureau of Investigation, and the U.S. Marshal's Office, that restored law and order to the Virgin Islands following Hurricane Hugo (York 1989; Branigin 1989a, 1989b; Peterson 1989). Military involvement was also essential to the response efforts in south Florida after Hurricane Andrew: both the Florida National Guard and the U.S. military (which included personnel from the army, the navy, the air force, and the marine corps) helped stabilize local conditions, airlifted food and supplies into the damaged communities, created temporary shelter (tent cities), dispensed needed medical care to storm victims, and removed tons of hurricane debris (U.S. General Accounting Office 1993a).

Clearly, the military plays a critical role in emergency relief operations. But the armed forces should not be placed in charge of the nation's disaster-response system. There are several major reasons why emergency relief should remain a civilian undertaking in the United States. First, the military's primary mission is to maintain the country's warfare capabilities. Responding to natural disasters is, at best, a secondary concern. If a natural catastrophe occurs at the same time as an international conflict, the military must focus on the latter, not the former. Who, then, would mobilize the governmental response to the natural disaster?

Second, putting the military in charge just does not address many of the nation's emergency management problems. The current disaster-response system operates on the basis of intergovernmental cooperation. Local, state, and national authorities must work together to provide the most efficient utilization of governmental resources during a natural disaster. It is assumed that subnational governments will handle many situations without the help of the national government. Even when a major disaster strikes, state and local governments must still coordinate and direct the flow of federal assistance into the affected areas. The national government does not have the authority to step in and take control of an entire relief effort. Instead, it must work with state and local governments throughout the entire process. As several of the case studies presented in this book demonstrate, problems can and do occur at state and local levels. When this happens, the intergovernmental response stalls or in some situations completely breaks down. Placing the military in charge of disaster relief simply does not address this problem.

Third, there is a more fundamental issue about the role of the military in this policy area. There is a long-standing constitutional principle in the United States that the responsibility for public policymaking remains firmly in the hands of civilian agencies and organizations. Placing the military in control of disaster-relief operations would directly contradict this central component of American democracy. A civilian-run disaster-response system was created and developed precisely because it reflects the general orientation of civilian control over governmental operations (Popkin 1990). Clearly, the military can play an important role in this process, but it must remain subordinate to higher *civilian* authorities (Peterson 1992). It would be a dangerous precedent to initiate a system where the military has the power to tell civilian agencies what to do.[1] This is true even though disaster situations— where such military control would be asserted—occur only infrequently and for limited periods of time. Thus, placing the military in control of the nation's disaster-response system is not really a viable option.

Create a New Federal Agency

A second recommendation is to abolish FEMA and create another federal (civilian) agency to head the governmental disaster-response system. This idea has been proposed by the congressional committees with oversight responsibilities for emergency management operations (see for example, U.S. House 1990 and 1993; Claiborne 1994). Once a natural disaster has reached the federal level of the response structure, FEMA is supposed to mobilize and coordinate the entire relief effort. But the agency has so many internal and external problems that it is unable to perform this function. Therefore, this perspective holds that FEMA has become more of a bureaucratic obstacle than a focal point for leading disaster relief efforts (Lippman 1992b).

FEMA's internal problems are obvious. As federal agencies go, FEMA is extremely small. During the disaster situations discussed in this book, FEMA had an annual operating budget of about $450 million to $500 million and a staff of about 2,000–3,000 full-time employees located in offices throughout the country (Peterson 1992).[2] These are paltry figures by the standards of the federal government, and the agency's lack of resources makes it difficult for FEMA to respond to large-scale disaster situations quickly (U.S. General Accounting Office 1993b). In addition, the agency's mission is itself somewhat ambiguous (National Academy of Public Administration 1993). Most of its planning, resources, and activities are focused on coping with the consequences of nuclear attacks against the United States. From 1982 to 1992, FEMA spent twelve times more money on preparing for the possibility of nuclear war than on preparing for natural disasters such as hurricanes, earthquakes, and floods (Peterson 1992; Lipman and Jaspin 1993). Obviously and fortunately, the latter occur far more frequently than the former. Moreover, FEMA has a large number of political appointees within its ranks. As is true in any governmental bureaucracy, these people are viewed with some skepticism by career employees (Wamsley 1993). Added to this, the political appointees' relatively short tenure in office and their lack of disaster-related expertise ensured that FEMA did not have consistent or effective leadership during the 1980s and early 1990s (Bandy 1989a; Lippman 1992c).[3] In summary, FEMA has been routinely exposed to internal stresses and strains that would have a detrimental impact on any organization's effectiveness.

FEMA's inability to lead is also the result, in part, of external factors. FEMA's lines of responsibility are unclear. The agency reports to twenty-five different congressional committees and subcommittees (Peterson 1989). Instead of one taskmaster, FEMA has many. This places it in direct contrast to most state emergency-preparedness agencies, which report directly to their respective governors. Furthermore, FEMA cannot operate alone. It depends heavily on state and local officials, as well as other federal agencies, to implement disaster assistance. As a result, FEMA does not control the process: the agency's job is merely to respond to state and local needs and to coordinate the efforts of the federal government. This inevitably places FEMA in a difficult spot. In order to be successful, FEMA must rely on assistance from other governmental agencies whose self-interests frequently lead them in other, potentially conflicting directions. Taken together, these external pressures make it difficult for FEMA to respond to large situations quickly and effectively.

Given FEMA's many internal and external problems, it may seem an expedient course of action simply to abolish the agency and create a new one. Presumably, such a new entity would have its mission, powers, and responsibilities articulated clearly and directly. But this course of action probably would not achieve lasting success.

Initially, a new federal disaster-response agency would have more drive and more energy than the tired, old Federal Emergency Management Agency. The officials in such an agency would be eager to demonstrate the effectiveness of their new organizational procedures. They would try to take bold, pathbreaking steps and thereby bring a new sense of commitment to their activities. But this initial spurt would probably not last very long. All organizations tend to become routinized and conservative over time (Downs 1967). New organizations quickly lose their initial burst of energy and enthusiasm; they develop standard operating procedures and policies; and they increasingly concentrate their efforts on preserving their own operations and spheres of responsibilities (Rourke 1984).[4] A new federal disaster-response agency would almost certainly follow this pattern of organizational development. It would be confronted with the same operating conditions and external demands that FEMA currently faces: periods of inactivity punctuated by intense, stressful, and demanding disaster situations. So, in the end, any new agency would probably possess many of the same bureaucratic characteristics and problems—for example, the obsession with paperwork, red tape, and the inability to handle nonroutine situations—as the old FEMA. Replacing the latter with a new organization would probably not lead to any lasting improvements in the system.

Adding a Special Mechanism for Catastrophic Events

Most scholars and experts in the field recognize that the governmental response to natural disasters is sometimes inadequate. But they do not believe that the military should assume control of the process, nor do they think that FEMA should be abolished. Instead, they want to retain the basic framework of the nation's current emergency management system. But they also want to add mechanisms that will enable the government to respond quickly and effectively to the kinds of major natural disaster situations that have proved most troublesome under the current system. The National Academy of Public Administration (1993), the U.S. General Accounting Office (1993b), and the Federal Emergency Management Agency (1993) itself have all advocated this approach. Although the recommendations come from several sources, they all tend to focus on a few specific components.

First, state and local governments must be better prepared to handle natural disasters. For some time, analysts have complained that most lower-level officials simply do not have the resources, training, and experience to perform emergency management responsibilities. After all, disasters are relatively rare events in most areas of the country. Local and state officials have many other duties and responsibilities to perform. Similarly, state and local financial resources tend to be expended on other, more immediate social problems and are not committed but unused in anticipation of future events that may never occur. As a result, little, if any, attention, is typically devoted to emergency management functions. The problem is that the quality of governmental disaster response is a direct by-product of state and local capabilities. The case studies in this book clearly demonstrate that disruptions at state or local levels subsequently affect the entire process, far beyond the jurisdictions where the breakdowns originally occur. Efforts to strengthen the emergency management functions of state and local governments can have beneficial consequences only further upward along the line.

Second, the role of the federal government in the nation's emergency management system must be reevaluated. The Federal Emergency Management Agency was created in 1979 to consolidate emergency preparedness and management activities at the national level. It was hoped that FEMA would be the coordinator, mobilizer, and catalyst for the nation's disaster-response system. Unfortunately, the agency has not lived up to this image. As the National Academy of Public Administration reports, "FEMA is like a patient in triage" (1993, ix). It has no unifying vision of its own activities, it has no agencywide planning or management processes, and it has suffered from ineffective leadership. Moreover, it has not been given the legislative or executive support it needs to perform all of its emergency management responsibilities. Therefore, all these facets of organizational mission, responsibility, and activity need to be reconsidered, with an aim toward articulating them more clearly.

Third, the federal government should have the authority to take an earlier and more commanding role than it does at present during unusually severe disasters. It is simply unrealistic to expect that state and local authorities will be able to carry out their preestablished duties when there is chaos and extreme disruption permeating the environment. In such situations, it would be better to develop a mechanism that allows the federal government to assume direct control of the response process. A special emergency response unit, or strike team, could be created to perform this activity. This federal entity should have the authority and the capability to supersede state and local officials temporarily in disaster-stricken areas. Its responsibilities would be to assess the extent of the damages, mobilize necessary resources, and provide immediate emergency relief. Establishing a powerful strike team of this sort may seem like an extreme measure. But it does appear to be completely justified in some situations. It could operate more quickly than state and local emergency response agencies. As we have seen, the latter are often crippled by the very disasters to which they are trying to respond. With its status as an arm of the federal government, the strike team would also have the ability to act across state and local jurisdictions. Moreover, a federally supported unit would have far more resources than any other institution—public or private. Thus there is ample justification for a more active and aggressive federal presence during extreme, catastrophic situations. The key is to create the kind of agency that emerges *only* during such circumstances. It would not be activated during the routine situations that constitute the vast majority of disasters in the United States.

The general approach of modifying the current system has a number of strengths. First, it leaves the organization and focus of the current emergency management system intact. Public organizations at local, state, and national levels would still constitute the basic infrastructure of the response system. Very few resources would be expended on reorganizational activities. Second, this approach preserves certain fundamental tenets of American politics. It is still based on civilian control over the nation's disaster-response system. It also conforms to the values of federalism by dividing important responsibilities between local, state, and national authorities. Third, this approach reflects the realities of the contemporary policymaking process by giving the federal government greater authority and control during extreme crisis situations. There are clearly imbalances in resources, power, and expertise across the three levels of government. This causes problems and breakdowns in the current system as a result of misperceptions and overreliance on higher-level authorities. Under the proposed modifications, the federal government's position would be used to greater advantage. It could step in quickly, making a preemptive strike against the conditions following the disaster. By doing so, it would short-circuit the criticisms and problems that often arise under the current framework.

The idea of modifying the present disaster-response system has substantial merit. But there is also a problem in that it places too much emphasis on *governmental* actions. Certainly, public organizations play an extremely important role in the process. But the government is not solely responsible for the way the system operates. As this study has shown, the degree of discrepancy or consistency between governmental actions and human behavior accounts for the effectiveness of disaster-relief efforts. Consequently, recommendations that focus exclusively on improving the government's internal operations miss a key element of the process: the collective behavior that inevitably occurs in the aftermath of a natural disaster. Of course, governmental activities have an impact on what the affected population will do. If public officials can quickly restore communication and supply channels, then the disaster victims will probably return to traditional patterns of behavior as well. But it is important to emphasize that emergent norms inevitably occur after natural disasters, and their exact nature is impossible to predict beforehand. Therefore it is unlikely that any governmental response system will ever be able fully to anticipate and deal with the human behavior that follows a natural disaster.

Reinvent the Governmental Response

Recently, a great deal of attention has focused on "making government work better" (Osborne and Gaebler 1992; National Performance Review 1993; DiIulio, Garvey, and Kettl 1993; U.S. General Accounting Office 1993c). Of course there are always demands for the reform of the public sector. But the decades since the 1960s have seen unusually broad public dissatisfaction with the operations of government institutions (Hill 1992). This has intensified demands for reform almost to the point at which they constitute a social movement, which is often characterized as "reinventing government" (Osborne and Gaebler 1992).

The problems identified by the reinventing government movement are all too well known. Public agencies respond too slowly and haphazardly to pressing social issues, and they deal with most concerns in an uncoordinated, disorganized manner. Government officials are overly concerned with preserving their own jobs and positions and are unable (or unwilling) to develop innovative, creative solutions to major public policy problems. All in all, government performs in an uncaring, lackadaisical, and inefficient fashion.

The basic premise of the reinventing government movement is that the system is broken and in need of repair (Moe 1994). Therefore it is time to rethink what the government does, how it operates, and how its activities have an impact on society. Spokespersons for this movement almost invariably articulate their objectives in broad generalities: rethink, reinvigorate, and refocus public-service activities in order to improve governmental performance (Osborne and Gaebler 1992).

The principles of reinventing government can be applied to the disaster-response system. In fact, the current director of FEMA, James Witt, has advocated exactly this approach. And he has already initiated a number of reforms in this area. First, he has clearly articulated an overriding mission for the agency: our job is to provide leadership and support "for all hazards, comprehensive emergency management" (Witt 1993, 1). As simple as this may appear, such a statement has never before been clearly, directly, and forcefully articulated (National Academy of Public Administration 1993). Second, FEMA has undergone extensive internal restructuring. Here the objective is to remove ambiguities and clarify the specific responsibilities associated with each bureau, office, and unit ("Witt Reinvents FEMA" 1993). Third, Director Witt has actively promoted cooperation between FEMA and other federal agencies, such as the Small Business Administration, the Department of Transportation, and the Department of Health and Human Services. As explained earlier, FEMA acts as a conduit for channeling the resources that other agencies provide to needy citizens. In the past, FEMA officials simply assumed that these other agencies would cooperate. Now FEMA is taking positive steps to try to ensure their cooperation in an ongoing manner. Fourth, FEMA is relying more heavily on public information campaigns to sensitize American citizens to the realities of disaster situations. These publicity campaigns are aimed at (1) preparing citizens for the possibility of disaster and (2) reassuring people that government assistance will be available if and when a disaster strikes (Ingwerson 1993). Finally, Director Witt has tried to "empower" agency employees. He has tried to instill a new sense of dedication and self-worth, both of which were sorely lacking under previous FEMA directors. The low morale within FEMA was exacerbated by the widespread public criticism of the agency. Current efforts try to convince employees that this criticism is not inevitable: they are valuable and essential arms of the federal government's disaster-relief effort (Witt 1993, 3). In general, James Witt has tried to refocus and sharpen FEMA's mission, make the agency more consumer oriented, streamline its operations, and establish an esprit de corps among its employees. All these objectives are taken directly from the principles of the reinventing government movement.

The reinventing government approach has several obvious advantages. First, it builds on the existing structural framework. It does not require dismantling the response system and starting anew. It takes advantage of the technical expertise, operating procedures, and structural relationships that have already proved successful in many disaster situations. This leaves policymakers free to focus exclusively on the problematic aspects of the response system.

Second, the reinventing government approach is politically expedient. The movement clearly has the active support of President Bill Clinton. He established the National Performance Review Task Force headed by Vice-President Al Gore. Stated bluntly, the presidential commission tried to proselytize the central ideas of the reinventing government movement. Clearly, any federal agency that actually tries to operationalize these principles, as FEMA has recently done, will receive political support. This is a far cry from the agency's fortunes under the Reagan and Bush administrations, during which it was often viewed with disfavor.

Third, the reinventing government movement is the only approach that emphasizes the connection between government activity and citizen reactions. And, as the present study amply demonstrates, the degree of correspondence between the two is absolutely crucial for the success or failure of any disaster response. Of course the reinventing government literature does not employ exactly the same concepts that have been utilized in this study. For example, it does not speak about the gap between bureaucratic norms and collective behavior. But it certainly does emphasize that public administrators must be attentive to the needs of their constituents. To the extent that this general objective can be institutionalized within the governmental response system, it will tend to reduce the size of the gap in future disasters.

Another telling point in favor of the reinventing government movement is that its reforms seem to be working in the area of disaster response. James Witt assumed office as the director of FEMA in early 1993 and implemented his reform initiatives almost immediately. Since that time, the agency has handled dozens of routine disasters in its normally smooth manner. But, more important, it has been faced with two major disasters and has carried out its responsibilities relatively effectively and efficiently. The Great Floods of 1993 caused major disruptions and affected thousands of lives in the Midwest. Similarly, the Los Angeles earthquake of January 1994 brought extensive structural damages and forced thousands of people out of their homes. In both situations, FEMA worked in concert with other governmental agencies to react quickly, efficiently, and responsively (Claiborne 1993; Ingwerson 1993; Ayres 1994). As a result, there was almost no public criticism of FEMA's actions, personnel, or policies after either of these major natural disasters. Why were these operations more successful in comparison with earlier efforts, such as the response to Hurricane Andrew and Hurricane Hugo? The basic structure of the governmental response system has remained the same, as has FEMA's formal place within the federal government. Therefore, it seems reasonable to say that the improved performance reflects, at least in part, the reforms brought about by the reinventing government movement.

While the reinventing government reforms have so far been successful in the area of disaster relief, a number of weaknesses should also be considered. First, there is the previously mentioned difficulty in sustaining organizational energy and initiative. New leaders can revitalize bureaucratic personnel, but organizational constraints invariably limit the duration of administrative enthusiasm.

Second, administrative leaders serve only for relatively short periods of time. When new administrators take over, they may have different ideas, objectives, and approaches. This could create particularly severe problems within the reinventing government framework, precisely because the latter is often vague and ambiguous about the details and specific changes necessary to obtain governmental reform. New leaders may agree in principle with their predecessors but still institute internal changes that impair the effectiveness of the disaster-response system.

Third, the linkage between a government agency and the public it serves is extremely fragile. This is particularly the case with emergency management institutions. Disasters are, by their very nature, unpredictable events. So the collective behavior that follows a catastrophic situation may proceed in directions that are completely unanticipated by public officials, no matter how closely the latter try to stay in touch with their constituencies. Added to this is the ongoing fact that citizens' postdisaster expectations are often at odds with the immediate capabilities of government institutions. Thus, relations between response agencies and disaster victims will inevitably remain somewhat troublesome, no matter what reforms are instituted.

And finally, the reinventing government reforms may go too far. It is true that the reforms may be effective when dealing with the most pronounced disaster situations, in which the gap between bureaucratic norms and emergent norms is particularly large. But this represents a fairly unusual situation. The results from this study emphasize that currently existing bureaucratic procedures and routines work very well in the vast majority of disasters that occur in the United States. They allow public agencies to cope with situations in a fairly routine, methodical, and consistent fashion. Any modifications to this basic system would be gratuitous, unnecessary, and probably detrimental to the effectiveness of the response. For almost all the work carried out by FEMA and the overall governmental response system, one could paraphrase the old adage and say, "It ain't broke, so don't fix it."

All in all, the reinventing government movement does not provide a panacea for improving governmental performance during natural disasters. But it does present some useful ideas for strengthening the response system's internal operations, public perceptions of this system, and linkages between government policy and citizen reactions. These are all important components that have been neglected or downplayed in other policy recommendations aimed at improving the governmental response to natural disasters.

Combining Recommendations: A Set of Changes in the System

After detailed consideration of the U.S. disaster-response system, its performance in a range of disaster situations, and a number of proposals for "fixing" or changing the system, we are still left with a single overriding question: what should be done to strengthen the disaster-response system? Although each proposal described earlier in this chapter contains some useful, thought-provoking ideas, no single recommendation provides an ideal solution. Nevertheless, suggestions from several different proposals can be combined to produce one fairly straightforward set of recommendations that would correct the most tangible problems.

First, the basic organizational structure of disaster assistance should be retained. The results from this study suggest that the current system has certain obvious advantages: it allows the government to handle the vast majority of natural disasters quietly, smoothly, and successfully. Consequently, there is no need to dismantle the current governmental framework and replace it with an entirely new structure. Putting the military in charge might facilitate faster emergency responses, but it would generate a host of other, potentially severe problems—conflicts between civilian and military officials and the role of the military in long-term recovery efforts. Similarly, the abolishment of FEMA and the creation of a new federal agency to lead the response and recovery charge is also not the solution. At worst, this would substitute one set of organizational problems for another; at best, it would only delay the onset of the same bureaucratic pathologies that have hindered the performance of the existing system.

Second, it is clear that the existing intergovernmental-response process needs to be strengthened. The quality of the entire response is a direct by-product of local, state, and national governmental actions. Weaknesses at any level can have a negative impact on the relief effort. The results of this study clearly indicate that hazard mitigation and disaster relief need to become higher priorities throughout the governmental system. At the local level, it is simply too easy for city and county personnel to forget about their emergency management responsibilities, particularly when they are confronted with more pressing and immediate community problems. Moreover, there is a natural temptation for local officials to view emergency management as "someone else's responsibility," and usually this "someone else" is the state or national government. Hence, steps must be taken to strengthen the emergency management efforts of *local* governments across the nation, particularly those in high-risk, disaster-prone areas.

Improvements also need to be made at the state level. Statewide hazard mitigation plans need to be prepared more carefully and conscientiously; state emergency management agencies need to be given the requisite resources (e.g., funding, personnel, and authority) to fulfill important responsibilities; and other state-level personnel need to be better equipped to perform critical supportive emergency management functions. In sum, state governments need to take their disaster-relief responsibilities more seriously.

Finally, the federal government's responsibilities in natural disaster situations need to be both clarified and strengthened. First, a distinction should be made between the role of the federal government during *catastrophic* disasters versus its role in *major,* noncatastrophic situations. This would enable the federal government to develop a set of policies and procedures specifically tailored for two different scenarios. In catastrophic events, the federal government should be given "first-response" capabilities; for non-catastrophic but major disasters, the federal government should retain its supplementary role, stepping in when state and local resources have been exhausted. This suggestion corresponds with the recommendations of the General Accounting Office and the National Academy of Public Administration. It also matches the administrative changes (i.e., the Federal Response Plan) already being implemented within the federal government.

A clarification of the federal government's role in the process will not, by itself, ensure a smoother, more effective federal response to natural disasters than we currently have. Several other changes must be made at the top of the system. Specifically, something must be done with the Federal Emergency Management Agency. FEMA cannot mobilize an effective response to natural disasters if the agency itself is unclear or confused about its mission. Similarly, agency personnel will not be proactive if they are unsure of their duties or hesitant to assume responsibilities. Clearly, steps must be taken to improve FEMA's internal operations. And, as previously mentioned, the current director, James Witt, is apparently trying to do precisely this: he is attempting to restructure, refocus, and revitalize the beleaguered agency and remotivate its personnel.

Internal changes will not solve all of FEMA's problems. The agency's credibility and influence throughout the entire governmental system must also be enhanced. After all, how can FEMA mobilize and implement a credible response if it continues to be viewed as the laughingstock of the federal bureaucracy? How can the agency provide effective leadership if it continues to be the dumping ground for political hacks and political patronage paybacks? And how can FEMA provide emergency relief to disaster victims in a timely and effective manner without adequate financial support from Congress and appropriate administrative support from other relevant federal agencies? Some of FEMA's problems can be corrected quite easily. For example, Congress can drastically reduce the number of political appointees within FEMA's administrative ranks,[5] and it can clarify FEMA's roles and responsibilities vis-à-vis other federal agencies involved in disaster relief.[6] FEMA's other internal problems may not be resolved in the near future, given the pressures of the current economic and political climate to curtail government spending and reduce the size of federal agencies.

In sum, several direct, tangible modifications can be made in the governmental response system. These changes would not require a complete overhaul of the existing governmental apparatus. If these changes are made, however, they would allow the government to respond quickly and effectively to natural disaster situations.

Final Thoughts

It is important to remember that some aspects of the governmental response process will be difficult, perhaps even impossible, to change. This study makes it quite clear that the components of the system that most need to be altered are relatively intangible: the perceptions, feelings, attitudes, and morale of everyone involved in the disaster-response process, both private citizens and public officials. This underscores the difficulties facing the disaster-response system, precisely because it is hard to effect meaningful change in psychological orientations.

Different perspectives can and often do develop within the governmental response system itself—particularly across the three levels of government. This usually takes the following form: Local and state officials feel that their responsibilities have ended once they pass on the response to the national government; their feeling is that federal agencies should be in charge of the relief effort and totally responsible for its operations. Conversely, federal officials do not view their role as one of taking over the responsibilities of state and local governments. Instead, they see the system as a team effort in which the three units of government have separate but clearly interdependent responsibilities. These differing role perceptions emerged in varying degrees across all the disasters discussed in this study. In the Caribbean Islands, local and territorial governments were initially unable to respond to the disaster. In the South Carolina and Florida hurricanes, state and local officials started the process but expected the federal government to take over as soon as the magnitude of the situation became clear. In California, there was some tendency toward this same view on the part of local officials; however, it was not nearly as widespread as in South Carolina during Hurricane Hugo or in Florida during Hurricane Andrew. In North Carolina, Louisiana, and South Carolina (during the 1990 floods), local, state, and federal officials all had a shared view of their responsibilities; there was virtually no difference in their role perceptions. There is a clear pattern here. When all three governmental levels have the same view of their role, the system works better. When there are differences, the disaster response produces confusion and conflict, or even stalemate. It is essential that officials from each level of government understand their own duties in order to handle disasters successfully. But again, achieving this understanding will be very difficult.

Problems can also arise when other actors develop unrealistic or inappropriate expectations about governmental activity. In at least four of the six case studies considered in this book, serious breakdowns in the system occurred precisely because nongovernmental actors, elected officials, or both intervened in the response process. Political leaders, the media, and individual citizens all have their own reasons for circumventing standard operating procedures. Senators, governors, and presidents all want to undertake actions that benefit their own careers, and natural disasters provide excellent opportunities for doing so. Network news organizations, along with print journalists, want to report items that will appeal to the widest possible audience. Stories about unmanageable disaster conditions, bureaucratic indifference to human suffering, and the sheer human chaos produced by natural catastrophes are attractive scenarios from a journalistic perspective. This remains true even though such images rarely convey a balanced or accurate picture of a disaster's aftermath. Finally, disaster victims naturally want to obtain essential relief for themselves and their families. Time-consuming paperwork and apparently nonsensical administrative procedures seem to hinder their access to the food, shelter, and medical supplies they require, rather than serve any useful purpose. Hence, activities that circumvent these procedures appear rational and almost necessary to many people.

Once again, the problem is that such actions by public or private participants will invariably hinder the overall effectiveness of the disaster response. This study has demonstrated that such phenomena are a natural by-product of any disaster situation. Thus, disaster response will probably remain a problematic element of public policymaking in the United States.

In conclusion, the governmental response to natural disaster is an extremely important topic. From a scholarly perspective, the government's ability to respond to disasters reveals a great deal about public policymaking under extraordinarily stressful conditions. From a more practical viewpoint, it is essential that the public and government officials (including those not directly involved in the response process) have a clear understanding of what to expect in disaster situations. Natural disasters provide a real-world laboratory for dealing with extremely trying circumstances. If the government can improve its performance here, it may be able to do so elsewhere as well. I hope that this analysis will not only increase our understanding of natural disasters and the effectiveness of emergency management procedures but will also stimulate further research on the linkages between governmental activities and human behavior in other important areas of public policymaking.

Notes

1. There are other problematic and potentially dangerous aspects of allowing the military to assume primary responsibility for disaster relief. These include the military's ability to control the release of information about disaster situations to the general public and the mass media; their ability to declare martial law, taking over the authority of civilian authorities; and their standing with respect to liability and damage issues.

2. FEMA's operating budget has increased over the last few years. For example, in fiscal year 1993, the agency's budget was about $790 million. These numbers are still quite small relative to those of other federal agencies.

3. These problems are not unique to FEMA. See Ingraham (1987) for a general discussion of how similar internal problems (i.e., political appointees) have plagued other federal agencies.

4. New organizations may also lack expertise and experience; consequently, they can also make monumental mistakes. For example, see Shaffer (1977) and Thompson (1982) for an account of OSHA's blunders during the early years of its existence.

5. The number of political appointees in FEMA's administrative ranks has already been reduced. In 1992, Congress cut funding for twenty politically appointed jobs within the agency.

6. The Federal Response Plan attempts to clarify the roles of various federal agencies. But this is an administrative plan formulated by the agencies directly involved in disaster relief. It has yet to be codified in federal statutes or regulations.

References

Aberbach, Joel D., Robert D. Putnam, and Bert A. Rockman. 1981. *Bureaucrats and Politicians in Western Democracies.* Cambridge: Harvard University Press.

Abney, F. Glenn, and Larry B. Hill. 1966. "Natural Disasters as a Political Variable: The Effect of a Hurricane on an Urban Election." *American Political Science Review* 60 (December): 974–81.

Alford, Robert. 1969. *Bureaucracy and Participation.* Chicago: Rand McNally.

And Hugo Was His Name: Hurricane Hugo—A Diary of Destruction. 1989. Sun City West, AZ: C.F. Boone Publishers.

Andrew: Savagery from the Sea. 1992. Fort Lauderdale, FL: Sun-Sentinel.

Andrews, Edmund L. 1992. "Bush Sending Army to Florida amid Criticisms of Relief Effort." *New York Times,* August 28, A1, A10.

Anton, Thomas J. 1989. *American Federalism and Public Policy.* New York: Random House.

Apple, R.W. 1992. "Politicians Warily Gauge the Effects of Los Angeles's Rioting at the Polls." *New York Times,* May 17, A20.

Applebome, Peter. 1989. "For Survivors of Hurricane, Relief Is Giving Way to Despair." *New York Times,* September 27, A1, A12.

Archea, John. 1990. "Immediate Reactions of People in Houses." In Bolin, *The Loma Prieta Earthquake,* 56–64.

Arrow, Kenneth. 1963. *Social Choice and Individual Values.* 2d ed. New York: Wiley.

Ayres, B. Drummond, Jr. 1994. "Los Angeles Is Taking Rapid Road to Recovery." *New York Times,* March 17, A20.

Bandy, Lee. 1989a. "Bungled Management, Disrespect, Scandal Mark Relief Agency's Past." *The State,* October 29, A1.

———. 1989b. "South Carolina Seeks Inquiry into FEMA." *The State,* October 4, B2.

———. 1990. "FEMA's Needs Outlined." *The State,* January 14, B1.

Baratz, Morton, and Peter Bachrach. 1963. "Decisions and Non-Decisions: An Analytic Framework." *American Political Science Review* 57: 632–42.

Bardach, Eugene. 1977. *The Implementation Game: What Happens after a Bill Becomes a Law.* Cambridge, MA: MIT Press.

Barron, James. 1992a. "Hurricane Roars across Gulf—Toll Is at 12." *New York Times,* August 26, A1, A14.

———. 1992b. "At Least 8 Killed—Houses Left in Splinters." *New York Times,* August 25, A1, A12.

Barton, Allan. 1969. *Communities in Disaster.* Garden City, NY: Doubleday Anchor.

Barzelay, Michael. 1992. *Breaking Through Bureaucracy: A New Vision for Managing in Government*. Berkeley: University of California Press.

Baumgartner, Frank R. 1987. "Parliament's Capacity to Expand Political Controversy in France." *Legislative Studies Quarterly* 12: 33–54.

Baumgartner, Frank R., and Bryan D. Jones. 1993. *Agendas and Instability in American Politics*. Chicago: University of Chicago Press.

Beckham, Tom. 1989. Deputy director, South Carolina Emergency Preparedness Division, Office of the Adjutant General. Personal interview, Columbia, SC, September 23.

Bendix, Reinhard. 1947. "Bureaucracy: The Problem and Its Setting." *American Sociological Review* 12: 493–507.

Bennett, C. Scott. 1990. *Heavy Rains, Flooding Hit Central South Carolina*. Columbia, SC: U.S. Department of Interior, Geological Survey.

Bennett, Lance W. 1988. *News: The Politics of Illusion*. 2d ed. New York: Longman.

Bennis, Warren G., ed. 1970. *American Bureaucracy*. Chicago: Aldine.

Benthall, Jonathan. 1993. *Disasters, Relief, and the Media*. London: I.B. Taurus.

Benveniste, Guy. 1977. *Bureaucracy*. San Francisco: Boyd and Fraser.

Berger, P.L., and T.L. Luckmann. 1967. *The Social Construction of Reality*. New York: Aldine de Gruyter.

Berk, Richard. 1974. *Collective Behavior*. Dubuque, IA: William C. Brown.

Berry, John M. 1994. "In Case of Emergency, Call Uncle Sam." *Washington Post National Weekly Edition,* February 7–13, 20.

Best, J. 1989. *Images of Issues: Typifying Contemporary Social Problems*. New York: Aldine de Gruyter.

The Big One: Hurricane Andrew. 1992. Kansas City, MO: Andrews and McNeal.

Blau, Peter M. 1955. *The Dynamics of Bureaucracy: A Study of Interpersonal Relationships in Two Government Agencies*. Chicago: University of Chicago Press.

Blumer, Herbert George. 1957. "Collective Behavior." In *Review of Sociology,* ed. Joseph B. Gittler, 127–58. New York: Wiley.

Bolin, Robert. 1990. "The Loma Prieta Earthquake: An Overview." In *The Loma Prieta Earthquake: Studies of Short-Term Impacts*, ed. Robert Bolin, 1–16. Boulder: University of Colorado, Institute of Behavioral Science, Program on Environment and Behavior. Monograph #50.

Booth, William. 1992a. "Hurricane Pounded 165 Square Miles of Florida into the Ground." *Washington Post,* August 30, A1, A18.

———. 1992b. "Next Survival Test: Anger and Anomie." *Washington Post,* September 4, A1, A18.

Booth, William, and Mary Jordan. 1992. "As Tempers Shorten, Miamians Get Unruly." *Washington Post,* August 27, A1, A21.

Booth, William, and Christina Sherry. 1993. "Picking Up the Pieces One Year after Andrew: Communities Are Slowly Rising from the Rubble." *Washington Post National Weekly Edition,* August 30–September 5, 31.

Bourgin, Frank R. 1983. *A History of Federal Disaster Relief Legislation, 1950–1974*. Washington, DC: Federal Emergency Management Agency.

Branigin, William. 1989a. "A Slow Recovery from '12 Hours of Terror.' " *Washington Post,* October 31, A1, A8.

———. 1989b. "In San Juan, Poor Still Feel Hugo's Wrath." *Washington Post,* October 30, A1, A10.

Brown, JoAnn. 1990. "The Social Construction of Invisible Danger: Two Historical Examples." In *Nothing to Fear,* ed. Andrew Kirby, 39–52. Tucson: University of Arizona Press.

Browning, Robert X. 1986. *Politics and Social Welfare Policy in the United States.* Knoxville: University of Tennessee Press.

Bruner, Jerome. 1983. *Child's Talk: Learning to Use Language.* New York: Norton.

Burke, John P. 1986. *Bureaucratic Responsibility.* Baltimore: Johns Hopkins University Press.

Carter, L. Fred. 1989. Special assistant to Governor Carroll Campbell. Personal interview, Columbia, SC, September 23.

Christian, Cora L.E. 1992. *Hurricane Hugo's Impact on the Virgin Islands.* Boulder: University of Colorado, National Hazards Research and Applications Information Center, Institute of Behavior Science. Working paper #73.

Chubb, John E. 1985. "Federalism and the Bias for Centralization." In *The New Direction in American Politics,* ed. John E. Chubb and Paul E. Peterson. Washington, DC: Brookings Institution.

Cigler, Beverly A. 1988. "Current Policy Issues in Mitigation." In *Managing Disaster,* ed. Louise K. Comfort, 39–52. Durham, NC: Duke University Press.

Claiborne, William. 1992a. "Paperwork Slows Storm Relief; Complaints Called Overstated." *Washington Post,* September 7, A11.

———. 1992b. "After Storms and Controversy, What's in Store for FEMA?" *Washington Post,* October 6.

———. 1993. "More Welcome Than Disaster: For Once—in Midwest—FEMA Is Relatively Well Received." *Washington Post,* August 13, A23.

———. 1994. "Doling Out Praise, FEMA Critic Presses for Reform at Hearing." *Washington Post,* March 25.

Clary, Bruce B. 1985. "The Evolution and Structure of Natural Hazard Policies." *Public Administration Review* 45 (January): 20–28.

Cobb, Roger W., and Charles D. Elder. 1983a. *Participation in American Politics: The Dynamics of Agenda-Building.* 2d ed. Baltimore: Johns Hopkins University Press.

———. 1983b. *The Political Uses of Symbols.* New York: Longman.

Cochrane, Hal. 1975. *Natural Disasters and Their Distributive Effects.* Boulder: University of Colorado, Institute of Behavioral Science, Program on Environment, Technology and Man. Monograph #NSF-RA-E-75-003.

———. 1990. "A Preliminary Analysis of Damages and Economic Dislocations." In Bolin, *The Loma Prieta Earthquake,* 25–32.

Comfort, Louis K. 1985. "Integrating Organizational Action in Emergency Management: Strategies for Change." *Public Administration Review* 45 (Special Issue, January), 155–64.

———. 1988. "Designing Policy for Action: The Emergency Management System." In *Managing Disaster,* ed. Louis K. Comfort, 3–21. Durham, NC: Duke University Press.

Conlan, Timothy. 1988. *New Federalism: Intergovernmental Reform from Nixon to Reagan.* Washington, DC: Brookings Institution.

Cook, Michael L. 1989. "FEMA: Bureaucratic Disaster Area." *The State,* November 1.

Cottingham, Phoebe H., and David T. Ellwood. 1989. *Welfare Policy for the 1990s.* Cambridge: Harvard University Press.

Couch, Carl J. 1968. "Collective Behavior: An Examination of Some Stereotypes." *Social Problems* 15: 310–22.

———. 1970. "Dimension of Association in Collective Behavior Episodes." *Sociometry* 33: 457–71.

Crozier, Michael. 1964. *The Bureaucratic Phenomenon.* Chicago: University of Chicago Press.

Davis. Bob. 1992a. "Federal Relief Agency Is Slowed by Infighting, Patronage, Regulations." *Wall Street Journal,* August 31, A1, A12.

———. 1992b. "Federal Response to Hurricane Andrew to Be Costly, Critical to Bush Campaign." *Wall Street Journal,* August 28, A2.

Democratic Study Group. 1989. "Short-Handed at FEMA: Fighting Disasters without Leaders." U.S. House of Representatives.

DeNeufville, Judith I., and Stephen E. Barton. 1987. "Myths and the Definition of Policy Problems: An Exploration of Home Ownership and Public-Private Partnerships." *Policy Sciences* 20: 181–206.

Dilulio, John J., Jr., Gerald Garvey, and Donald F. Kettl. 1993. *Improving Government Performance: An Owner's Manual.* Washington, DC: Brookings Institution.

Donahue, John D. 1989. *The Privatization Decision.* New York: Basic Books.

Downs, Anthony. 1957. *An Economic Theory of Democracy.* New York: Harper & Row.

———. 1967. *Inside Bureaucracy.* Boston: Little, Brown. Reissued by Waveland Press, Prospect Heights, IL, 1994.

———. 1972. "Up and Down with Ecology: The Issue Attention Cycle." *Public Interest* 28: 38–50.

Drabek, Thomas. 1968. *Disaster in Isle 13.* Columbus: Disaster Research Center, Ohio State University.

———. 1970. "Methodology of Studying Disasters." *American Behavioral Scientist* 13: 331–43.

———. 1984. *Some Emerging Issues in Emergency Management.* Emmitsburg, MD: National Emergency Training Center, Federal Emergency Management Agency.

———. 1986. *Human System Responses to Disasters.* New York: Springer-Verlag.

Drabek, Thomas, and John Stephenson. 1971. "When Disaster Strikes." *Journal of Applied Social Psychology* 1: 187–203.

Durkheim, Emile. 1895. *The Rules of Sociological Method.* New York: Free Press.

———. 1912. *The Elementary Forms of Religious Life.* Translated by Joseph Ward Swain, 1915. New York: Macmillan.

Dynes, Russell R. 1970. *Organized Behavior in Disasters.* Lexington, MA: Heath Lexington Books.

Dynes, Russell R., and E.L. Quarantelli. 1968. "Group Behavior under Stress: A Required Convergence of Organizational and Collective Behavior Perspectives." *Sociology and Social Research* 52 (July): 416–29.

———. 1977. "Organizational Communications and Decision Making in Crises." Report Series #17. Disaster Research Center, Columbus, OH.

Edelman, Murray. 1964. *The Symbolic Uses of Politics.* Urbana: University of Illinois Press.

———. 1977. *Political Language: Words That Succeed and Policies That Fail.* New York: Academic Press.

———. 1989. *Constructing the Political Spectacle.* Chicago: University of Chicago Press.

Eichel, Henry. 1989. "Relief Effort Faulted: Experts Say South Carolina System Lacked Coordination." *The State,* October 22, A1, A17.

Elazar, Daniel. 1962. *The American Partnership: Intergovernmental Cooperation in the Nineteenth-Century United States.* Chicago: University of Chicago Press.

Enos, Gary. 1993. "Disaster Response Improves." *City and State,* December 6, 23.

EQE International. 1992. *Hurricanes Andrew and Iniki 1992.* San Francisco: EQE International.

Eyestone, Robert. 1978. *From Social Issues to Public Policy.* New York: Wiley.

Fairweather, V. 1990. "The Next Earthquake." *Civil Engineering,* March, 54–57.

Faust, Roland. 1989. Federal Emergency Management Agency, Region IV. Phone interview, November 12.

Federal Emergency Management Agency. 1988. *Federal Catastrophic Earthquake Response Plan.* Washington, DC: Government Printing Office.

———. 1989a. *Interagency Hazard Mitigation Team Report.* Prepared by the Region IV Interagency Hazard Mitigation Team in Response to the September 22, 1989, Disaster Declaration, State of South Carolina. FEMA-843-DR-SC.

———. 1989b. *When Disaster Strikes.* Washington, DC: Office of Public Affairs, Federal Emergency Management Agency.

———. 1990a. *Interagency Hazard Mitigation Team Report.* Prepared by the Region IV Interagency Hazard Mitigation Team in Response to the October 22, 1990, Disaster Declaration, State of South Carolina. FEMA-881-DR-SC.

———. 1990b. Public Information Office. Phone interview.

———. 1992a. *Briefing Reports on Recent Disaster Activity.* Washington, DC: Federal Emergency Management Agency.

———. 1992b. *Federal Response Plan: For Public Law 93-288, As Amended.* Washington, DC: Federal Emergency Management Agency.

———. 1993. *FEMA's Disaster Management Program: A Performance Audit after Hurricane Andrew.* Washington, DC: Office of Inspector General.

Fenno, Richard F., Jr. 1978. *Home Style: House Members in Their Districts.* Boston: Little, Brown.

Fensch, Thomas. 1990. *Associated Press Coverage of a Major Disaster: The Crash of Flight 1141.* Hillsdale, NJ: L. Erlbaum Associates.

Fesler, James W., and Donald F. Kettl. 1991. *The Politics of the Administrative Process.* Chatham, NJ: Chatham House.

Fiedler, Tom, and Peter Slevin. 1992. "Military Comes to Florida's Aid." *Charlotte Observer,* August 29, A1.

Fitzpatrick, Colleen, and Dennis S. Mileti. 1990. "Perception and Response to Aftershock Warnings during the Emergency Period." In Bolin, *The Loma Prieta Earthquake,* 75–83.

Fox, Gerald C. 1990. "Evaluation of FEMA's Performance in Responding to Hurricane Hugo in N.C." Testimony before the Subcommitee on Investigations and Oversight, Committee on Public Works and Transportation, U.S. House of Representatives, May 2.

Fretwell, Sammy. 1989a. "Frustration Rises as Victims Await Help." *The State,* October 23, A1, A4.

———. 1989b. "S.C. Homeless in FEMA Limbo." *The State,* October 12, A1, A8.

Friesema, H. Paul, James Caporaso, Gerald Goldstein, Robert Lineberry, and Richard McCleary. 1979. *Aftermath: Communities after Natural Disasters.* Beverly Hills, CA: Sage.

Fritsch, Jane. 1994. "U.S. Is Setting Up Tent Cities as Nerves Fray after Quake." *New York Times,* January 22, A1, A24.

Fritz, Charles. 1957. "Disasters Compared in Six American Communities." *Human Organization* 16 (Summer): 6–9.

———. 1961. "Disaster." In *Contemporary Social Problems: An Introduction to the Sociology of Deviant Behavior and Social Organizations,* ed. Robert K. Merton and Robert A. Nisbet, 651–94. New York: Harcourt, Brace and World.

Gawthrop, Louis. 1969. *Bureaucratic Behavior in the Executive Branch: An Analysis of Organizational Change.* New York: Free Press.

Ginsberg, Benjamin. 1976. "Elections and Public Policy," *American Political Science Review* 70 (March): 41–49.

Gitlin, T. 1989. "Gauging the Aftershocks of Disaster Coverage." *New York Times.* November 11.

Giuffrida, Louis O. 1983. *Emergency Management: The National Perspective.* Emmitsburg, MD: National Emergency Training Center.

———. 1985. "FEMA: Its Mission, Its Partners." *Public Administration Review* 45 (Special Issue, January): 2.

Goggin, Malcolm L., Ann O'M. Bowman, James P. Lester, and Laurence J. O'Toole, Jr. 1990. *Implementation Theory and Practice: Toward a Third Generation.* Glenview, IL: Scott, Foresman/Little, Brown Higher Education.

Goldman, Kevin, and Patrick Reilly. 1992. "Untold Story: Media's Slow Grasp of Hurricane's Impact Helped Delay Response." *Wall Street Journal,* September 10, A1, A9.

Goodsell, Charles. 1985. *The Case for Bureaucracy.* 2d ed. Chatham, NJ: Chatham House.

Gore, Rick. 1993. "Andrew Aftermath." *National Geographic* 183 (April): 2–37.

Gormley, William. 1989. *Taming the Bureaucracy: Muscles, Prayers, and Other Strategies.* Princeton, NJ: Princeton University Press.

Governor's Disaster Planning and Response Review Committee. 1993. Tallahassee, FL: Governor's Disaster Planning and Response Review Committee.

Grodzins, Morton. 1966. *The American System: A New View of Government in the United States.* Chicago: Rand McNally.

Gross, Jane. 1990. "Pressured Agencies Alter Post-Quake Relief Policy." *New York Times,* March 6.

———. 1994. "Los Angeles Drivers Try New Ways on Old Roads." *New York Times,* March 1, A16.

Guider, E. 1989. "Stations, Networks Ponder Lessons Learned in Quake." *Victory,* October, 45–46.

Gulick, Luther, and L. Urwick. 1937. *Papers on the Science of Administration.* New York: Institute of Public Administration.

Haas, Eugene, Robert W. Kates, and Martyn J. Bowden, eds. 1977. *Reconstruction following Disaster.* Cambridge, MA: MIT Press.

Hall, Paul. 1989. Federal coordinating officer for Hurricane Hugo in the Carolinas, Federal Emergency Management Agency. Personal interview, Washington, DC, December 15.

Hamilton, Dane, and Gregory S. Johnson. 1992. "Hurricane Aid Proves Logistical Nightmare." *Journal of Commerce,* September 2, 1A, 3A.

Hamilton, William. 1994. "L.A.'s Unspoken Rule: Positively No Pessimists Allowed." *Washington Post,* January 27, A1.

Hamner, Thomas. 1990. Federal coordinating officer for the Loma Prieta response, Federal Emergency Management Agency. Phone interview, January 31.

Hancock, David, and Anthony Faiola. 1992. "Bigger, Stronger, Closer: South Florida Bracing for Hurricane Andrew." *Miami Herald,* August 23, 1A, 19A.

Harrison, Carlos. 1989. "St. Croix Collapses in Hugo's Wake." *The State,* September 20, A9.

Harvey, Carol D.H., and Howard M. Bahr. 1980. *The Sunshine Widows: Adapting to Sudden Bereavement.* Toronto: Lexington Books.

Heflin, Frank. 1990. "FEMA Finally Gets Relief." *The State,* March 17, A1, A4.

Hill, Larry B. 1992. "Taking Bureaucracy Seriously." In *The State of Public Bureaucracy,* ed. Larry B. Hill, 15–58. Armonk, NY: M.E. Sharpe.

Hodgkinson, Peter E., and Michael Stewart. 1990. *Coping with Catastrophe: A Handbook of Disaster Management.* New York: Routledge.

Hugo. n.d. Columbia, SC: State Publishing Company.

Hurricane Hugo: Storm of the Century. 1990. Mount Pleasant, SC: BD Publishing.

Hy, Ronald, and William Waugh, 1990. "The Function of Emergency Management." In *Handbook of Emergency Management,* ed. William Waugh and Ronald Hy, 11–26. New York: Greenwood Press.

Hyneman, Charles S. 1950. *Bureaucracy in a Democracy.* New York: Harper.

Ibarra, P.R., and J.I. Kitsuse. 1993. "Vernacular Constituents of Moral Discourse: An Interactionist Proposal for the Study of Social Problems." In *Constructionist Controversies: Issues in Social Problems Theory,* ed. G. Miller and J.A. Holstein, 21–54. New York: Aldine de Gruyter.

Ingraham, Patricia. 1987. "Building Bridges or Burning Them? The President, the Appointees, and the Bureaucracy." *Public Administration Review* 47 (September/October): 425–35.

Ingwerson, Marshall. 1993. "FEMA Is 'Not Waiting' for the Winds to Die Down." *Christian Science Monitor,* September 1, 6.

Iyengar, S. 1991. *Is Anyone Responsible? How Television Frames Political Issues.* Chicago: University of Chicago Press.

Jordan, Mary. 1992a. "After Andrew: Protecting What's Left and Wondering Why." *Washington Post,* August 30, A18.

————. 1992b. "Local Relief Officials Fault Federal Response to Hurricane." *Washington Post,* August 28, A1, A14.

Kasperson, Roger E., and K. David Pijawka. 1985. "Societal Response to Hazards and Major Hazard Events: Comparing Natural and Technological Hazards." *Public Administration Review* 45 (January): 7–19.

Katz, Daniel, and Robert L. Kahn. 1978. *The Social Psychology of Organizations.* 2d ed. New York: Wiley.

Katz, Michael B. 1989. *The Undeserving Poor.* New York: Pantheon.

Kaufman, Herbert. 1969. "Administrative Decentralization and Political Power." *Public Administration Review* 29 (January/February): 3–15.

Key, V.O. 1961. *Public Opinion in American Democracy.* New York: Knopf.

Kilborn, Peter T. 1992. "Snarl of Red Tape Keeps U.S. Checks from Storm Areas." *New York Times,* September 6, A1, A13.

————. 1993. "Flood Victims Find Tortuous Path to U.S. Relief Agency Money." *New York Times,* August 9, A10.

Kingdon, John. 1984. *Agendas, Alternatives, and Public Policies.* Boston: Little, Brown.

Kirby, Andrew, ed. 1990. *Nothing to Fear.* Tucson: University of Arizona Press.

Kreimer, Alcira, and Mohan Munasinghe. 1990. "Managing Environmental Degradation and Natural Disasters." In *Managing Natural Disasters and the Environment,* ed. Alcira Kreimer and Mohan Munasinghe, 31–51. Washington, DC: World Bank.

Kreps, Gary A. 1986. *Structure and Disaster.* Newark: University of Delaware Press.

Lancaster, John. 1989. "The Storm after the Hurricane: South Carolinians Say Federal Relief Is Too Slow." *Washington Post National Weekly Edition,* October 9–15, 32.

Lewis, Michael. 1989. "Some Disaster Victims Can't Get Federal Help." *The State,* September 28, B5.

Lewis, Ralph G. 1988. "Management Issues in Emergency Response." In Comfort, *Managing Disaster,* 163–79.

Light, Paul C. 1982. *The President's Agenda.* Baltimore: Johns Hopkins University Press.

Lindblom, Charles E. 1959. "The Science of 'Muddling Through.' " *Public Administration Review* 19: 79–88.

Lipman, Larry, and Elliott Jaspin. 1993. "Top-Secret Obsession Slows FEMA." *The State*, February 22, A1, A8.

Lippman, Thomas W. 1992a. "Hurricane May Have Exposed Flaws in New Disaster Relief Plan." *Washington Post*, September 3, A21.

———. 1992b. "One Disaster Followed by Another?" *Washington Post National Weekly Edition*, September 7–13, 31.

———. 1992c. "Wounded Agency Hopes to Heal Itself by Helping Hurricane Victims." *Washington Post*, August 28, A21.

Lipsky, Michael. 1978. "Standing the Study of Policy Implementation on Its Head." In *American Politics and Public Policy*, ed. Walter D. Burnham and Martha W. Weinberg. Cambridge, MA: MIT Press.

Livingston, Mike. 1989. "FEMA Documents Swallow Small Staff." *The State*, October 7, 1B, 4B.

Lofland, John. 1981. "Collective Behavior: The Elementary Forms." In *Social Psychology*, ed. Morris Rosenberg and Ralph H. Turner, 411–46. New York: Basic Books.

———. 1985. *Protest: Studies of Collective Behavior and Social Movements*. New Brunswick, NJ: Transaction Books.

Lowi, Theodore. 1969, 1979. *The End of Liberalism*. New York: Norton.

McAda, William. 1989. Public information officer. Federal Emergency Management Agency. Personal interview, Washington, DC, November 9.

———. 1990. Public information officer. Federal Emergency Management Agency. Phone interview, Washington, DC, January 13.

McKay, John. 1992. Federal Emergency Management Agency. Personal interview, Washington, DC, December 27.

McLoughlin, David, 1985. "A Framework for Integrated Emergency Management." *Public Administration Review* 45 (Special Issue, January): 163–72.

McPhail, Clark. 1991. *The Myth of the Madding Crowd*. New York: Aldine de Gruyter.

Magnuson, Ed. 1989. "Earthquake." *Time*, October 30, 29–40.

Majone, Giandomenico. 1989. *Evidence, Argument, and Persuasion in the Policy Process*. New Haven, CT: Yale University Press.

Manegold, Catherine S. 1992a. "What Was Once Home Is Foreign Landscape." *New York Times*, August 31, A1, A9.

———. 1992b. "Amid Wreckage, Survivors Tell Their Stories." *New York Times*, August 25, A1, A13.

———. 1992c. "In Migrant Labor Camp, Relief Is Slow and Chaotic." *New York Times*, September 1, A8.

———. 1992d. "Restoring Power after Storm to Take Months and Millions." *New York Times*, September 5, A1, A6.

Maraniss, David. 1992a. "As Hurricane Crosses Gulf, Pounds at Louisiana." *Washington Post*, August 26, A1, A26.

———. 1992b. "Dwindling Andrew Partly Pulls Punch along Gulf Coast." *Washington Post*, August 27, A1, A21.

March, James G., and Johan P. Olsen. 1989. *Rediscovering Institutions: The Organizational Basis of Politics*. New York: Free Press.

Marcus, Frances Frank. 1992. "Louisianians Calm about Storm but Fear Their Turn May Come." *New York Times*, August 25, A12.

Marvick, Dwaine. 1954. *Career Perspectives in a Bureaucratic Setting*. Ann Arbor: University of Michigan Press.

Mathews, Tom, 1992. "The Siege of L.A." *Newsweek*, May 11, 30–38.

Mathews, Tom, Peter Katel, Todd Barrett, Douglas Waller, Clara Bingham, Melinda

Liu, Steven Waldman, and Ginny Carroll. 1992. "What Went Wrong?" *Newsweek,* September 7, 22–27.

May, Peter J. 1985a. "FEMA's Role in Emergency Management: Recent Experience." *Public Administration Review* 45 (Special Issue, January): 40–48.

————. 1985b. *Recovering from Catastrophes: Federal Disaster Relief Policy and Politics.* Westport, CT: Greenwood Press.

May, Peter J., and Walter Williams. 1986. *Disaster Policy Implementation: Managing Programs under Shared Governance.* New York: Plenum Press.

Mayhew, David R. 1974. *Congress: The Electoral Connection.* New Haven, CT: Yale University Press.

Mazmanian, Daniel A., and Paul A. Sabatier. 1983. *Implementation and Public Policy.* Glenview, IL: Scott, Foresman.

Mead, George Herbert. 1936. "The Problem of Society." In *Movements of Thought in the Nineteenth Century,* ed. Merritt H. Moore, 360–85. Chicago: University of Chicago Press.

Medsger, B. 1989. "Earthquake Shakes Four Newspapers." *Washington Journalism Review,* December, 18–20.

Meier, Kenneth J. 1993. *Politics and the Bureaucracy.* 3d ed. Monterey, CA: Brooks/ Cole.

Merton, Robert K. 1940. "Bureaucratic Structure and Personality." *Social Forces* 18: 560–68.

————. 1957. *Social Theory and Social Structure.* New York: Free Press.

Miller, Dan, Robert Hintz, and Carl Couch. 1975. "The Structure of Openings." *Sociological Quarterly* 16: 479–99.

Miller, Jeff. 1989a. "FEMA Shuns Hurricane Drills." *The State,* November 6, B1.

————. 1989b. "Storm Surge: Mass of Aid Requests Overwhelmed FEMA." *The State,* October 23, A1, A4.

————. 1992. "Emergency Agency Tries to Aid Itself." *The State,* November 24, 1B, 3B.

Mittler, Elliott. 1988. "Agenda-Setting in Nonstructural Hazard Mitigation Policy." In Comfort, *Managing Disaster,* 86–107.

Moe, Ronald D. 1994. "The 'Reinventing Government' Exercise: Misinterpreting the Problem, Misjudging the Consequences." *Public Administration Review* 54 (March/April): 111–22.

Moniz, Dave. 1992. "Military of '90s May Fight Domestic Battles." *The State,* September 13, 1A, 6A.

Morganthau, Tom, and Karen Springen. 1992. "Storm Warnings." *Newsweek,* September 14, 24–28.

Morrill, Jim, Paige Williams, and John York. 1989. "Carolinians Line Up for Aid." *Charlotte Observer,* October 1, A1.

Mosco, Frank. 1989. Public information officer. Federal Emergency Management Agency. Personal interview, North Charleston, SC, November 7.

Mushkatel, Alvin, and Louis F. Weschler. 1985. "Emergency Management and the Intergovernmental System." *Public Administration Review* 45 (January): 47–58.

Mydans, Seth. 1994a. "Angry Crowds Besiege U.S. Agency for Quake Aid." *New York Times,* January 21, A1, A18.

————. 1994b. "Tallying Losses from Quake, Los Angeles Stirs and Hopes." *New York Times,* January 19, A1.

Nakamura, Robert T., and Frank Smallwood. 1980. *The Politics of Policy Implementation.* New York: St. Martin's Press.

Nathan, Richard P. 1993. "The Role of the States in American Federalism." In *The*

State of the States, ed. Carl E. Van Horn, 15–30. Washington, DC: CQ Press.

National Academy of Public Administration. 1993. *Coping with Catastrophe: Building an Emergency Management System to Meet People's Needs in Natural and Man-made Disasters.* Washington, DC: National Academy of Public Administration.

National Performance Review, Executive Office of the President. 1993. *From Red Tape to Results: Creating a Government That Works Better and Costs Less.* Washington, DC: Government Printing Office.

National Research Council. 1991. *Reducing the Impacts of Natural Disasters.* Washington, DC: National Academy Press.

Niskanen, William. 1971. *Bureaucracy and Representative Government.* Chicago: Aldine/Atherton.

Northcott, H.C. 1992. *Aging in Alberta: Rhetoric and Reality.* Calgary, Alberta: Detselif Enterprises Ltd.

The October 17, 1989, Loma Prieta Earthquake. 1989. San Francisco: EQE Engineering.

Olson, Mancur. 1965. *The Logic of Collective Action.* Cambridge: Harvard University Press.

Osborne, David, and Ted Gaebler. 1992. *Reinventing Government: How the Entrepreneurial Spirit Is Transforming the Public Sector from Schoolhouse to State House, City Hall to Pentagon.* Reading, MA: Addison-Wesley.

O'Toole, Laurence J. 1993. *American Intergovernmental Relations.* 2d ed. Washington, DC: CQ Press.

Page, Benjamin I., and Robert Y. Shapiro. 1983. "Effects of Public Opinion on Policy." *American Political Science Review* 77 (March): 315–25.

Panetta, Leon E. 1990. *Testimony before the Subcommittee on Investigations and Oversight Regarding the Response of FEMA Following the Loma Prieta Earthquake.* U.S. House of Representatives. 101st Cong. May 1.

Parker, Laura, 1989. "Hugo's Swirl of Paperwork." *Washington Post,* October 29, A1, A24.

Pear, Robert. 1992. "Clinton, in Attack on President, Ties Riots to Neglect." *New York Times,* May 6, A1.

Perry, Ronald W., and Marjorie Greene. 1983. *Citizen Response to Volcanic Eruptions.* New York: Irvington.

Perry, Ronald W., and Alvin H. Mushkatel. 1984. *Disaster Management: Warning Response and Community Relocation.* Westport, CT: Greenwood Press.

Perry, Ronald W., and Joanne M. Nigg. 1985. "Emergency Management Strategies for Communicating Hazard Information." *Public Administration Review* 45 (Special Issue, January): 72–76.

Petak, William J. 1985. "Emergency Management: A Challenge for Public Administration." *Public Administration Review* 45 (Special Issue, January): 3–7.

Petak, William J., and A. Atkisson. 1982. *Natural Hazard Risk Assessment and Public Policy: Anticipating the Unexpected.* New York: Springer-Verlag.

Peters, B. Guy. 1981. "The Problems of Bureaucratic Government." *Journal of Politics* 43 (February): 65–66.

———. 1989. *The Politics of Bureaucracy.* New York: Longman.

———. 1993. *American Public Policy: Promise and Performance.* Chatham, NJ: Chatham House.

Peters, B. Guy, and Brian W. Hogwood. 1985. "In Search of the Issue Attention Cycle." *Journal of Politics* 47 (February): 238–53.

Peterson, Grant C. 1989. Associate director, State and Local Program and Support Agency, Federal Emergency Management Agency. Personal interview, Washington, DC, December 7.

———. 1992. Associate director, State and Local Program and Support Agency, Federal

Emergency Management Agency. Personal interview, Washington, DC, December 27.

Peterson, Paul E. 1981. *City Limits*. Chicago: University of Chicago Press.

Peterson, Paul E., and Mark Rom. 1990. *Welfare Magnets: A New Case for a National Standard*. Washington, DC: Brookings Institution.

Piacente, Steve. 1989. "In the Eye of the Storm." *Government Executive* 21 (December): 24–33.

Popkin, Roy S. 1990. "The History and Politics of Disaster Management in the United States." In Kirby, *Nothing to Fear*, 101–29.

Pressman, Jeffrey L., and Aaron Wildavsky. 1984. *Implementation*. 2d ed. Berkeley: University of California Press.

Quarantelli, E.L. 1983. *Emergent Citizen Groups in Disaster Preparedness and Recovery Activities*. Columbus: Ohio Disaster Research Center.

———. 1988. "Local Emergency Management Agencies: Research Findings on Their Progress and Problems in the Last Two Decades." Newark, DE: Disaster Research Center. Preliminary paper #126.

———. 1990. "Disaster Response: Generic or Agent-Specific." In Kreimer and Munasinghe, *Managing Natural Disasters and the Environment*, 97–105.

———. 1991. "Different Types of Disasters and Planning Implications." Newark, DE: Disaster Research Center. Preliminary paper #169.

Quarantelli, E.L., and Russell R. Dynes. 1972. "When Disaster Strikes (It Isn't Much Like What You've Heard and Read About)." *Psychology Today* 5 (February): 67–70.

———. 1977. "Response to Social Crisis and Disaster." *Annual Review of Sociology* 3: 23–49.

Reicher, S.D. 1984. "The St. Paul's Riot: An Explanation of the Limits of Crowd Action in Terms of a Social Identity Model." *European Journal of Social Psychology* 19: 1–21.

Riker, William. 1986. *The Art of Political Manipulation*. New Haven, CT: Yale University Press.

Riley, Joseph P. 1989. Mayor of the City of Charleston. Personal interview, Charleston, SC, November 7.

Ripley, Randall B., and Grace A. Franklin. 1991. *Bureaucracy and Policy Implementation*. Homewood, IL: Dorsey Press.

Rivlin, Alice M. 1992. *Reviving the American Dream: The Economy, the States, and the Federal Government*. Washington, DC: Brookings Institution.

Rochefort, David A., and Roger W. Cobb. 1994. "Problem Definition: An Emerging Perspective." In *The Politics of Problem Definition*, ed. Rochefort and Cobb, 1–31. Lawrence: University Press of Kansas.

Rockman, Bert A. 1992. "Bureaucracy, Power, Policy, and the State." In *The State of Public Bureaucracy*, ed. Larry B. Hill, 141–70. Armonk, NY: M.E. Sharpe.

Rogers, Everett M., Matthew Berndt, John Harris, and John Minzer. 1990. "Accuracy in Mass Media Coverage." In Bolin, *The Loma Prieta Earthquake*, 44–55.

Rohter, Larry. 1992a. "A Million Are Told to Flee Hurricane in South Florida." *New York Times*, August 24, A1, A8.

———. 1992b. "As Army Gears Up, Floridians Rely on Private Relief." *New York Times*, August 30, A1, A12.

———. 1992c. "President Pledges Money to Rebuild in South Florida." *New York Times*, September 2, A1, A11.

———. 1992d. "Rumors Abound of Storm Deaths Going Untallied." *New York Times*, September 5, A6.

———. 1992e. "Survey Shows Bush Weak in Republican Stronghold." *New York Times*, September 17, A1, A10.

Rossi, Peter H., James D. Wright, and Eleanor Weber-Burdin. 1982. *Natural Hazards and Public Choice: The State and Local Politics of Hazards Mitigation.* New York: Academic Press.

Rossi, Peter H., James D. Wright, Eleanor Weber-Burdin, and Joseph Pereira. 1983. *Victims of the Environment: Loss from Natural Hazards in the United States, 1970–1980.* New York: Plenum Press.

Rourke, Francis E. 1984. *Bureaucracy, Politics, and Public Policy.* 3d ed. Boston: Little, Brown.

Rubin, Claire B., and Daniel G. Barbee. 1985. "Disaster Recovery and Hazard Mitigation: Bridging the Intergovernmental Gap." *Public Administration Review* 45 (Special Issue, January): 59–63.

Rubin, Claire B., and Roy Popkin. 1990. *Disaster Recovery after Hurricane Hugo in South Carolina.* Final report to the National Science Foundation. Washington, DC: George Washington University.

Rubin, Claire B., Martin D. Saperstein, and Daniel G. Barbee. 1985. *Community Recovery from a Major Disaster.* Boulder: University of Colorado, Institute of Behavioral Sciences.

Sabatier, Paul A. 1986. "Top-Down and Bottom-Up Approaches to Implementation Research: A Critical Analysis and Suggested Synthesis." *Journal of Public Policy* 6: 31–48.

Sanchez, Rene. 1992. "Tough Times in the Bayou 'Nothing New for the Cajun People.'" *Washington Post,* August 28, A14.

Savas, E.S. 1982. *Privatizing the Public Sector.* Chatham, NJ: Chatham House.

———. 1987. *Privatization: The Key to Better Government.* Chatham, NJ: Chatham House.

Scanlon, Joseph T. 1977. "Post-Disaster Rumor Chains: A Case Study." *Mass Emergencies* 2: 121–26.

Scanlon, Joseph T., Suzanne Alldred, Al Farrell, and Angela Prawzick. 1985. "Coping with the Media in Disasters: Some Predictable Problems." *Public Administration Review* 45 (Special Issue, January): 123–33.

Schmidt, William E. 1990. "Cleanup Begins at Tornado Site Where 25 Died." *New York Times,* August 30, A18.

Schnattschneider, E.E. 1960. *The Semisovereign People.* New York: Holt, Rinehart and Winston.

Schneider, Ann, and Helen Ingraham. 1993. "Social Construction of Target Populations: Implications for Politics and Policy." *American Political Science Review* 87: 334–47.

Schneider, Saundra K. 1989. "South Carolina, FEMA, and the Response to Hurricane Hugo." *South Carolina Forum* 1 (April/June): 16–23.

———. 1990. "FEMA, Federalism, Hugo and 'Frisco." *Publius: The Journal of Federalism* 20 (Summer): 97–116.

———. 1992. "Governmental Response to Disasters: The Conflict between Bureaucratic Procedures and Emergent Norms." *Public Administration Review* 52 (March/April): 135–45.

Schoettler, Jim. 1992. "The Cheers Turned to Tears at Jeanerette Gym." *Florida Times-Union,* August 27, A9.

Schon, Donald A., and Martin Rein. 1994. *Frame Reflections: Toward the Resolution of Intractable Policy Controversies.* New York: Basic Books.

Seidman, Harold, and Robert Gilmour. 1986. *Politics, Position, and Power: From the Positive to the Regulatory State.* 4th ed. New York: Oxford University Press.

Selznick, Peter. 1943. "An Approach to a Theory of Bureaucracy." *American Sociological Review* 8: 47–54.

Shaffer, Helen B. 1977. "Job Health and Safety." In *Earth, Energy and Environment,* ed. CQ Press, 189–208. Washington, DC: CQ Press.

"Shattered." 1994. *Newsweek* (Special Report after the L.A. earthquake), January 31, 16–37.

Sherif, Muzafer. 1936. *The Psychology of Social Norms.* New York: Harper.

Silverstein, Martin E. 1992. *Disasters: Your Right to Survive.* Riverside, NJ: Macmillan.

Simon, Herbert. 1976. *Administrative Behavior.* 3d ed. New York: Free Press.

Sinclair, Barbara D. 1977. "Party Realignment and the Transformation of the Political Agenda." *American Political Science Review* 71 (September): 940–53.

Singer, Eleanor. 1993. *Reporting on Risk.* New York: Russell Sage Foundation.

Skocpol, Theda, and Edwin Amenta. 1986. "States and Social Policies." *Annual Review of Sociology* 12.

Smelser, Neil. 1963. *Theory of Collective Behavior.* New York: Free Press.

———. 1964. "Theoretical Issues of Scope and Problems." *Sociological Quarterly* 5: 116–21.

Smith, Steve. 1990. "Severe Storms Hit, Injuring Four and Destroying Houses." *The State,* October 23, 1B, 2B.

Sontag, Deborah, 1992. "Life on Fringes of Ruin Makes Cautious Comeback." *New York Times,* September 7, A1, A7.

Sponhour, Michael. 1989a. "Coastal South Carolina Gears Up for Hugo." *The State,* September 20, B5.

———. 1989b. "Federal Red Tape Hinders Aid Distribution in Charleston." *The State,* September 28, B1.

———. 1989c. "Forgotten Residents Fend for Themselves." *The State,* October 29, A1, A4.

Stallings, Robert A., and E.L. Quarantelli. 1985. "Emergent Citizen Groups and Emergency Management." *Public Administration Review* 45 (Special Issue, January): 93–100.

Stanley, Harold W., and Richard G. Niemi. 1994. *Vital Statistics on American Politics.* 4th ed. Washington, DC: CQ Press.

"State of Shock." 1994. *Time* (Special Report), January 31, 26–46.

Stevenson, Jennifer L., Henry Kaylois, and David Barstow. 1992. "We're Lucky—It Could Have Been Like Florida." *St. Petersburg Times,* August 27, 1A, 2A.

Stillman, Richard J., II. 1987. *The American Bureaucracy.* Chicago: Nelson-Hall.

Stone, Deborah. 1988. *Policy Paradox and Political Reason.* Glenview, IL: Scott, Foresman.

Stratton, Ruth M. 1989. *Disaster Relief.* Lanham, MD: University Press of America.

Sugiman, Toshio, and Jyuji Misumi. 1988. "Development of a New Evacuation Methodology for Emergencies: Control of Collective Behavior by Emergent Small Groups." *Journal of Applied Psychology* 73 (February): 3–11.

Suleiman, Ezra. 1974. *Politics, Power, and Bureaucracy in France: The Administrative Elite.* Princeton, NJ: Princeton University Press.

Sundquist, James L., with David W. Davis. 1969. *Making Federalism Work.* Washington, DC: Brookings Institution.

Suro, Robert. 1992a. "Despite the Devastation, Louisianians Feel Lucky." *New York Times,* August 28, A11.

———. 1992b. "When Storm Got Tough, the Women Got Tougher." *New York Times,* September 10, A8.

"Task of Pulling Survivors from Debris Creating New Class of Heroes." 1989. *The State,* October 19, 10A.

Taylor, Frederick W. 1911. *Principles of Scientific Management.* New York: Harper & Row.

Thompson, Frank J. 1982. "Deregulation by the Bureaucracy: OSHA and the Augean Quest for Error Correction." *Public Administration Review* 42: 202–12.

Thompson, Victor A. 1961. *Modern Organizations: A General Theory.* New York: Knopf.

Thrift, Ashley. 1989. Adviser to Senator Ernest F. Hollings. Personal interview. Office of Senator Hollings, Washington, DC, November 9.

Tierney, Kathleen. 1980. "Emergent Norm Theory as 'Theory': An Analysis and Critique of Turner's Formulation." In *Collective Behavior: A Source Book,* ed. Meredith Pugh, 42–53. St. Paul, MN: West.

Tilly, Charles. 1978. *From Mobilization to Revolution.* Reading, MA: Addison-Wesley.

Toulmin, Llewellyn M., Charles J. Givans, and Deborah L. Steel. 1989. "The Impact of Intergovernmental Distance on Disaster Communications." *International Journal of Mass Emergencies and Disasters* 7 (August): 116–32.

Treaster, Joseph B. 1992a. "Price Gouging Is Widely Cited in Storm Region." *New York Times,* August 30, A1, A11.

———. 1992b. "Troops Begin Work in Storm-Hit Area, but Misery Mounts." *New York Times,* August 31, A1, A8.

Turner, Barry A. 1976. "The Organizational and Interorganizational Development of Disasters." *Administrative Science Quarterly* 21 (September): 378–97.

Turner, Ralph H. 1986. *Waiting for Disaster.* Berkeley: University of California Press.

Turner, Ralph H., and Lewis Killian. 1972. *Collective Behavior.* 2d ed. Englewood Cliffs, NJ: Prentice Hall.

———. 1987. *Collective Behavior.* 3d ed. Englewood Cliffs, NJ: Prentice Hall.

Tuten, Jan. 1989. "Some Victims Still Await Help." *The State,* November 24, 1B.

———. 1990. "City Could Have Avoided Flood Deaths, Expert Says." *The State,* October 23, 2B.

U.S. Bureau of the Census. 1952. *Statistical Abstract of the United States: 1952.* Washington, DC: Government Printing Office.

———. 1994. *Statistical Abstract of the United States: 1994.* Washington, DC: Government Printing Office.

U.S. Congress. 1974. *The Disaster Relief Act Amendments of 1974.* 93d Cong. Public Law 93-288.

———. 1988. *The Robert T. Stafford Disaster Relief and Emergency Assistance Act.* 100th Cong. Public Law 100-707.

U.S. Department of Commerce. National Oceanic and Atmospheric Administration and National Weather Service. 1993. *Some Devastating North Atlantic Hurricanes of the 20th Century.* Washington, DC: U.S. Department of Commerce, National Oceanic and Atmospheric Administration and National Weather Service.

———. 1994. *The Great Flood of 1993.* Rockville, MD: U.S. Department of Commerce, National Oceanic and Atmospheric Administration and National Weather Service.

U.S. General Accounting Office. 1989. *Disaster Assistance: Timeliness and Other Issues Involving the Major Disaster Declaration Process.* Washington, DC: General Accounting Office.

———. 1991. *Disaster Assistance: Federal, State, and Local Responses to Natural Disasters Need Improvement.* Washington, DC: General Accounting Office.

———. 1993a. *Disaster Assistance: DOD's Support for Hurricanes Andrew and Iniki and Typhoon Omar.* Washington, DC: General Accounting Office.

———. 1993b. *Disaster Management: Recent Disasters Demonstrate the Need to Improve the Nation's Response Strategy.* Washington, DC: General Accounting Office.

———. 1993c. *Disaster Relief Fund: Actions Still Needed to Prevent Recurrence of Funding Shortfall.* Washington, DC: General Accounting Office.

————. 1993d. *Management Reform: GAO's Comments on the National Performance Review Recommendations.* Washington, DC: General Accounting Office.

————. 1994. *Los Angeles Earthquake: Opinions of Officials on Federal Impediments to Rebuilding.* Washington, DC: General Accounting Office.

U.S. Geological Survey. 1990. "The Loma Prieta, California, Earthquake: An Anticipated Event." *Science* 247: 286–93.

U.S. House. 1990. Subcommittee on Investigations and Oversight, Committee on Public Works and Transportation. *Hearing on the Federal Emergency Management Agency's (FEMA) Response to Natural Disasters.* 101st Cong., 2d sess. May 1 and 2.

————. 1993. Subcommittee on Investigations and Oversight, Committee on Public Works and Transportation. *Hearing on Federal Emergency Management Agency's Disaster Assistance Program.* 103d Cong., 1st sess. March 2.

U.S. Senate. 1988. Committee on Environment and Public Works. *Report on the Disaster Relief Act Amendments of 1988.* 100th Cong., 2d sess. September 22.

————. 1993a. *Subcommittee Hearings on VA HUD-Independent Agencies.* 103d Cong., 1st sess. January 27.

————. 1993b. Committee on Agriculture, Nutrition, and Forestry. *Hearing on Flood and Disaster Relief in the Midwest.* 103d Cong., 1st sess. July 16.

————. 1993c. Committee on Governmental Affairs. *Hearing on Rebuilding FEMA: Preparing for the Next Disaster.* 103d Cong., 1st sess. May 18.

————. 1993d. Subcommittee on Toxic Substances, Research and Development, Committee on Environment and Public Works. *Hearing on Lessons Learned from Hurricane Andrew.* 103d Cong., 1st sess. April 19.

————. 1994a. Committee on Environment and Public Works. *Hearing on Federal Response to the Midwest Floods of 1993.* 103d Cong., 1st sess. November 9.

————. 1994b. Committee on Environment and Public Works. *Hearing on Response to the California Earthquake.* 103d Cong., 2d sess. January 27.

Van Meter, Carl E., and Donald S. Van Horn. 1976. "The Implementation of Intergovernmental Policy." In *Public Policy-Making in a Federal System,* ed. Charles Jones and Robert Thomas. Beverly Hills, CA: Sage.

von Mises, Ludwig. 1944. *Bureaucracy.* New Haven, CT: Yale University Press.

Wagar, Linda. 1990. "Hugo and the Earthquake: Lessons Learned." *Council of State Governments* 33: 11–33.

Walden, Richard M. 1992. "The Disaster after the Disaster." *New York Times,* August 28, A15.

Waldo, Dwight. 1961. "Organization Theory: An Elephantine Problem." *Public Administration Review* 21: 210–25.

Walker, Jack L. 1977. "The Diffusion of Innovations among the American States." *American Political Science Review* 68 (September): 880–99.

Walters, Lynne Masel, Lee Wilkins, and Tim Walters. 1989. *Bad Tidings: Communication and Catastrophe.* Hillsdale, NJ: Lawrence Erlbaum and Associates.

Wamsley, Gary L. 1993. "The Pathologies of Trying to Control Bureaucracy and Policy: The Case of F.E.M.A. and Emergency Management." Blacksburg: Virginia Polytechnic Institute and State University, Center of Public Administration and Policy.

Warwick, Donald P. 1973. *A Theory of Public Bureaucracy: Politics, Personality and Organization in the State Department.* Cambridge: Harvard University Press.

Waugh, William L. 1990. "Emergency Management and State and Local Government Capacity." In *Cities and Disaster,* ed. Richard T. Sylves and William L. Waugh, 221–38. Springfield, IL: Charles C. Thomas.

————. 1994. "Regionalizing Emergency Management: Counties as State and Local Government." *Public Administration Review* 54 (May/June): 253–58.

Waxman, Jerry J. 1973. "Local Broadcast Gatekeeping during Natural Disasters." *Journalism Quarterly* 50 (Winter): 751–58.

Weber, Max. 1958. *From Max Weber: Essays in Sociology.* Translated by H.H. Gerth and C. Wright Mills. New York: Oxford University Press.

Weiss, Janet A. 1989. "The Powers of Problem Definition: The Case of Government Paperwork." *Policy Sciences* 22: 97–121.

Weller, Jack, and Enrico L. Quarantelli. 1973. "Neglected Characteristics of Collective Behavior." *American Journal of Sociology* 79 (November): 665–86.

Wildavsky, Aaron. 1964. *The Politics of the Budgetary Process.* Boston: Little, Brown.

Wilkerson, Isabel. 1992. "Giant Worries Are Stalking Hurricane's Smallest Victims." *New York Times,* September 4, A1, A8.

Wilkins, Lee. 1987. *Shared Vulnerability: The Media and American Perceptions of the Bhopal Disaster.* New York: Greenwood.

Williams, Walter. 1980. *The Implementation Perspective.* Berkeley: University of California Press.

Wilson, James Q. 1989. *Bureaucracy: What Government Agencies Do and Why They Do It.* New York: Basic Books.

Wines, Michael. 1992. "President to View U.S. Relief Efforts in Storm-Hit Areas." *New York Times,* September 1, A1, A10.

Witt, James L. 1993. "Foundations of the Future." *National Hazards Observer* 17, no. 6 (July): 1–3.

"Witt Reinvents FEMA." 1993. *National Hazards Observer* 18, no. 2 (November): 3.

Wolensky, Robert, and Edward Miller. 1981. "The Everyday versus the Disaster Role of Local Officials." *Urban Affairs Quarterly* 16 (June): 483–504.

Wolensky, Robert, and Kenneth C. Wolensky. 1991. "American Local Government and the Disaster Management Problem." *Local Government Studies,* March/April, 15–32.

Wolf, Charles. 1988. *Markets or Governments: Choosing between Imperfect Alternatives.* Cambridge, MA: MIT Press.

Woll, Peter. 1963. *American Bureaucracy.* New York: Norton.

Wright, Deil S. 1988. "Models of National, State, and Local Relationships." In *Understanding Intergovernmental Relations,* ed. Deil S. Wright. Pacific Grove, CA: Brooks/Cole.

Wright, James, and Peter Rossi. 1981. *Social Science and Natural Hazards.* North Scituate, MA: Duxbury Press.

Wright, James D., Peter H. Rossi, Sonia R. Wright, and Eleanor Weber-Burdin. 1979. *After the Clean-Up: Long-Range Effects of Natural Disasters.* Beverly Hills, CA: Sage.

Wright, Sam. 1978. *Crowds and Riots: A Study in Social Organization.* Beverly Hills, CA: Sage.

Yates, Douglas. 1982. *Bureaucratic Democracy: The Search for Democracy and Efficiency in American Government.* Cambridge: Harvard University Press.

York, Michael. 1989. "Making Sense Out of St. Croix: Why Did Order Collapse Completely after Hugo?" *Washington Post National Weekly Edition,* October 9–15, 32–33.

Zensinger, Larry. 1992. Program coordinator, Federal Emergency Management Agency. Personal interview. Washington, DC, December 27.

Index

About the Author

Saundra K. Schneider is Associate Professor and Director of the Master of Public Administration Program in the Department of Government and International Studies at the University of South Carolina. Her general research interests focus on the role of the bureaucracy in public policy development. Her articles have appeared in *Public Administration Review, Comparative Politics, Publius: The Journal of Federalism,* and *Policy Studies Journal.*